Red Handed 56 · Keating

Nuristan Forest

Bostick

Kalagush

Pech River · · ABAD

Mehtar Lam

Kunar River

PAKISTAN

Jalalabad

Tora Bora Caves

PAKISTAN

RC - North

RC - West

RC - East

AFGHANISTAN

RC - South

T0265493

WAR &
COFFEE

WAR &
COFFEE

CONFESSIONS OF AN AMERICAN
BLACKHAWK PILOT IN AFGHANISTAN

Joshua Havill

SCHIFFER MILITARY
4880 Lower Valley Road   Atglen, PA 19310

Other Schiffer books on related subjects

Crazyhorse: Flying Apache Attack Helicopters with the 1st Cavalry Division in Iraq, 2006–2007, Daniel M. McClinton, ISBN 978-0-7643-6494-5

Along the Tigris: The 101st Airborne Division in Operation Iraqi Freedom, February 2003 to March 2004, Thomas L. Day, ISBN 978-0-7643-2620-2

Designed by Christopher Bower
Cover design by Justin Watkinson
Type set in Futura/Minion Pro

ISBN: 978-0-7643-6702-1
Printed in India

Published by Schiffer Publishing, Ltd.
4880 Lower Valley Road
Atglen, PA 19310
Phone: (610) 593-1777; Fax: (610) 593-2002
Email: Info@schifferbooks.com
Web: www.schifferbooks.com

For our complete selection of fine books on this and related subjects, please visit our website at www.schifferbooks.com. You may also write for a free catalog.

Schiffer Publishing's titles are available at special discounts for bulk purchases for sales promotions or premiums. Special editions, including personalized covers, corporate imprints, and excerpts, can be created in large quantities for special needs. For more information, contact the publisher.

We are always looking for people to write books on new and related subjects. If you have an idea for a book, please contact us at proposals@schifferbooks.com.

FSC
www.fsc.org
MIX
Paper from
responsible sources
FSC® C016779

For absent friends, Kyle Jackson and Gene DeCrisci

CONTENTS

PREFACE

I came from a middle-class family in upstate New York. My dad was a carpenter, and my mom was a deputy sheriff. I grew up in the country, in a house that used a woodburning stove for heat, and by the age of twelve knew my way around a chain saw. I rode motorbikes and crashed remote-controlled airplanes. I was a country kid fascinated by anything mechanical. I worked part-time as an apprentice in a machine shop after school each day and used my earnings to take lessons at the local flying club. Within two weeks of graduating from high school, I passed the check ride for my private pilot's license and left for boot camp.

My military career began at the age of seventeen; I remember turning eighteen during boot camp. It was 1991 in Orlando, Florida. I served my first nine years in the US Navy submarine service and was the only person on either side of my family to ever serve in the military. My main job was to navigate the submarine, and I had a secondary function as one of the ship's divers. During the early years of evolving into a military person, I enjoyed multiple deployments on two fast-attack submarines: USS *Hammerhead* and USS *Philadelphia*. I went around the world on those two boats, and beyond the classified content of various deployments, I'm proud to say I've been north of the Arctic Circle, south of the equator, through the Panama Canal, through many of the oceans and seas and made port in seven different countries. I've eaten fish and chips in Scotland, and I've swum on the 1,000-fathom curve at Tongue of the Ocean. I've seen massive rats in Curaçao, I've been to Guantánamo Bay, I've eaten fresh cinnamon rolls in Norway, and I've been to Alcatraz.

When I reached the end of my second enlistment in 1999, the ending of the Cold War had caught up with the submarine force, and for a while there were very few worthy submarine missions. Slowly but surely, the Russian navy withdrew their side of the cat-and-mouse game, which had been the bread and butter of naval strategy for decades. Until the submarine force reinvented itself for a new political season, submariners would endure a lot of fire and flooding drills, torpedo evasion drills, painting, and upkeep.

Because there was no real fight out on the high seas, after nine years I got out of the Navy and was drawn back to working as a machinist and a welder, which I did for three years at various machine and fabrication shops in southeastern Connecticut. I didn't realize it for a few months, but *the normal life* of not wearing a uniform, not requiring frequent haircuts, not saluting everyone, and not having to comply with the uniform code of military justice gave me perspective about the hidden stresses of being institutionalized in the military. This allowed me to recage my interpretation of what might be stressful, and what didn't *need* to be; as a mindless recruit, I had bought into robotic obedience, and compliance with all things written and stated. I really "drank the Kool-Aid" as they say. I had soaked up the words of the oath like gospel, and I wore my uniform inspection-ready at all times. Anything else would have been akin to blasphemy. Returning later, after those years as a civilian, I began to understand that some who served continuously for twenty years (or more) potentially never recalibrated themselves from the initial programming and endured a career saturated with artificial stressors.

Around Y2K, I had a small apartment and two cats and enjoyed the basic routine of going to work every day and making things with my hands. I made things people needed day by day, and I enjoyed the instant gratification. Civilian life is quite different from military life in how immediately tangible or relevant everything can be. Being a Cold War submariner always had a very intangible sense of purpose—like we were always there to make sure nothing ever happened. As a machinist, if a farmer came in and needed a new shaft machined for his hay baler, that was real, he needed it right then, and he was immediately thankful when it was fixed. I enjoyed that tangible sense of purpose compared to being in the military.

On the side, I began using the GI Bill benefit from my enlisted service to take helicopter lessons. At that time, flying a helicopter was just a fun hobby. When I wasn't at the machine shop, I was at the airport, a parallel to my life in high school. I enjoyed flying helicopters for the way they move and the feeling of controlling one, and for the machinery itself: a tricky collection of physics problems solved through engineering.

Even with the GI Bill, the fantastic expense of renting helicopters was causing me to run out of money. A friend of mine by the name of Tony Chirillo, aware of my struggle, asked why I didn't join the Army and become a warrant officer. That way I would get paid instead of going broke, and I would get to fly impressive military machines. "The Army?!" I said, *"Fuck that!* I was in the Navy! I'm not joining the Army! All the Army is is a bunch of dorks walking around with backpacks and machine guns."

For the sake of being open minded, I began taking steps with a recruiter to determine if becoming an Army aviator was even a possibility. It was. I shifted gears once again and moved forward with reenlistment and flight school. Even though I had been out for three years, nine years in the Navy had fully conditioned me for stepping easily back into military service. My fitness level from being a Navy diver was more than adequate for keeping up with Army service, which is quite a bit more physically demanding than Navy service, and my navigational expertise from the Navy and flying experience from being a private pilot in airplanes and helicopters gave me great advantage in flight school. I was able to complete the fourteen-month course as the distinguished honor graduate before choosing the Blackhawk as my preferred helicopter. I then chose the most powerful division in the world as my first assignment, the 101st Airborne Division at Ft. Campbell, Kentucky.

By the time of the events in this book, I had been back in for seven years, including a deployment to Iraq for a year and a handful of short deployments to other areas.

Without consciously processing it too much, my break in service grounded me against the temptation to be an automaton; not only was I aware of the threat of blind obedience accumulating poorly in my persona, but I was just older and more laid back. I had been around the world, had time to reflect on it, and came back in of my own volition. I wasn't cornered by debt or family responsibilities; I had neither. I was also not driven by the events of 9/11. I was simply at one of those junctures in life where an opportunity came up, and taking it seemed more intriguing than what I had been doing. When I came back in, because of the contrasting perspective of being a civilian for three years, I was more aware of what made sense about the military and what didn't, and significantly less affected by it than I had been as a younger enlisted man.

Rank structure in the military also required pilots to be officers, and during what would become the second half of my military career, I served as a warrant officer: A bizarre half-breed provision within the rank and pay-grade structure, above enlisted status but below line-officer status. A notable portion of the military demographic will ponder how to interact with a warrant officer if they ever see one. Generically, warrant officers have all the privileges of a line officer with little of the responsibility. Of the five chief warrant officer ranks, I was right in the middle as a CW3.

I had flown UH-60L "Lima"-model Blackhawks for a year in Iraq before my unit had been outfitted with the newest, most powerful Sikorsky Blackhawk, the new "Mike" model (M is the model that came after L), and we had completed all the required training and ramp-up for deployment to Afghanistan.

At the time of this deployment, I was a middleman, neither upper management nor new guy, not senior enough to do any paperwork, and not junior enough to do any real work. I was merely a helicopter commander, and a conscious player in the mission.

This account contains the observations of an alert attendee, sitting 500 feet above the longest-lasting war in American history.

CHAPTER 1
FREIGHT TRAIN

December 13, 2008. Day 1. There is the sense that a freight train is coming, and you're standing on the tracks. The freight train won't hit you tomorrow or the next day, so you don't think about it too much. As the date approaches, you might have heard an air whistle in the distance, but then nothing. It gets stronger and stronger, though, you're hearing it, only a bend away. You're still standing there, and then you can see it. You begin to accept that the train will hit you. You start saying goodbye to people for real.

After all the packing and parties, you show up on schedule. After everyone and everything you know getting shut up, shut down, packed away, or told goodbye, you realize you've crossed a threshold of some sort; time is no longer running out. *The train must have hit you . . .* You're at a beginning now, wearing some new sort of skin. Everything you ever loved or cherished in life is no longer reachable. Your only option is to take a seat.

D-day is just another day where you stow your anxiety, show up in uniform to do your job, meet up with your best friends as usual, and start trading sarcastic little jokes. *Alright already. Get on the fuckin' plane.*

Showing up two hours prior to takeoff would have been fine, but it ended up being nine; the huge aircraft didn't lift off until 5:03 the next morning. By then everyone was exhausted, which is how we stayed for the next six days. There was a going-away ceremony at 11:00 p.m. for the families, then we stood around all night long. Whoever planned that one should get a swift kick in the crotch.

The other tedious decision was for everyone to wear body armor and Kevlar helmets on the plane. It's stupid enough that we're all carrying machine guns with no bullets to look cool for anyone who might see us, but what's the point in making us uncomfortable for the two-day trip? I imagined some insecure major having to make the big decision about what we'd look like and basing none of it on common sense. Like, *it's a fuckin' commercial airliner.* The Army has a contract with World Airways to fly this circuit almost continuously. The flight attendants don't carry body armor, so why do we? Just so on every landing the overhead bins can pop open under the strain of someone's ballistic plates and dump all contents onto the skull of some exhausted soldier who just left his wife and kids behind? *Enjoy your deployment!*

The flight surgeon had issued three tablets of Ambien to everyone, thinking if we slept throughout the morning on our way across the Atlantic Ocean, we would wake up in the correct circadian rhythm once we got there. Some of the guys wouldn't take Ambien and were willing to give the pills away. Others wanted a whole stash for future use and went about covertly collecting. My friend Joe Farwell and I each decided to take all three tablets immediately to see who could stay awake the longest. For fifteen minutes there wasn't much of a contest, but when the megadose hit us, neither one could tell who fell asleep first. We were knocked out.

The first stop was in Shannon, Ireland, which was a three-hour refueling layover. We were wakened by shouting friends in a nearly empty plane. We hadn't felt the landing. We came around like tranquilized gorillas, uncoordinated and drooling, and eventually zombied our way into the terminal for some food. It was our last chance for restaurant food. We found out later the flight surgeon got in a little bit of trouble for what he did, because if there had been any emergency situations where we had to respond, we would have been as useless as the luggage. I ordered a cup of coffee from the bar just before the announcement that we were reboarding, and after very little negotiating, the bartender generously allowed me to keep the porcelain mug. The mug would be saved for my eventual quarters. We went back to the cramped and stuffy airplane, tripping over machine guns and brain buckets[1] on our way to Romania.

Romania was no Ireland and offered no stroll through a pleasant international terminal to break up the confinement. We weren't even allowed off the plane, and the refuel truck ran out of fuel and had to go get itself refueled before coming back. It was three hours again, with no AC running inside the cramped DC-10, with three hundred tired and sweaty people either snoozing or complaining. I had never wanted to reach a combat zone so badly in my life.

Five hours after departing Romania, with only a foggy concept of space and time, we landed in Manas, Kyrgyzstan. Manas was the staging post within what I consider to be "Rural Russia." That was the end of service on World Airways, and the beginning of service from the United States Air Force. In Manas, some folks would make an immediate transfer onto a military transport, and some folks would wait days or weeks for their turn to go "in country." My group was lucky enough to get on board the mighty C-17 Globemaster within four hours. From there in, it was military air. Only then did we realize why we were carrying our body armor; it was a requirement for flying into a war zone. I hadn't remembered this small detail from Iraq because we had staged in Kuwait, suited up, and flown across the border into Iraq in the helicopters. That was a much more conscious feeling than being flown to our base by the Air Force.

Riding in the back of a military transport plane is a bit sportier than flying commercial. It is purely a cargo plane, but instead of cargo pallets, the cargo bay gets configured with seat pallets. Seat pallets are five-by-three-seat aluminum rectangles that get secured to the same floor track system as any other standard Air Force pallet, and that's about all they do. The crew chiefs of the massive aircraft also had to manage the entire waste disposal, so it is considered bad form to use the limited facilities. It would take great effort and disturbance to get out from under your gear and ask the guys in the seats next to you to do the same, so forget it. Your body is wedged into pitch-black confinement with no hope of comfort. There aren't any windows or light. There is also not an overhead bin, because you are riding "down in baggage," and all your gear is on your lap. Since cargo doesn't need individual air vents or reading lamps, these accommodations are absent even if seat pallets are installed. The seats don't recline, and there is not a magazine pouch. There is no stewardess call button; there is no stewardess. There is no drink service, there are no peanuts.

Somewhere in the middle of this miserable four-hour flight, a crew chief shouted over the massive, droning engines to put on body armor as we crossed the wire inbound.[2] I complied with this requirement before falling asleep and later awoke in complete darkness, under my 50 pounds of gear, to the sensation that we were falling. I waited for impact with the ground for at least twenty minutes while I struggled for any sense of spatial orientation in the darkness.

With a sense of finality, ten time zones from home, my face slammed into my duffel bag. We had landed in Bagram, Afghanistan.

Thirty-three hours from initial departure. Lindbergh himself would have passed out.

CHAPTER 2
PLYWOOD CAMPING

Day 2. It's hard to comprehend anything on the first night, no clue about time; I just wanted someone to direct me to the showers and show me an available mattress. We were met instead with a series of highly emphasized, "Welcome to Afghanistan" briefings, none of which we could quite latch on to. Perhaps the most important thing we were told and told again was to always be wearing a bright-yellow reflective belt, and that the sergeant majors of the camp would even write us a ticket if we were found without. It was a big issue. *Right. We'll wear reflective belts in a combat zone. Got it.* How the hell this type of logic prevails is unknown. It felt like a weakness from insecure leadership that some-one couldn't tell people, "Don't get run over," on the most brightly illuminated air base in the country.

I was in the submarine force in the waning years of the Cold War, in the early 1990s, and on deployment we wore whatever footwear, T-shirts, ball caps, hairdo, beard, or mutton chops we liked, including dyed, shaved, or mohawk. The em-phasis was on the mission. The threat in Afghanistan was a lot more tangible than it had been in the Cold War, and yet the briefings appeared to be purely focused on superficial bullshit and garrison appearances.

After conceding to the distinct possibility that some nearsighted sergeant major might engage me, which wasn't a fight I had the energy to be in, I donned my bright-yellow reflective device. Then my friend and company commander, Bob Massey, drove me to my quarters in a John Deere Gator, the Army's store-bought combat golf cart. Bob had been at Bagram two weeks already, afforded the extra time to get his bearings before the rest of his unit arrived. He was a young, skinny, blonde-haired captain; had a very easygoing demeanor for a commander; and made his way around on the Gator getting his people settled in.

Within minutes, we were introduced to our new dwellings. "B-huts," as they were called, would certainly amuse a building codes inspector. B-huts were haphazardly pounded-together shacks made of "Haji-plywood," a low-grade sheet product floating somewhere on the durability scale between cardboard and Luan. Each 20-by-30-foot building, marginally level and plumb, was divided into eight rooms with a 2-foot-wide hallway down the middle, with electricity and AC but no plumbing. Each room comes out to about 7 by 8 feet, with a haji-wood door. The lap of luxury! We had to concede, it was far better than a tent.

The room of the B-hut I was assigned to lent itself easily to a Turkish prison cell joke at first glance: a dirty little plywood room with exposed two-by-fours, dusty and cold. There the bed I was after, though, a gray metal frame and two greasy-looking, stained, gray mattresses. I was going to sleep in my clothes anyway, so all of this somehow felt acceptable. There were no lights, but there was an outlet in case I traveled with my own lamp. The gun with no bullets was logical enough; why didn't they deploy us with our own lamps with no bulb? The think tank may have been too busy getting a budget increase for the reflective belts.

I gave up on all levels of hygiene and conceded to sleep, allowing my carcass to mold into the lumps of the two stacked mattresses, fully dressed. This moment was comparable to wandering lost in the wilderness, becoming disoriented, and slumping into a thicket of brush to pass out.

A few minutes or a few hours later, I woke up. My phone gave up nine time zones ago, and the room was completely black. Figuring it was the middle of the day, I wandered outside to use the facilities and met the dead of night and the confusing artificial illume[1] coming from the stadium lighting of the central airfield. *Huh. Still nighttime.* I quickly found a "blue canoe," one of our terms to describe the portable plastic outhouse. I was vaguely hopeful then that I would find a more decent place to go to the bathroom, but I lacked the energy to go searching. In the long run, a blue canoe wouldn't do. It worked at that moment only to hurry me back into my contorted slumber in *The Twilight Zone.*

The morning eventually sliced in through a few cracks in my plywood room. I awoke with the desire to take off my boots and let blood flow through the waffled skin of my ankles, and lay pondering the lack of craftsmanship surrounding me. *What the fuck am I doing here?* I guessed the inside of that shack was going to be my home for the next year. It was quiet enough at that moment to accept that I had made it; the exercises, the workup, all the prep; it was over. We had arrived. The countdown to return home could begin.

My first agenda was a simple but important one: find a shower and establish—and maintain thereafter—a high level of hygiene. I didn't have so much as an end table to unpack on and was hesitant to dump my bags on the bed. My stuff was sacred and clean, and the bed was a swampy hive. I dug into the bag instead, finding my navy-blue towel and my shower kit, a clean T-shirt, and some shower shoes, and even a pair of sunglasses.

My first look outside in the daylight brought with it a fresh breeze of cold mountain air, and a striking view of snowcapped mountains in all directions. Invigorating! Bagram is surrounded by the Hindu Kush Mountains, which taper down into a patchy bowl of dirt and mud huts. In the middle of "the Bowl" were three high courses of concertina wire on Hesco barriers,[2] punctuated with guard towers every half mile or so. In the middle of the perimeter was the enormous runway of Bagram Air Base, surrounded by hundreds of plywood shacks.

The showers were close, only a one-minute walk. Like much of my new world, the showers were container based, the type of large shipping containers that go all over the world on truck, train, or cargo ship. The lower steel containers held the potable and gray water tanks, and some type of boiler. The upper containers (which seemed to be welded into one large room) contained the plumbing and a series of shower stalls. The stalls were the kind with plastic curtains sliding on galvanized steel pipes, a pair of Third World knobs on two valves, and a poorly chromed shower head. The hot water available ranged from icy to boiling, depending on how many people had used it, and was usually scalding but adjustable. A makeshift row of slats nailed together composed the floor, and they ranged from recently installed and clean looking, to needing replacement, black and green with various and slippery forms of algae. The shower helped me.

With a new outlook on life, and new hope that I could somehow resurrect what had been a grubby experience, I strayed from the shower on my way home and quickly found some restrooms. Whoa! A real place with real toilets! Another temporary welded-steel structure; I stepped inside and found the keys to happiness, as far as deployment goes—bright lighting, air-conditioning, and real, flushing, porcelain toilets. A sense of peace came over me. I was going to be able to stay comfortably civilized.

The latter portion of the morning heard mention of brand-new mattresses still wrapped in plastic, in one of the shipping containers. I had to have one. *Immediate acquisition was critical.* So much of deployed status can be stolen in a war zone; how one lives, what one eats or drinks, and various levels of comfort. In this case it wasn't stolen. Someone in the S-4[3] shop had apparently been thinking ahead, but the early bird would get the worm. Scrounging, scurrying, I had to find that container. It was one more anonymous container among dozens, but several people were on the same mission I was, including the first sergeant. He knew the way. He had the keys! There, behind dusty, creaking steel doors, stacked up to the ceiling, was a pile of brand-new, thick, blue mattresses in plastic wrap.

Like a child trying not to share a new toy, I grabbed one, scurried back to my B-hut, unlocked my door, and wrestled the precious commodity into my room.

It was a simple decision then: in with the new, out with the old. Wishing for a protective suit, I began the decontamination process by moving the diseased sacks of musty stuffing into the hallway, then to the nearest dumpster. The old-school steel bed frame seemed awkward, but I would keep it until I acquired the necessary materials to sculpt a fresh motif in the tiny cell.

I suppose this sounds like an unusual level of concern over what should be a minor footnote to any report of war, but the fact of the matter is that conditions can be a lot worse. I've been through plenty of monthlong exercises sleeping on back-twisting, Vietnam-era cots with no shower to soak it out. I've eaten for days and days out of the heavy plastic sack of an MRE (Meal, Ready to Eat) and spent weeks at a time wishing for things like laundry service or any sort of plumbing at all. If you can imagine bad camping, then air-conditioning, hot showers, and new mattresses become quite precious when you're looking at the next year of your life.

Personal effects being shipped at different times, parts of my unit arriving at different times, the level of required scavenging, and portions of company equipment still en route reminded me of the stark contrast between Army and Navy deployments. In the Navy, you know months ahead of time which bunk is yours, and if you tilt it up there is about 6 cubic feet of storage directly under the mattress for *all* your belongings. The day a deployment starts, you walk down the pier with your seabag and get on board. When the mooring lines get cast off, that's it; you're on deployment with all your stuff. The whole crew is there simultaneously, all the equipment is built into the ship and functioning, and it is literally a well-oiled machine from that first minute. A unit is 100 percent together and functioning *immediately*. In the Army, the personnel, equipment, and schedule all move as if fragments of a tornado, to the same effect. It's a powerful force, the amount of energy is unstoppable and does damage, and fragments of the main body fling off in unexpected directions. Each individual is allowed to pack multiple tuff boxes for a container that departs several months ahead of the personnel. The same is true for unit-level packing; many deployment supplies such as printers, printer paper, computers, office chairs, maintenance luxury items, generic support tools, huge boxes of coffee, hundreds of DVDs, and certain combat-unattainable but shelf-stable food items get sent ahead of time, to traverse the old-school trade routes. The containers get filled up in the parking lot of the unit's home base, then transported via truck to a railhead, then via train to a shipyard, then via ship to the other side of the world. Somehow, on the other end, American logistics personnel attempt to facilitate the reverse order, but with foreign assets! A similar thing happens with the helicopters: They get flown to port, taken apart, put on a ship, offloaded in a foreign port, put back together, and flown into theater. Certain specialists and equipment reach the battlefield via military air transport, and finally, weeks or months later, various portions of the unit traipse in at different times on different airlines, arriving randomly with only hope that their personal belongings eventually find them. From the moment that first container leaves the parking lot, until the entire unit and all the equipment come back into mission-ready focus at the FOB, is months.

Behind this main difference in how the Army and Navy deploy, essentially, is that in the Navy, the ship is the asset; the members of the unit have only to bring their personal effects on deployment, and any other equipment is built into the ship and ready to be operated. War planners move a ship icon into the virtual theater model, and it is one item. In the Army, or in any army, a plural presentation of individual fighters is the asset, and each individual is issued large piles of different types of uniforms for different occasions, different types of accessories for different situations, and different types of tools and weapons to be universally effective against the average threat. Based on different body sizes and different specialties, this gear is individually issued, and only the individual is responsible for getting his or her own mountain of crap to the fight. As you can imagine, it doesn't go smoothly. Somehow, most of the tornado eventually touches down.

At lunchtime I walked to the DFAC,[4] and in a connected room I noticed many stacks of 1-inch Styrofoam sheet, most likely acquired to carve reindeer or huge snowflakes for the upcoming Christmas party. *Insulation!* Santa Claus delivered early. I could fill in between the studs with the Styrofoam panels, then add another layer of plywood over that for some peace and quiet. I procured the Styrofoam along with some lumber, and over the course of the next four days I was able to remodel my shed into a modern-looking apartment, complete with desk, storage, and lighting. A cozy little dwelling then, with a two-by-four bed frame elevated 24 inches above the floor for storage beneath, custom-made to fit the new mattress. The final touches came when our company's personal shipping container eventually arrived and I got my two tuff boxes, which I had packed and shipped months prior. Thankful to get them, I unpacked a quilt from home, set up my coffeepot, and hung three of my father's paintings on the wall, which I unrolled from a tube and restretched. It was a personal space then, I had transformed the dungeon into a clean and cozy quarter worthy of mention in the tiny-homes movement. It was my own asylum of privacy and comfort, just a little bit bigger in all dimensions than the captain's stateroom on a submarine.

Stretching out on the fresh, cool bed with the homemade quilt, it finally settled on me that I was on the other side of the world again. In this first moment of thoughtful consciousness, I reflected vulnerably on our particular mission. Oddly enough, I hadn't really thought about being *in* Afghanistan until that moment. It was a different culture, and even further removed from Western life than Iraq. There we were, but *why* I wondered. Not a classic linear battlefield by any means, but another mottled guerrilla conflict like Iraq and Vietnam. It wasn't the citizens of Afghanistan we were there to fight, but either al-Qaeda or the Taliban, depending on who you talk to, all of whom had a similar appearance, and many of whom *were* Afghan. It didn't feel like combat. There were occasional engagements created by one side or the other, but never a deciding battle. What was it? We found out one mission at a time.

CHAPTER 3

MONOXIDE CHOKE

Day 4. This was the final deployment of my military career: Operation Enduring Freedom (OEF). I had been in the military for fifteen years. I had been on four major deployments, meaning they required a defined period of mission-specific training, followed by a series of inspections by higher authority to check for readiness, followed by a distinct departure from home base with a return date too far in the future to care about. Of these, three were with the US Navy Submarine Force and one was with the US Army to Iraq, and I had been on several minor deployments in between. I was one of the senior line pilots in my unit, and my function was simply to transport passengers or cargo around the battlefield, on time. I was a utility asset.

Who, exactly, was commanding your helicopter? Just a nondescript American yokel. I barely graduated high school, no college; I was poor at sports, attempting only bland track events without ever winning. I had a noteworthy collection of reference points in life, all largely physics-based observations in the first person: I knew what woodworking smelled like, since I had grown up with it in my dad's shop; I knew what work-related stress looked like, since I had watched my mother's career as a deputy sheriff; I had raced a handful of seasons as a flat-track motorcycle racer and had the respective number of crashes and broken bones; I was an established private pilot with as much single-pilot experience in single-engine, low-powered aircraft as I had in two-pilot, twin-engine, turbine-powered military aircraft; I was a civilian diver and a Navy diver and had negotiated near-death experiences with each; I was a capable metalworker, comfortable with everything from a lathe to a TIG welder; I dated a huge list of different women and had no preference over race, nationality, or hair color; I preferred cats over dogs but still loved any dog I met; and I could drink tanks of beer and bourbon. Despite these reference points, I was still notably bland in a lot of ways: I was a late bloomer socially, thirty-five years old with no marriages or offspring. My dog tags had the letters NORELPREF stamped into them, meaning "no religious preference," though I do consider myself to be Christian-like and God fearing. Of the few times I officially voted, I voted only for whoever I thought was the smartest, and any party affiliation remained blurry. I feel like I was just as generic or neutral as the designers of boot camp could ever have hoped for. I was the ultimate piece of trainable putty. I was good at accumulating skills, with few preconceived notions hampering my potential.

So, as I sat in the cockpit, it was without agenda. I was no more than a component, programmed to respond to a set of variables with predetermined actions, based on instrumentation. I was the unremarkable thing the designers of unmanned aerial vehicles sought to replace. Sure, there were times when I thought of creative solutions to unexpected situations, but those situations were seldom.

The real fighters, the ones who deserve the most appreciation for their service, are the ones on patrol every day who mix it up with the locals; convoys driving the IED-dotted highways; squad-sized elements that patrol through local villages on foot; dudes on the ground getting into firefights with machine guns and body armor. That's where the real action is, the real fight, if any. My part was a notably wimpier one: fly over the action in a thirteen-million-dollar, bulletproof helicopter. It was the best job of the war, mostly out of harm's way, with cushy seats, a powerful communication suite, and 4,000 horsepower at my command. Looking down at potential danger on missions could remind me of looking down into a lion's cage at the zoo. Certainly, if I fell into the cage, I would be terrified, adrenaline spiked, and looking desperately for a way out or maybe even paralyzed with fear, but from the relative safety of the railing, 12 feet up, I can look down into the cage while enjoying a slushy. Perhaps the lions could jump 12 feet, but they probably wouldn't try; maybe insurgents can hit a helicopter 500 feet up in the air with something, but probably not, and they usually won't try. So, with great fascination, I enjoyed the privilege of looking down into the lion's cage for a year. I even had the tranq darts if I needed them.

Occasionally we would fly troops into the objective, with an unknown threat but the potential for grave danger. Mostly, my job was to fly from A to B, moving anything or anyone not on a convoy. We would fly resupply, medevac, downed-aircraft recovery team (DART), convoy security, VIPs, quick-reaction force (QRF), search and rescue, and a few occasional assaults. In Army jargon, an assault is the rapid insertion of combat troops onto the objective at the moment of the fight. We call ourselves *assault pilots*, referring to what historically would be the most gung-ho piece of our mission, as well as our historical lineage, even though assaulting is what we did the least of in Operation Enduring Freedom. It was still important to keep the label of our lineage though. A more accurate label would be helicopter utility pilots, since we would do almost anything someone asked for with a helicopter. *But what the fuck were we doing there*, I had to ask myself.

The absence of daily fighting, and the absence of an occasional strategic-overview briefing, made it obvious that this wasn't exactly Operation Overlord.

Basic human nature had me wondering if this deployment would be similar to my last deployment in the Middle East. My unit flew in Iraq for a year in 2005, under a mission represented by the acronym SASO: Stability and Support Operations. We had a temporary patch on our shoulder with the letters SASO. We flew back and forth, here and there, carting around a lot of troops—not too many combatants, mind you, just soldiers needing to get to another location, people working on commerce, supply, and public affairs. We flew senators and congressional members who came over so they could see the country firsthand. We flew movie stars, football players, and singers on the USO tour. We flew dignitaries and ambassadors. We flew the FBI's explosive-sniffing dogs.

We flew a lot of things, every day. Iraq was never from the sky what cable news tried to convince us it was on the ground. On the *supposedly* bloodiest day of Operation Iraqi Freedom (OIF), I flew over Baghdad at 200 feet, looking down into the streets, and saw nothing more than people going to market, children playing, people on cell phones, and a shepherd herding his goats through the city. At the end of a long, quiet day, I returned to Balad Air Base to catch cable news reporting bloody battles *erupting* in the streets of Baghdad, and flashing to scenes of dusty desert warfare; never showing the plush, green side of Iraq's agricultural belt, or excited children running into the meadow waiting for another candy drop from American helicopters, or a solitary shepherd in the middle of a peaceful plain with his flock. They preferred to show brown dirt, American troops in body armor and Kevlar, the aftermath of a roadside bomb, and some added footage of an old firefight. I found myself thinking, *Wait a minute; I flew over that spot all day at 200 feet. I didn't see anything!* There were times when I thought maybe the Army had paid the media to glorify what happened day by day, but the media needed no help with that. There was already enough ambiguity about why we were in Iraq.

This was Afghanistan, though. Afghanistan held a defendable agenda.

We were in Afghanistan for so long, it was underway even before Iraq. Once we were fighting two wars simultaneously with divided resources, Afghanistan went clearly to the back burner. To confuse things further, we were also interested in Afghanistan long ago, helping the Mujahedeen against the Soviets. For some reason we keep trying to affect this patchy, tribal country. Our current attendance was no longer just a response for 9/11. It evolved into stabilizing the government, while making a nearsighted attempt to catch Afghanistan up with modern civilization. Afghanistan could be great, maybe, if we could inject them with a huge shot of good ol' American initiative and democracy and pull them up by their bootstraps.

That can't be right. I knew I wasn't the strategist for this thing, so I would just do what I was told, and eventually our purpose might settle on me. I mean *really*. The job of a helicopter pilot is not grossly affected by politics. We moved people from A to B, either way. I worked for someone who didn't know the overarching strategy, but he was my comrade, and I was going to do what I was told. He worked for someone who probably didn't know but was also obedient, who worked for someone who did know, disagreed, but was obedient. That guy worked for someone who knew, agreed, was effective, and might have been wrong about the strategy, but he also might have been right. No one knew at that point. Either way, we all had basic work ethic, so there really weren't too many objections.

My part in Iraq or Afghanistan was the same, regardless of strategy or status: move passengers and cargo from one point to the next, on time. This time we had a patch on our shoulders that read ISAF, which stands for "International Security Assistance Force," which is disturbingly reminiscent of *Team America, World Police*. I soon learned that the troops with more time on station came up with a variety of other interpretations, all based on the sarcastic constant of our military. *I See Americans Fighting* and *In Support of Afghan's Fuckup* were prime examples of the creative power of our uniformed services. Why we had to be so sarcastic is a good question, but a combination of extra time on our hands and a lack of information may have been the answer. The version of this futile exercise that rolled off the tongue easiest was *I Suck at Fighting*. Once again, we wore the patch on our shoulder all year, along with its embroidered Arabic translation, as a required uniform item with no emotional significance.

I had three or four days without any assignment to get my bearings, set up my living quarters, find the chow hall, take a few showers, and get used to the time zone. Bagram, Afghanistan, lies in a bizarre half time zone, 4½ hours ahead of Zulu time and 10½ hours ahead of Central Standard Time. I had more of a problem with the ten hours than I did with the half, but after a few days I felt awake during the day again. I was ready to get to work.

The walk from my B-hut to the CP[1] was less than five minutes along a crushed gravel road, in between rows of similar plywood buildings, and parallel to runway 3, from which one jet after another landed or launched into the sky. The fighter jets could be deafening, taking off on full afterburner, and their noise mixed with the constant *duke duke duke* of helicopters hovering nearby. The loud and dusty gravel road seemed swarming with all types of people, military and civilian, men and women, many different nationalities, all living in Bagram and working with the coalition. There were lots of folks, but any level of people-watching soon revealed an incongruity; this colony lacked children and senior citizens. It made rational sense, of course, but in the basic human leaning toward normalcy, the adjusted cross section on an active military airbase conveyed a slight enigma. Like walking through a dense forest and realizing there wasn't a single leaf on the ground. At an instinctive level, the absence of children felt wrong, somehow, but everyone seemed content. Transient people walked here and there with luggage, boxes, or bags in between steel containers being moved by large, off-road forklifts.

This seemed to be a place where stuff was really happening, though I didn't know exactly what. The air was cold, and in between the exhaust cloud of heavy trucks going by, there was still the feel of crisp mountain air. Bagram was a tremendous base, the size of Boston Logan Airport, with hundreds of different types of aircraft and vehicles coming and going every day, every minute: massive cargo planes, tanker trucks, attack helicopters, heavy-lift helicopters, tractor-trailers, unmanned drones, Toyota minivans, the huge Russian Antonovs, FedEx planes, Honda scooters, Pizza Hut delivery four-wheelers, and jingle trucks with pallets of bottled water. The jingle trucks were beautiful! Bagram was a clump of 26,000 people and hundreds of cars and trucks, right in the middle of tiny local villages and farming communities. It was bizarre that the dirt roads of the surrounding villages did not lead to the military metropolis; we seemed to exist beyond a barrier that was more than just sandbags and wire.

My short walk under the huge blue sky brought me to the CP.

After another intermediate airfield gate, I was introduced to the Lighthouse, a small coffee shop that offered free, round-the-clock coffee, brewed in a pair of Bunn-O-Matic coffee machines. *Not too bad*, I thought, as I helped myself to a cup that began a ritual I would repeat many times a day for the year. Families from all over the United States must have mailed coffee to the Lighthouse, because under the counter were several large cardboard boxes full of shiny new bags of Starbucks and other delightful coffees. No one manned the Lighthouse; there was a simple *you kill it, you fill it* rule in place, which seemed to be working.

I had found Main Street. At the top of the street was the Lighthouse, and out toward the runway was a line of brand-new Sikorsky Blackhawk helicopters. In this case, different from my experience in Iraq, the helicopters had stayed on the ship all the way to Rota, Spain, then were transferred onto Air Force C-17 and C-5 aircraft and flown to Bagram. They were taken out of the plane, unfolded,[2] put back together again, and test-flown before being put on the line. One more nondescript plywood building on the right was our command post, and walking with a cup of coffee in one hand and plugging my left ear with the other hand as a skull-rattling fighter jet took off, I stepped inside to see what was up.

The nature of the place became apparent as soon as I stepped inside: temporary. The inside of the CP was very similar to my B-hut, an unfinished plywood building. It seemed like any craftsman with an extra hour would have at least found some colorful stain for the place, but maybe that wasn't the point. I wasn't about to go looking for any either, even though this place was my new office. Early on, I felt a defense mechanism: *It's not really mine . . . I just have to tolerate it for a year.*

The CP was an area assigned specifically to the company, for the pilots to plan and brief missions and for the chain of command to perform administrative functions. Along one side was a small room for the commander and another small room for the first sergeant, good enough to qualify the shack as a command post. There were the usual things in the CP: a coffeepot, a planning table, schedules, charts, landing diagrams, computers and printers that would gradually object to the dust and be cursed for it, and posters of various sorts. Beneath it all lay a sort of . . . indefinable funk, probably the collection of overdue laundry, sweaty missions without enough deodorant, spoiling milk in the fridge, and many parts per million of unclaimed flatulence.

In between the rumble of a pair of F-15s taking off, the noise in the CP that prevailed was the constant hum of an ancient refrigerator, coils covered in heavy dust, full of items people had stored with good intentions but had been abandoned and became creaturely. It was a big fridge, stainless steel with two doors. The only part of the fridge that mattered was the front few inches of each shelf, just enough for current items. There was little chance of anyone performing a refrigerator audit. There was a coffeepot in the CP, or maybe only a coffeepot-shaped item covered in dust. There was no reason to conduct an archeological dig for the device, since there was no way it could compete with the Bunn-o-Matics next door.

A look at the flight schedule suggested I would be going out for "dust qualifications" in a few days, along with a local-area orientation. We trained often for landing in the dust, a skill that would come in very handy on certain missions. A landing helicopter blows downward tremendously, stirring up anything available. Depending on how a Blackhawk is loaded, the downwash can exceed 60 mph, and landing on plain dirt or in the sand causes a condition known to pilots as "brownout." In the last few seconds of landing, the ground (along with any visible horizon) completely disappears, luring the pilot to contact the ground incorrectly. Many helicopters have rolled over due to brownout, and many more have landed on huge rocks or in ditches, damaging the aircraft.

After "dust quals," I was on the flight schedule to begin flying missions the following day. I didn't know what to expect, having landed *in country* at night and possessing no knowledge of Afghanistan whatsoever, but the local-area orientation flight would fix that. The best thing to do in the meantime was to sit in the CP, observing.

At that moment, activity in the CP mostly comprised the junior pilots trying to figure out how to use the planning computers, how to generate the required paper products for each mission (maps and informational packets), and how to get information into the required format for each mission briefing. Daily, my company would support two quick-reaction force (QRF) shifts, one "med chase" aircraft (a medevac escort), and a handful of AMR[3] support missions. All missions would be briefed discreetly except for the QRF missions, which briefed generically every day at 6:00 a.m. and 6:00 p.m. The QRF mission was random in its own way, tending to be the catchall for anything the battalion hadn't planned for. The QRF would be two Blackhawks, with two pilots and two crew chiefs each, capable of supporting any mission that came along. Since it was the quick-reaction force, it required the least amount of planning but the highest level of readiness. There would sometimes be only a three-minute launch window for urgent medevac flights. Initially, my company was clumsy at the daily grind of things, and the morning struggles centered more on what font to use, how to get the printers to work, finding more rolls of paper for the plotter, and figuring out where the replacement ink cartridges were.

Members of the outgoing unit still saturated our ranks, at times seeming annoyed with our presence, other times being exceptionally courteous and helpful. They were cool operators, totally comfortable with whatever it was, having flown in Afghanistan for a year. In that sense it did feel like we were in their space and, to a great extent, getting in their way. They were tolerant of us, though; they had to help us figure everything out if they wanted to go home. My perspective from having spent a year in Iraq informed me that within a few days, this deployment would start to feel comfortable. Within a few weeks it would feel familiar, and within a few months we'd be in the danger zone of being so comfortable we would grow careless. The number of months remaining in the deployment would become a dismal thought to avoid, but within a year we'd be *these guys*, partially patient and partially annoyed by our replacements.

Leaning back in a dusty, high-backed leather office chair the previous unit was leaving behind, I casually sipped my coffee and tried to gauge the stress level of each of the junior pilots. Some were nearly in a frenzy trying to meet requirements in time for the briefing, noticeably voicing their problems with "the fucking printer," for example, while others were less concerned. Some were even standing in a daze, trying to figure out how to look like they knew what was going on. I set my cup down on the planning table, which was a large Plexiglas-covered table made of two-by-fours and plywood. You could always tell which things were made with American plywood that units had brought over in the many containers, and which things were made with Haji-wood. Some soldiers had deployed so often in their careers that they became experts at it, even having the presence of mind to bring their own construction materials and tools. This particular table could have withstood a big-block V-8 engine rebuild and had the autographs of every pilot ever attending boldly signed on it. In certain cases, pocketknives had done the work.

Finally, the team had all their products printed, rounded up their crew members, and briefed their mission. Within five or six seconds of listening to the same old stuff we always briefed, I started to zone out and imagine as much of their mission going wrong as possible. Any egotistical pilot in command would imagine getting shot at, having hydraulic lines rupture, conducting an emergency landing, leaping out with a machine gun, and being fulfilled with the glory of raw combat. Back to reality, though, you had to always be running scenarios in your mind to figure out your position on various issues in case something ever did happen. You must already *know* how you want to react, so actions during unexpected scenarios can happen more smoothly. Real operators want to get the mission accomplished, regardless of permission; anytime something happens that wasn't briefed or approved, they get it done, *then* defend their actions as being required by circumstance. It's something senior leadership in the Army hopes for, whether they can say it out loud or not. *Operators*: people who get the job done, allowing the colonel to shape the fight without feeling like he must hold anyone's hand. He should know, from the nerve center of the battlespace, when he looks at certain icons on the Blue Force Tracker,[4] that the job is getting done effectively, by someone operating more from ingrained instinct than regulation.

Who was the colonel? In the case of this deployment, for my unit, it was a Wilmington, Delaware, native by the name of Rob Dickerson. On the fourth major deployment of his career, Dickerson brought with him a background in special operations. With more than half of his service to date being with the Night Stalkers, orchestrating a regular line unit didn't appear to give him much logistical or tactical challenge. His physical stature could be intimidating to some; at 6-foot-4 and 250 pounds, he wasn't particularly heavy, he was just a *big dude*. The eighth of nine children, he had been recruited to West Point as a football player and spent four years as a starting tight end before going to flight school at Ft. Rucker, then on to a string of different assignments. At the street level, some combination of his pragmatic decision-making style, his tactical demeanor, and his physical presence earned him the nickname "Heavy D." At the twenty-year point in a thirty-year career, Lt. Col. Dickerson departed Ft. Campbell as the 7th Battalion commander and arrived at Bagram Air Base as the Task Force Eagle Lift commander, with 55 aircraft, 210 pilots, and 760 total personnel. The group comprised mostly original members of 7-101 (7th Battalion of the 101st Airborne Division). My assigned company from 4-101 was attached to provide a Blackhawk assault component, and elements of two battalions combined equals a task force. We had been made to feel welcome by the members of 7th Battalion, and it was going to be fun to see how it ran under the command of "Lift 6."[5]

As muscle memory brought another semiconscious sip of coffee to my mouth, I awoke back into the monotonous briefing and realized that one of the junior pilots was paying homage to the required words, saying the things he was expected to say while reading them from a cue sheet, investing in the prescribed litany of the thing. Nothing at all original. Whatever, though, it was appropriate for their mission. I must admit, I've given the same exact briefing a hundred times. Being able to snap out of it was an art form.

At the end of it, they disbanded unceremoniously, grabbed their gear, and went thumping out the door and down a short boardwalk toward the flight line. For all that formality and protocol, they had a twelve-minute flight to Kabul and back to pick up some major. As the eight of them left, the CP was quiet again, the air seemed to stagnate, and the place quickly felt stale. The hum of computers became apparent, the compressor in the fridge rattled back to sleep, and one of the computer screens switched over to a screensaver loop of stick people having sex until their crotches ignited and they burned to ashes, again and again. With an appreciative snort, I departed for lunch.

CHAPTER 4
FRANKENSTEIN'S CHAIR

Day 7. My walk to lunch was colored in many shades of tan. Everything in the apparent foreground was either dirty or dusty, and there must have been a massive surplus of tan or beige paint during the initial construction of Bagram, since every shack in the great sea of plywood B-huts was the same basic color. Some had faded to awkward tones of mustard or even salmon somehow, and the more recent paint jobs could be butterscotch, but every variant was matte with dust. The roads were gravel, so every Gator cruising by kicked up more dust, and dust blew in from around the countryside in the summer. There is a season in Afghanistan referred to as "120 days of wind," during which the afternoon wind would routinely sail above 15 miles per hour or so, sentencing every paint color to fade from abrasion.

Three years earlier during a deployment to Iraq, in the northern part of the country, I saw Kurdish villages from the sky—those folks knew about color! I'm sure they didn't have a Home Depot, but somehow they managed to create a vibrant array of pastels. Many houses in the desert are made of mud brick, which, left unpainted, end up the same sandy tones as the desert. Several of the houses had not been painted, but with many houses painted in bright pastels, each Kurdish village looked surprisingly like a bowl of Lucky Charms cereal from the sky. It was an exact match from a distance. In Bagram, Afghanistan, there had been no such imagination. The only place to see any color variety was down container alley, where multicolored shipping containers from around the world sat, and even they had lost any vibrancy.

Another abundant commodity around Bagram was sandbags. Every structure was surrounded up to 4 feet high with stacked sandbags. Perhaps the apparently biodegradable bags had initially been the same color, a dark OD (olive drab) green. Some appeared freshly stacked, but the majority had been there a long, long time. Some had even been there long enough for the plastic to decompose, so the only thing remaining was the sand, somehow standing naked and shaped like bags, waiting only for a catalyst to crumble. Bagram was subject to the occasional mortar attack, and the sandbags were intended to prevent shrapnel from flying through someone's B-hut, at least up to the 4-foot mark. Either it was too much work to stack them any higher, or they just can't be stacked that high without running two courses, which would have been much more work. For the most part when a mortar round hits, basic ground level is the terminus, and most secondary action projects horizontally from the impact point.

Various shapes of crude furniture were also featured along the road, mostly Frankenstein-looking junk pounded together by well-meaning people with an endless supply of two-by-fours. Some were comfortable looking, though most appeared torturous. Occasionally, a well-crafted Adirondack chair would join the lineup, even looking out of place next to clunkier mutations.

The dining facility was a "hardstand" building. Bagram Air Base was an old facility, originally built by the US decades ago and later occupied by the Russians during their unsuccessful time in Afghanistan, all of which came full circle again in the ironic revolving conflict there. There were a lot of permanent buildings from long ago with typical concrete-and-plaster construction, and the DFAC was one such building. Painted white, air-conditioned, and with polished asbestos tile on the floors, walking into the DFAC could snap you back to Western life, like the feeling of being drawn into the plot of a great old war movie on TV, then being snapped out of it by a fabric-softener commercial. I had been having this Korean War–feeling stroll, then was jolted back to modern civilization: florescent lighting, glass-topped salad bars, fake flowers for décor, and elevator music seeping in somehow through invisible speakers. A pleasant young woman scanned my ID card, the process somehow collecting data to justify the operating costs of the DFAC.

The DFAC had two main lines, one for entrées and one for fast food. It was possible to eat hamburgers and french fries for the whole year with ice cream for dessert, which no one attempted. The main line advertised forty-eight different entrees, while the fast-food line always had the same thing: hamburgers, french fries, small pizzas, corn dogs, and sometimes fish sticks. There were additional bars for salad, fruit, and cereal, and full-size display fridges for various deserts, yogurts, and pudding. An ice cream bar with an Indian server standing behind it was available for lunch and dinner, offering the most-recent flavors of Baskin-Robbins ice cream for free. They had this thing all set up to help someone gain 5 pounds a month.

I settled for a huge plate of cabbage, some deep-fried mozzarella sticks with marinara sauce, and a foil-covered tub of fruit loops and milk, then picked an anonymous seat on the side of the DFAC for some people-watching.

People from all over the world were there to be part of the coalition. There were forty-six different countries participating. I saw a lot of Italians, French, Dutch, British, Germans, and some nationalities I didn't recognize, as well as unknown contractors and locals. The mix of US military was also unusual, with all four branches present. There is a competitive tension between US military branches, which can make it almost more awkward than sitting with someone from another country. Mostly we just wouldn't look at each other, like pretending the other branches weren't there. I'm sure some of it came from a jaded sense of unfairness that the Army deploys for twelve to fifteen months, and the Air Force deploys for only four months. The Army lives in tents and B-huts, and the Air Force lives in new and improved "hardstand" barracks. Army pilots preflight their own aircraft, Air Force pilots don't. That last part might not even be true, but that's what we're going with. Either way, the DFAC welcomed a large group of people from all over the world, all looking for a satisfying meal. We shared a common bond, unified as a coalition: no one could find a single gourmet item as we worked together through another forgettable meal. It wasn't bad, though, and it would take a long time to get through all forty-eight entrées.

I dropped my tray in the unmanned stainless-steel booth, with a faded green conveyor belt taking it into a dark, steamy tunnel toward the sound of water spray and clanking. I pulled my hat out of a leg pocket and went back out to the harsh sunlight. My B-hut was a two-minute walk through the dusty gravel, stacks of dissolving sandbags, and mustard-colored shacks. All these low-tech structures were adorned with strands and bunches of blue CAT-5 and co-ax cable, piping satellite-dish internet into each air-conditioned room that helped each displaced occupant stay in touch with the outside world and home. Ironically, within the little wires, electrons flow at the speed of light and allow access to the most-high-tech things in the world, but the wires themselves were crudely stapled, zip-tied, and in some cases duct-taped haphazardly to one of the lowest-tech styles of construction ever assembled. The place had a real temporary feel to it but was obviously decades old. Some of the structures looked so pathetic, maybe the CAT-5 cable was even holding them together.

Back in my room, I relaxed my uniform, took off my shoes, sat on my bed, and turned on my computer. The outside world was muffled then, but I also had a pair of headphones with a 20-foot cord, which allowed me to watch a movie on the computer at the foot of my bed without blasting noise throughout the B-hut. I picked *First Blood*, with Brian Dennehy and Sylvester Stallone. I settled in for a lazy, quiet afternoon of being entertained on my custom 2-by-4 bed, in my 7-by-8-foot room, cozy and content. Inside the headphones I was transported out of Afghanistan, and it was a fine little getaway.

CHAPTER 5
MINEFIELDS

Day 9. After that first week of settling in, I woke up early to get ready for environmental training. It's not really training, but more of a final check that each pilot is ready to fly at higher altitudes and land in the dust as well as make pinnacle approaches and fly with good power management. Being one of the pilots in the unit with previous deployed experience, it was really a casual flight with one of the instructors to "check the block." This would continue to be true; the longer I flew without making any noticeable mistakes, the less I would go through any critical evaluations during my career. Not that there weren't mistakes—certainly there were, but there was always someone swimming slower for the shark to get. It's typical that when the senior pilots of a unit are in the same peer group as the instructors, evaluation flights end up being perfunctory. You would think with two seasoned pilots the inclination would be to work on riskier techniques, but the opposite sometimes prevails. It's more like, *We both know this is pointless, so let's just enjoy ourselves.*

I showered and then ate breakfast, noting the same things as before, with no change, no new excitement and no sense of danger, but ended up sharing a table with Bob Massey.

"Cap'n," I said.

"Mr. Havill! How is charming Bagram Airbase treating you this morning?" He asked with mock enthusiasm.

"Fine, I suppose; delighted to be here. Yourself?"

"Can't complain. You headin' out with Bill this morning for dust quals?"

"Yup. Should be big fun." I responded flatly, both of us knowing it would be unremarkable. I considered trying to work in some sort of dirty joke to hear Bobby's jovial laugh but defaulted to quietly enjoying my omelet. The commander usually tried to maintain a professional demeanor, but it was easy to break him out of it. He was in his late twenties, but his optimism and persistent smile made him seem like a kid, and his laugh could be downright comical if you caught him off guard. It was fun to bust him up laughing, but it was too early in the morning to throw him the catnip.

Bob had an interesting life since departing high school in 1998. Originally from Elizabeth, Colorado, he was invited to Metropolitan State University in Denver on a baseball scholarship. While getting ready to start with Metro State, he attended an open tryout for the AA farm team with the Los Angeles Dodgers and made it as a walk-on. He played in the farm system for two years as a shortstop, and it was obvious that this experience as a competitive team member was a component of his command ability and natural sense of esprit de corps. In 2001, he traded the mountains of Colorado for the flatlands of Grand Forks to attend the University of North Dakota, where he acquired a bachelor's degree in commercial aviation, earned his commission from the ROTC program, and added another three hundred hours to his logbook. By the time he went into Army flight school at Ft. Rucker, Alabama, he was already a comfortable and confident pilot. For this year, he was the receipt holder of twelve brand-new Blackhawk helicopters, and in command of thirty-two crew chiefs and twenty-eight pilots.

We finished breakfast, exchanged a "*See you in the CP*" with each other, and took our trays up.

The air was clear and the sky was huge and blue, and I strolled carefree into the CP. If there was a war, maybe it was mutually understood by both sides to be only an afternoon thing. The whole base seemed as quiet and snuggly as Christmas morning, but that wouldn't be for a few more days. Maybe it was just the Christmas spirit calming everyone down. Either way, it was a nice morning to go flying, especially with no mission. All we had to do was drift around the Bowl, demonstrate a few tasks, and come back in for lunch.

After a quick stop at the Lighthouse, I went into the briefing, which was run by the standardization pilot, or SP, Bill Westerguard. Bill was no more or less of a pilot than the other instructors but outranked them by a few months. Getting promoted just a few months earlier put him in charge of just about every procedural flying decision that would be made within the company. Seniority could be like that in the military. The thing about Bill that lent a good deal to his charisma was his accent. Originally from southern Georgia, every other word had a heavy *gall-dang* sound to it. Sometimes it could be hard not to smile at certain words he said, and he was fun to talk with. At times he could sound just about like a pair of springs being plucked. Nevertheless, he explained the route we would be flying to accomplish the various tasks required for the environmental qualification, and we were on our way.

That first flight was fun. The lower elevations inside a circle of mountains that we referred to as "the Bowl" were considered low threat, even though the base would frequently get mortared from somewhere within the valley. A large geographical area, the Bowl was roughly crescent shaped, bordered with mountains, some farmland to the north, mostly dirt to the south, and various passes leading out. To the south were the fewest mountains, and it was easy to wander south toward Kabul without any serious navigation. In contrast, Panjshir Valley to the north would require more attention to get through, especially in the windier seasons, since the entrance was a tight draw. The Bowl supported a full array of training activities, and previous units had mapped out good locations for practicing dust landings, pinnacle landings, and test firing of weapons.

The pronounced ridgeline to the northwest, which led the way out to Bamiyan, was especially fun to land on, and a low-enough risk that it was OK to get out of the helicopters if someone needed to relieve themselves or wanted to gaze upon Bagram far below. There weren't any land mines up there, which was nice. At the lower-pinnacle landing site down in the Bowl, the land mines were so abundant that large areas of open land had been carefully marked with small piles of white-painted rocks to distinguish the mined areas from the unmined. It was wise to never trust *any* area, because according to one of the various threat briefings, the Russians had left over a quarter of a million mines in Afghanistan. It was something to remember. We had been reminded that if we ever had to do an emergency landing, not to even get out of the helicopter. There were certain options for evading on foot, such as walking only through plowed fields or streambeds, for example, but any sort of travel on foot was not to be taken lightly.

Bill and I had a leisurely trip around the course, a simple orientation of the airbase, a few dust landings, and a pinnacle landing or two, then back. That had been my first look at Afghanistan from the cockpit of a Blackhawk, and it was absolutely gorgeous. I walked back in from the ramp with a smile like I had just made it to third base on a date and was truly excited. To be there, fully acclimated, well rested, signed off to fly combat missions, in command of an awesome combat vehicle, and working with a pack of red-blooded, like-minded, badass American operators across such a landscape was the chance of a lifetime. I was looking forward to conquering whatever mission got thrown at us. A short walk over the asphalt ramp led me back to the dirty base.

There was a definable freedom that came with being outside the wire that could make the base feel cramped. It was a *huge* base, but I went from floating in the big blue sky over a majestic countryside, breathing fresh air, and feeling empowered in the floating lair, to being on foot again, scuffing through Gator dust, and walking in between Jersey barriers and mustard-colored shacks. I was trapped in the industrial funk of the airbase again.

Stopping at a line of Port-O-Potties before I reached the Lighthouse, I enjoyed graffiti inside the maturity-free zone. I turned to go and noticed, lower on the door, a large caption in black marker. Each plastic crapper was full of it, and I never missed an opportunity to reflect on the stagnant humor. "*OBJECTS GREATER THAN 8 INCHES IN LENGTH MUST BE HAND LOWERED DUE TO SPLASH HAZARD.*" This of course gave me a disgusted smile. I squeezed my eyes shut to try to eject the image from my mind. Yup, I was back on the FOB.[1] For lack of handwashing stations, on the outside of each unit was a hand sanitizer dispenser, which was bad form to skip.

When I walked back into the CP to hang out, I noticed my name on the board for a mission the following day. I found the mission request by number and read it: a straightforward flight from Bagram to JBAD,[2] pick up two pax,[3] and return. I was looking forward to it.

I walked back to my B-hut, gravel crunch, dust choke, sandbags, and people moving about under the dull roar of all types of vehicles. Nobody moving too fast, really, just moving. Deployment is more of a marathon than a sprint, so it's important not to get too stressed out. The short five-minute walk brought me back to my fortress of solitude, and I realized I was going to be comfortable there for the long run. It was the least military place I could find on the base, and that was important. As my plywood door swung shut and was locked, the room was dark except for one narrow strip of light slicing in from the window, a window that consisted of a pair of inward-swinging plywood shutters on the inside, and only a screen on the outside. The insulation I had stolen created a dulling of the noise, and it was peaceful inside. There was no war in my room.

No war outside, for that matter.

To say we were in a war zone felt like a stretch. There was no war there, in the linear sense, and barely even in the guerrilla sense, and it seemed like the only violence was directed at *us*, although I'm sure that wasn't true. I hadn't flown too far from base yet, but the region had been "at war" for so long, it was a sustained normalcy more than war. It's kind of like the South Side of Chicago of the world. There was certainly conflict, but far from anything requiring such a tremendous presence by the United States. It was just another political situation we were trying to find the least embarrassing way to end without it looking like we didn't need to be there in the first place.

There is certainly a difference between the security I felt on base and what the combatant fighters felt when they were out working. Being out and about on the Bagram Airbase is as worrisome as being at a busy marketplace; there is activity and some confusion, but no great threat. I would be substantially more nervous if

I was in a bad neighborhood of "Any City, USA." Outside the wire, I would be concerned. In the high-threat area where our soldiers patrolled and where our convoys rode, I would be apprehensive. On the huge base, it just wasn't that bad.

I set out to find a gym, and going to it became my daily habit for the year. There were a few residual hardstand buildings from times past, and one of them had been converted into a gym by the Army. But in a nicer part of the base, the Air Force had brought in a large Quonset hut, insulated it, and added modern air conditioners and lighting to create the nicest gym available. It was fun to go there and see the great variety of bodies evolving, from unmotivated, overweight people who didn't know where to start, to energetic young women bouncing from one machine to the next in trim bodies and ponytails. There were motivational posters of Arnold Schwarzenegger on the wall, coolers full of free bottled water, and music playing. This became a good daily escape from the dusty base.

Daily then the routine began, breakfast at the DFAC, stroll to work, fly, return, exercise, shower, dinner, gravel and sandbags, plywood fortress, sleep. As many times per day as one desired, the showers stood waiting, which was important to me—with so much dust and a variety of unsanitary conditions looming, it was critical to maintain the highest order of hygiene.

CHAPTER 6
MULE TRAIN

Day 10. Mission number 1 must have been hand-chosen as an initial mission for me. I wouldn't ask about it; I knew Bobby and Bill did their jobs well, and that they would be trying to make good decisions about what kind of flight someone had to manage from day one. They would have afforded any other pilot the same luxury, because managing crews and cultivating the development of theater-specific resilience was their job for the year. A no-brainer mission made sense for anyone's first time borrowing the keys to the car. It was daytime, it was finite, and there were no additional skills required, such as night-vision goggles or time-on-target landings. It was just an airport-to-airport flight. Normally the daytime QRF would absorb BS little missions like this. It was a coffee drinker, anyone knew it, and I accepted it like a box of chocolates on Valentine's Day; it was sweet. I didn't need it, but I was going to enjoy it because it was thoughtful and disarming.

Flights not part of the QRF were usually supported by an AMR, or *air mission request*, which doubled as the manifest. The AMR defined the required stops but not the route, as well as the suggested time of pickup. This was important to me, because it meant that a passenger was waiting in a pax terminal somewhere, uncomfortable and hoping the flight would happen on time. *It would*. As I read the incredibly short AMR, it left no room for interpretation and required no logistical skills:

1300	JAF	KHATUN, ASHOK	CIV	1400	BAF
1300	JAF	WILLIAMS, EDWARD	MAJ	1400	BAF

OK, then, nothing much to consider there; let's make sure we've landed by 1245, we have the frequency for the pax terminal, and everyone has a chance to get out and use the facilities if they want to prior to a 1300, on-time departure.

Jalalabad was a little bit intriguing. Units assigned there were closer to the valleys of the Kunar and Pech Rivers, where the threat level was higher, so at night, JBAD was a blackout airbase. In contrast to Bagram, which maintained massive stadium lighting at night, allowing pilots to land with the naked eye, JBAD required all aircraft and runway lights to be off, including building lights of any kind, which required the use of night vision goggles. It was also within fifteen minutes of the famous Tora Bora caves, where we once thought Osama Bin Laden was hiding. He was still hiding somewhere, but where we did not know.

For this flight, the other aircraft would be piloted by Tommy Ingram and his crew, and I would be flying with a good-natured guy by the name of Jasper Diego, who had a southern Pacific complexion and made easy friends with anyone in the unit. I thought he had a made-up name, like some cross between a baseball player and a ghost, until I asked him about it one day and he said his middle name was *Sol*. Apparently, he had one of those earthy, creative mothers. Certain people seemed to be driven by the requirement to be conveying happiness first, and doing whatever the mission required second, and Jasper was one of these guys. It was like his main focus was contributing to the energy of the team, and if he got to fly once in a while, he'd be happy. He was one of the newer pilots, a CW2 who had yet to be signed off as a pilot in command but had a true fondness for aviation and was already a commercial pilot in the civilian world. Once he carried as much equipment to the helicopter as he could and got as many crew members to laugh as he could, it was easy to miss the fact that somehow, he had also done an excellent job with his own duties.

I went to the TOC[1] for a weather brief and a threat brief, then came back and gave everyone in the formation a crew brief. My crew chiefs / gunners Victoria Burns and Ron Ecker began loading the M-240 machine guns, along with the required eight hundred rounds of ammo for each, or four cans. The guns connected to the helicopter via a pintle mount in the windows behind the pilots' seats, and the ammo cans were stored within arm's reach. The crew chiefs also loaded emergency rations, water, and a basic set of contingency maintenance items. Both teams climbed into their respective machines and got them fired up.

After a ship-to-ship comm check over the internal radio, I called Bagram Ground for taxi clearance. Both aircraft taxied out to the threshold, and we began our pretakeoff checks. All systems indicated normally; engine and rotor rpm were "in the green." We had enough fuel for the mission, and the final item in the before-takeoff checklist was "Crew, passengers, and mission equipment: SET." I heard the normal responses from the crew. "Left rear," "Right rear," "Right front," and I responded with "Left front." We didn't have any pax yet, and for mission equipment we wouldn't rack the slides on the 240s until we crossed the wire outbound, and we wouldn't turn off the safeties until there was a target. Victoria pulled the safety pin out of the CMWS[2] launcher relay, but I would not arm the flare system from the cockpit switch until we were outside the wire. The impressive flare-launching system had an array of five fish-eyes scanning all sectors of a hemisphere below the helicopter, could detect the exact heat signature of missile exhaust, and would automatically launch a countermeasure to defeat said missile, because any human pilot is too slow to make these calculations in time. Perhaps the pilot of a U-2 spy plane or an SR-71 Blackbird would have time to make a thoughtful decision about this sort of thing from much higher in the sky, or even a fighter jet flying at a more notable fraction of the speed of the missile itself. At the low speeds and altitudes we flew, there would be less than a second to outsmart a missile. With my own lightning-fast reflexes, I'd be wondering what the loud noise was long before I could reach for the "LAUNCH FLARES" button.

In the analysis of its automatic behavior, too many different light sources could cause an inadvertent launch of the CMWS system, and with as many fuel blivets and expensive aircraft as there were sitting around the ramp, it was a bad place to be shooting off cocktails of bright burning metal. The flare buckets on either side of the tail cone were programmed to shoot three flares each, with each flare burning in a different light or heat spectrum, on the basis of being compounded with different elements. A group of three flares was referred to as a cocktail, and at least one of the flares from each cocktail was hot enough to melt through anything but rock. Being launched with high-grain squibs, they could really reach out and do some damage if they went off anywhere below 100 feet or so, and several times I had seen flares bouncing down the ramp from other aircraft. It could be like watching the Fourth of July gone wrong, and according to the threat brief there were no heat-seeking missiles in this theater anyway.

I turned off the bright strobe light on the back of the vertical fin that would otherwise be distracting to chalk two, and transmitted over the internal radio, "1-1 is REDCON ONE," in a monotone but authoritative voice, and heard Tommy reply back immediately, "1-2 is REDCON ONE."[3]

Checking for landing traffic before calling the tower, I looked toward the approach end of the runway and thought to myself, *Yup, we are going to wait.* I transmitted again over *internal*, "Standby, flight," and enjoyed the view as I watched the largest military transport aircraft in the world during its approach, the mighty Antonov AN-124. Bigger than a 747, and sinister looking with anhedral, watching this beast land from where we sat conveyed the same sense of reverence as being out in a small boat whale-watching as one of the massive creatures got too close. I watched in awe as it seemed to land in slow motion, and was reminded there were other big countries with big toys in the world besides the United States. It was a treat to see the Russian Goliath in action. After touching down, it used the rest of the runway to stop, but I noted where it had touched down, which is also the point at which its huge wings would have stopped generating lift. That would be the same point that incredibly powerful vortices rolling off its wingtips would also have stopped, and seeing that we could take off without surfing through them, I called the tower for departure.

"Bagram Tower, this is Honcho 46 and flight, holding short at Foxtrot [taxi-way], ready for departure to the east."

The tower responded, "Honcho 46 and flight, you are cleared for a present-position departure to the east; caution wake turbulence."

I responded with a simple "46, cleared for takeoff," and told Jasper to have at it.

It was chalk two's responsibility to be ready back there, since they had announced REDCON ONE. It was also their job to be monitoring the tower frequency once we were at the hold-short line, and they were. For a considerate formation departure, we wouldn't yank our aircraft off the taxiway unexpectedly. I didn't need to say anything over the internal radio in this case, because they would have heard my conversation with the tower. Jasper added power gradually, so chalk two could see our aircraft "getting light on the skids" and mimic our application of power. If done correctly, both aircraft would depart simultaneously, then chalk two would immediately establish the correct formation angle and spacing, having matched altitudes from the moment of departure. Jasper made a smooth takeoff, and over the internal radio Tommy transmitted, "Bacon," which was his funny way of saying "beacon," which meant they were successfully in formation. I transmitted "ALPHA" to the TOC over the Air Battle Net, indicating our mission had begun.

We picked up a 130 heading, and as we crossed the wire outbound, I lifted the red cover of the military-grade CMWS toggle switch before placing it in the "ARMED" position. Once we were well clear of the airfield, Ron asked for permission to test-fire, which I granted, then he announced, "Test-firing right," followed by a short burst, followed by the report: "Test-fire complete." Victoria said, "Test-firing left," followed by three not-so-short bursts, before reporting, "Test-fire complete." I looked back at her quizzically and asked, "Did it work?," since everyone in the aircraft knew her test fire was contrary to SI guidance,[4] but let's face it, the thing is fun to shoot. She said, "Yes sir," with no further explanation, and caught everyone smiling. I think the basic gist of the guidance was to save ammo, but also not to make our presence in the country more menacing than it already was. If the 240 cycled through three or four rounds without jamming, it was good to go.

Jasper apparently wanted to hand-fly this leg, which I understood. There would be times on longer flights when we would turn on the "flight director," which is another name for autopilot, and while it flew straighter and stayed on altitude better than a human, it reduced the pilot to being a systems monitor instead of getting to fly. We crossed the ridgeline out of the Bowl, and as the terrain dropped off we assumed an en route altitude of 1,000 feet above ground level. This wouldn't be too high to enjoy the scenery, but it would put us out of range of small-arms and RPG fire.

The weather was gorgeous, and so was the scenery. It was wintertime, and being up high made it even colder in a vehicle notorious for freezing its occupants, but the coldness also made the coffee that much better. As we flew to the southeast, it was fascinating to look at rough terrain sloping gradually down toward the Kabul

River. Fifteen minutes southeast of Bagram, the Naghlo Dam on the Kabul River created a beautiful reservoir, and the intervening strip of farmland in the Tagab valley created a scene that could have been mistaken for Lake Mead on the Colorado River. The elevation was a few thousand feet higher than Lake Mead, but the latitude was right, so the climate would have been similar. From there the terrain flattened considerably but would still have been challenging on foot. Our flight continued with a gradual descent, on the basis of JBAD being about 3,000 feet lower than Bagram. In the final ten minutes, the ground flattened enough for the Alishing River to join the Kabul River prior to the Daronta Dam, creating hundreds of square miles of usable farmland, which was dormant for the winter. Beyond the dam was the small city of Jalalabad, and with our navigation equipment pointing to it, we spotted the airfield easily. Putting the safeties on all our weapons and countermeasure equipment as we crossed over the fence line, we touched down ahead of schedule. Recognizing the pax terminal from an airport diagram we had studied prior to departure, we rolled to a stop in front of it and set the parking brake.

Typical for this type of run, the crew chiefs hopped out and opened the cargo door on the terminal side of the aircraft and postured themselves to intercept anyone trying to walk around the back of the helicopter, thereby getting diced up by the tail rotor. Most pax would understand this formation, an obvious funnel, and walk between the two crew chiefs toward the open door. There would be a surprising number who had their mind set on walking behind the helicopter for some reason, and we would intercept them all year long. The other thing typical of this type of run was that we would have no idea who the pax were. On a manifested flight like this one, we had their names but little else, and in many cases there would be "space-A" pax[5] added that we knew absolutely nothing about. We were required to put our trust in the pax terminal to screen the passengers, as well as brief them on how to act in the helicopter; during hot stops, the volume of the engines' whine prevented the crew chiefs from effectively speaking to anyone without a headset. All passengers rode with body armor, a brain bucket, and earplugs.

Once the pax were secured, we went through the same checks and internal conversation as before and departed on the reverse route home. In this case, the forty-five-minute flight would be mostly uphill, and while we'd use more fuel to get home than it took getting to JBAD, we wouldn't notice a difference in time or speed. We had enough reserve power to maintain 110 knots ground speed in both directions.

Five minutes past the Naghlo Dam, or within ten minutes of Bagram, down in very rough terrain, I spotted a long mule train making slow progress to the west, and after five or six seconds of being fascinated by it, I asked the crew what they thought, and also asked Tommy over internal. True to form, Tommy suggested we "light them up without further ado," and added something about donkey meat for dinner, which was certainly a disturbing thought. It didn't seem like hostile activity, two or three guys walking a dozen mules along a trail, but it also didn't make sense to me. They didn't seem to be between two logical points for foot traffic, and the thought of someone hauling in munitions, RPGs, or some other sort of weapon hidden in plain sight became a concern to me. I decided not to slow down or circle, for a few reasons: We had pax aboard, neither of whom had agreed to any combat action. Chalk two didn't have pax, but splitting up the formation for one ship to go recon a threat wasn't a great idea. Our mission wasn't briefed or approved for that kind of activity, and if they got engaged, we'd have to explain to Heavy D why we decided to shift into an offensive posture without organizing gunship support. Furthermore, this mule train, which was most likely friendly, would lend more intel if we did not ruin the element of surprise. I told Jasper to call it in over SATCOM as an observation, after which the TOC could decide if they wanted to send the OH-58s out for a closer look or coordinate with ground elements to intercept the mule train for an inspection.[6]

In just a few minutes we popped over the final ridgeline on the southeast side of the Bowl, called the tower, and sequenced into the pattern for landing. The pax were able to get out of the helicopter at our own ramp to go wherever it was they needed to go, and Victoria and Ron allowed them to do so before we even completed the shutdown checklist. One of them looked back and gave us a thumbs-up, but like most passengers of the year, I'd never say a word to them. This could be what airline pilots feel like.

That wrapped up mission number 1. We transmitted "ZULU" to the TOC, shut down, and tied down, and the crew chiefs took the guns into the maintenance area for postmission cleaning and oiling. With a workday shorter than five total hours, and less than two hours in the cockpit, I had polished off the box of chocolates and walked home with a sweet aftertaste.

I had a few quiet days then, and the whole base seemed fairly peaceful for Christmas. Deployed Christmas was everything you'd expect: Christmas decorations here and there, some Christmas cards being received, and a lot of people missing their families. Bobby walked around possibly as the most cheerful one, wearing a Santa hat and genuinely conveying holiday spirit. He was another guy like me who didn't have any children at the time, and also was simply in his element to be in a war zone, commanding an assault helicopter company and contributing to morale. Little was done to make the CP more festive looking, but many folks exchanged holiday greetings in the typical manner. Perhaps the most festive place on the airbase was inside the DFAC, where notable effort had been made to add holiday cheer, including holiday music, special tablecloths, green and red stringers, bowls of candy and nuts, and a handful of Styrofoam snowflakes hanging from the ceiling. They could have used some more snowflakes.

The staff of the dining facility also wore Santa hats and seemed to put a great deal of emphasis on maintaining the right energy level for the holidays, since many of its customers' morale would be directly connected to the quality of food for a holiday spent missing loved ones.

I made sure to call my parents.

CHAPTER 7
MEETING IN THE CLOUDS

Day 20. For a flight on New Year's Day, I found myself scheduled with Todd "the Duke" Wolfe, a new pilot in the company, but a talented guy who was also a private pilot and persistently astute. The Duke became fascinated with aviation at the age of eight, after several flights with an uncle in a Bellanca Citabria, at a local airport in Marine City, Michigan, where he had been wedged into the back seat along with a cousin during two-for-one fun sessions. He flew whatever he could get his hands on and built model airplanes until the age of fifteen, when he began formal lessons for his pilot's license. After completing four years at Michigan State University for a bachelor's degree in communications, Todd enlisted in the Army and served one year in the tactical air traffic control field before being accepted to Warrant Officer Candidate School at Ft. Rucker, Alabama. The Duke eventually graduated as the distinguished honor graduate. After graduation he was assigned to the 101st Airborne Division and reported to the "Alpha" Co. "Comancheros" of 4th Battalion, where I met him in 2007, just a year or so before we were sloughed off into the Reapers. I was lucky he made the cut. He was fun to fly with because you didn't have to tell him anything twice. You just about didn't have to tell him anything at all.

The quick-reaction force is fun because it lacks the planning and staging of the more elaborate, formal air assaults our unit was famous for. The shift typically starts with a run-up, and the positioning of gear for "ready launch." That's it. No planning, no rehearsals. It also has a tendency to draw pilots into the fantasy that maybe they won't have to fly that day, and that makes it kind of a relaxed shift. Often, pilots get settled into other activities and start hoping they won't get interrupted from whatever they're doing to pass the time. Sometimes they don't get interrupted, but sometimes they have to snap out of watching a movie or playing a video game and rush out to the aircraft. The worst of this would be nighttime QRF, falling asleep in a chair at two in the morning when the phone rings for something urgent. It could be a rude awakening indeed, leaving the cozy CP to strike out into cold darkness and fire up such a contraption to fly toward danger in the mountains; it required *at least* the pilot in command to develop a mental posture to check for the many loose ends of the machine and crew, to say nothing of mission-specific dynamics. It could be very easy for vigilance to wane in the QRF scenario. The best was when the entire crew maintained battle-ready vigilance, each backing up the other. There would be plenty of flights where an excellent crew chief in the back had it together far more than the person controlling the vehicle, and on certain missions with this sort of person keeping tabs on the entire operation from the back, it could be best for the pilots to just listen and comply. In the combat efficiency discussion, what really matters is whether or not the passengers or cargo reach the appropriate destination on schedule. The person within the vehicle who is orchestrating the flight typically remains anonymous unless it goes wrong. Many times, I enjoyed the great luxury of merely being the engineer aboard a train being conducted smartly by an outstanding crew chief.

On this particular day, the Duke and I experienced the common occurrence of sitting around the table and sharing flying stories, when the phone rang. A passenger down at Orgun-East (locally known as "O-E") needed a ride up to FOB Airborne, and the QRF was tasked. There was no urgency, so we had ten or fifteen minutes to take a look at the route, develop a timeline, and inform the crews.

This would be another relaxed flight, in the daytime with good weather, crossing hundreds of miles of mountains and desert. We topped off our thermoses, got the last-minute weather brief with SWO,[1] and departed to the south.

On a normal flight in the "mike-model" Blackhawk, the pilots can get away with very little hand flying if they want to. With the software version of the time, it was necessary to take off and land by hand, but once the aircraft got above 60 knots the autopilot became active, and the rest of the flight could be accomplished by the simple twisting of small knobs on the dashboard. True to coffee-drinking form, for this flight we dialed the autopilot up to 120 knots (about 140 mph) and set the altitude for 1,000 feet above the ground. Again, well out of range of any shoulder-fired weapon, we engaged the flight plan feature, which would lock the Blackhawk on to a series of GPS waypoints we had created back at the CP. We had the potential of pushing the speed up to around 150 knots (about 175 mph), but this would cause our fuel burn to go through the roof and would also mean we had no power reserve for maneuvering. There was no good reason to go that fast. The mike model was truly a luxurious craft en route, not only with autopilot, but also a vibration-canceling system built into the airframe, comprising a series of "force generators," or weights slung around on different schedules, to cancel the normal vibrations of the machine on all three axes. It was smooth and hands off until landing, and even that could be pulled off if one were willing to manipulate the autopilot to its full extent, though no auto-landing protocol was advertised. Landing the craft by hand was best.

We enjoyed a scenic ride down through the snow-capped mountains, stopping at FOB Goode along the way for hot refuel,[2] and for the crew to get out and use the blue canoes. The rest of the flight to O-E went fine, but on short final, the TOC called to ask if one of our ships was available to escort a medevac aircraft that didn't have a wingman, from Sharona to Ghazni. Over the internal radio, we sort of flipped a coin about who would run the errand and who would get to shut down at Sharona and wait; we had been told the medevac bird would also need an escort back, so there was no need to fly three ships on the medevac run.

The Duke and I won the flip to go and, still on the ground at O-E, transferred our pax over to our sister ship. We proceeded to Sharona with no pax. Once we were within 5 miles of Sharona, we called the medevac aircraft over SATCOM[3] and told them we were in range if they were ready for departure. After establishing an internal FM frequency, they departed, our sister ship broke formation to land, and the Duke and I peeled off to fall in behind Dustoff 32 as they departed from Sharona. This would have appeared from the ground as it did from the air; we became a floating chaperone.

This was an unpredictable situation because we had no idea who we were flying with. Obviously an Army medevac unit, because they all use the same "Dustoff" call sign, but we had no idea which unit they were attached to. We were also flying in formation with someone we hadn't shared a formation briefing with, but that wasn't too concerning because we were the trail aircraft; we wouldn't have to worry about formation separation spacing or angle, landing distance, acceleration/deceleration rates, contingency maneuvers, or anything else, because we could set all of that from the back and be comfortable. Had we been in front with unknown operators behind us, we could only have wondered how closely they were following or how fast they could react if we did any evasive maneuvering. In this case they didn't seem to be worried about any of it, so I didn't bring it up. We just flew west, a random formation, en route to Ghazni.

This forty-minute flight went fine for the first half hour. In the ever-changing venture of flying in mountain weather, it became apparent that our path to FOB Ghazni was going to be obscured by huge cumulus clouds that defied normal behavior by sitting, white and puffy, all the way down on the ground.

Dustoff 32, no more concerned with the weather than they had been with any other details of an urgent medevac flight, maintained their speed and simply began descending toward the ground, apparently being wedged down by the shape of the clouds. The Duke and I decided to begin slowing down, since not only were there no instrument approaches in this neck of the woods, but we were also in a mountain range, where solid rock tends to hide in the clouds. We had a terrain-avoidance graphic in the M model, but I hadn't practiced with it, wasn't about to try, and wouldn't have trusted it if I had. It just wasn't a proven technique for maintaining separation between aluminum and stone.

Just as the Duke was about to squeeze the trigger to transmit to the mystery pilots that we were slowing due to weather, we saw them plunk right into a cloud. I directed the Duke to reverse course to the left, which he immediately began, but in a moment of unexpressed anxiousness, I took the controls to steepen the turn and pushed the nose down enough for the computer-generated attitude indicator to display large arrows pointing up to the sky. The Duke noted this to me and out of reflex more than anything pulled back on the cyclic, though neither of us was worried about it because the cheesy "arrows" graphic shows up and points up if you exceed a mere 30 degrees pitch angle; it was mainly a software feature. Having said that, the maneuver could also have been avoided, and in hindsight, any usage of crew coordination on my part prior to taking the controls had been absent—I could have just talked through what I wanted to happen instead of hastily groping the controls.

We had within seconds turned from the bad weather and dropped a few hundred feet, versus the option of decelerating to a hover to avoid going into the clouds. Either option would have been fine, because this wasn't a high-threat area, nor was the elevation too high to hover. In the middle of reversing course, however, we heard the Dustoff crew make the suggested radio call, with all the numbers in the wrong place. A frantic voice shouted, "THIS IS DUSTOFF 32; WE ARE INADVERTENT I-M-C, HEADING 7,300 FEET, AIRSPEED 2-8-0, CLIMBING TO 95 KNOTS!"

The Duke and I looked at each other and exchanged clenched teeth at the panic in the voice, but while concerned for their success, we also felt relieved we were not roving our way through the same cloud at the same time as they were. Replying, I said, "Dustoff 32, this is Honcho. We have remained VFR (visual flight rules). Over."

After a few moments with the feeling things had gone horribly wrong, we finally heard back from what sounded like a pair of drunken high-school students trying to coax someone to come out surfing: "Hey Honcho, it's Dustoff 32! We broke out, man! We broke out on top at 9,000 feet, and it's all good up here! Come on up! We got a line on Ghazni!"

Right . . . I'm about to climb up through some clouds and try to figure out where you are, and if we don't collide, we can try to get back down as a formation through whatever sucker hole you're looking at.

"Uh, yeah, Dustoff; uuuuuh, that's a negative on us punching in to link up. If you are landing assured Ghazni, we will RTB[4] Sharona."

Expecting some measure of further convincing from Dustoff 32, we were instead entertained by Jan and Dean's carefree reply: "Roger that, Honcho! We're good to go! Thanks for the lift over here, and we'll catch you next time!"

"All right, fellas; good luck."

We would never find out who the mystery pilots were, and never heard from them again.

There's a funny thing with formation discipline. In aircraft, the pilots almost have to be best friends to pull it off, or at least there is a required intimacy—it really comes down to just two humans, each controlling their own aluminum shredding machine with great regard for one another. If one pilot twitches and the two aircraft contact, both get ground up. It's almost never the case that they only get scuffed up, although it has happened: Two different instructors of mine during sixteen months in flight school had survivable helicopter-to-helicopter midair collisions, both of which happened in training. One had been about to be T-boned and pulled up hard on the collective just in time for the other aircraft to shear off the support tubes of his skids in an OH-58. He landed successfully in a ditch, which cradled the fuselage, while the other helicopter was totaled with no fatalities. In the other scenario, a different instructor of mine had been landing a Blackhawk at the airport in Florala, Alabama, as another was taking off; the departing aircraft's tail rotor was carving a notch in between my instructor's feet before he realized it and pulled away. Both aircraft landed safely, with damage. They were all lucky to be alive; usually midair collisions are violent and total.

It has been experimented with from time to time (only by the most audacious of pilots) to fly a tight formation into a cloud and see if the formation can be maintained. It seems as if only the eye is trusted; as soon as visual contact is lost, the notion that your aluminum shredder is about to contact another aluminum shredder becomes stronger than any mathematical equation or conclusion of physics. When you consider at times, from the comfort of your cabin-class seat on an airliner, that when you fly into a cloud you can't even see the wingtip, it would need to be a tight formation indeed for two helicopters to stay in formation in the clouds. Furthermore, since turbulence always doubles inside the cloud, attempting the maneuver is ill advised.

As such, we dared not cohabit the clouds with our medevac brethren.

In a transition contrary to the Aviation Procedures Guide for Afghanistan, we proceeded back to Sharona single ship, explaining our status to the TOC as we flew. We landed at Sharona and shut down for cold fuel on the basis of the other aircraft being shut down already, which would generally mean there was no way to contact them on the radio. With a very patient passenger, we got everyone refueled and fired back up, then proceeded north, up the valley to FOB Airborne, dropped the pax, and continued north past Kabul, finally arriving back in the Bowl, sequenced into the pattern, picked up the taxiway for our ramp, and rolled on home.

The transformation started then; even grabbing the shutdown checklist began a shift in behavior, the gradual but unstoppable venting of responsibility. *Focus for a few more seconds*, I told myself. I didn't want to let go of the vigilance until we got the rotor system stopped. Therein lies the key to me, *professionalism and poise for the complete duration of risk*. As long as the blades were turning, we could be chopping someone's head off. . . . It's happened to at least three Blackhawk crews I have heard of: with pilots casually shutting down, not paying attention to the position of the controls, not looking outside, then someone walks into the blades and gets decapitated; Blackhawk main rotor blades can easily get within 4 feet of the ground at the nose. I heightened my focus for just a few more seconds as we pulled the throttles back, shut the fuel valves, hit the rotor brake, and got the blades stopped. We shut down the auxiliary power unit (an additional, smaller turbine engine) and turned off the batteries, and with the last whiny turbine venting down, it was over. We could carelessly devolve back into booger-eating morons, and nobody would question us. We climbed out of our multimillion-dollar floating lair and onto the ramp, heading toward the dusty plywood hamlet. From the most advanced vehicle on the battlefield, we stepped into an environment of dirt roads and unremarkable shacks.

In the CP, I sat on a cloth-upholstered couch that had been a hand-me-down from previous units working in the same building, and realized it was capable of generating an unlimited number of stale dust clouds. Our QRF shift ended at 6:00 p.m., our replacements showed up, and we swapped our gear with them. After a high-five sort of handoff, the shift was over and I started the walk home, past the Lighthouse coffee shop, a hundred Jersey barriers, a thousand sandbags, and trillions of molecules of dust and carbon monoxide.

CHAPTER 8
ABSENT WITHOUT LEAVING

Day 35. It's essential during deployment to incubate a variety of mini escapes. We were there, trapped in this thing for a year that loosely paralleled a prison term. It wasn't bad, it wasn't suffering, but we were captive, even though we got into it voluntarily. Then again, so did prisoners. It was *a year*, and focusing on that for any length of time could induce some serious cabin fever. Somehow when you're in it, you become inured and don't think about it much, or at least you don't let the thought of it get to you. There is a routine between the plywood walls, the DFAC, the same walk across the gravel courtyard, wearing the same uniform, with the same people being in charge all year, which is at least comparable to being in prison.

While enduring this, I would sometimes check out mentally and imagine the feelings of normal life. It was pretty low level. I wasn't walking around disgruntled or miserable, but certain reminders of other times or places could suddenly dominate the conscious space of thought and seem captivating. Several times a month I tended to have these mental escapes, outside of the normal missions. Flying missions wasn't an escape so much as a totally different dimension. I found that when I was flying, I never made any of these sorts of comparisons. Floating around in the sky was a freedom, and a very grand one in a country as gorgeous as Afghanistan. Each minute of flying was a fascinating adventure that many personnel on the base never enjoyed. On the base, it's painfully apparent one has no choice but to continue to "embrace the suck" for many months. *Maintenance of optimism* requires a dedicated effort.

My own mental maintenance included going back to my room, closing the plywood door, hooking the little door hook, putting on PTs, and watching a movie. Keeping as few reminders of the Army in my room as possible, when the door shut, I could be transported to other places. That was my catharsis. On that particular day in mid-January, I was being transported with great fascination to the Hudson River in New York, as news of Sully Sullenberger making a successful water landing reached us.

Down the hallway, my buddy Chris Randle had offered me some of his stash of contraband bourbon, shipped from home, and I decided to take him up on it. I took my Irish coffee mug down the plywood hallway and knocked on his plywood door. He emerged from his equally low-rent cell and saw why I was there. His stash was poorly hidden because the entire chain of command partook of the same liberties, so inspections simply never happened. With no exchange of words required, he pulled out the biggest bottle of Woodford Reserve I had ever seen, big enough to make my eyebrows go up. I would have expected airline bottles. "I didn't know they made bottles that big!"

"Yup," he said with a smile, and served me a reckless portion.

I said, "Thanks, I owe you one," and slipped back into my cell. I mentally left the Hudson to put *First Blood* back on, climbed into bed, propped myself up on the pillow just right, and unlatched. Warmth began soaking into my veins, and quickly I was absorbed by the movie. Being about 10 percent conscious of reality, I smiled and thought, *This is all right. Commanding the newest helicopters on the battlefield, an easy mission, beautiful terrain, enjoying a cozy mug of bourbon, and listening to Col. Sam Troutman.* As a single guy with no children back home, I had the opportunity to be content.

Brian Dennehy's brilliant portrayal of Sheriff Will Teasle drew me in again, and I began a peculiar ritual of watching *First Blood* almost every day. It was a favorite of my father's and mine, and it seemed like it was always on the TV whenever I went home. We would watch it together and had almost every line memorized.

You got someplace I can eat around here?

There's a diner about 30 miles up the highway.

Is there a law against me getting something here?

Yeah. Me.

My favorite break from anything was being in my room, but there were others. During the making of the many pots of coffee, I always liked closing my eyes and smelling the inside of a fresh bag of coffee. It wasn't just a favorite smell, it was a time machine, or a portal. I had subconsciously programmed myself to go back to Italy, and in that singular moment I could enjoy an entire meal somehow, on the streets of Venice again, outside a small café for breakfast perhaps, enjoying the view of seven-hundred-year-old stonework and the taste of Cinque Terre marmalade on sourdough toast. Such singular moments of escape added up to the maintenance of optimism for me.

What is notable is not the mental escape but the fact that I was doing it, finding ways to daydream. I had it good. A lot of people had it rough, and it was very difficult for them and their families. I can only imagine how they must try to mentally go home to their families every single day, and that foundation of longing or regret being detrimental to the maintenance of mental health. When I imagine a family man who was also an infantry soldier dealing with the real stress of foot patrols or convoys, ambushes, or IEDs while badly missing his family, I know he had a much more challenging psychological riddle to solve. I know between the two of us he's more of a man and has the better stories, the more genuine levels of camaraderie, and greater vulnerability to PTSD. It makes me wish I could send him the marmalade and somehow have it work.

Eventually I was sleepy, turned off the movie, and put on my slippers to go brush my teeth. I saw people outside who were working the opposite shift, but I successfully maintained a barrier from any sort of vigilance kicking in. I was walking back to my room when I saw Chinook pilot Ryan Dechent walking home. Giving him the customary up-nod, he asked if I had heard about the Chinook crash.

"What Chinook crash?" I replied in oblivion. We both stopped walking for a few seconds.

"Yeah, just got shot down in the Pech. From Pale Horse. One person killed."

"Oh, fuck," I said, and waited for a further explanation he couldn't provide.

"Yeah," Ryan said as he continued walking, as if we had just concurred on a thorough review of the thing. The relevant details would float to the surface in the usual way over the next few days, more and more diluted, less and less personal feeling, but the immediate wash of emotion was one based purely on human compassion. There was no concern for victory or defeat, just a sense that they were part of our family, wearing the same uniform, and flying the same mission to the same places.

Despite the news of that particular evening, getting to talk with Ryan Dechent was always interesting. He was the senior pilot in his company, and one of the few guys who had impeccable professional demeanor while still being able to maintain that glint in his eyes that suggested he was ready for a fight. He was balanced, though, which for people in his position wasn't always the case; frequently caught laughing or having a smile on his face, he knew how to be disarming in conversation, even though he was an authority. He grew up in Elmira, Oregon, with an impressive lineage of military aviators from World War II forward, on both sides of his family. He had been instilled with a love of flying from a young age, and had his private pilot's license before graduating high school. He enjoyed the full spectrum of outdoor activity and was an Eagle Scout before going to college, where he earned a degree in flight technology. On one occasion while working at the airport in Eugene, Oregon, Ryan met a Lane County Sheriff's Department OH-6 pilot who was a Vietnam vet, who suggested a path Ryan decided to follow: becoming a warrant officer in the United States Army.

There was something different about Ryan, though. It might have been the lineage. I was the first and only person in my family to serve in the military, and I feel like I stumbled through my whole career, incidentally accumulating various qualifications and degrees of status. It's almost like my military career was happenstance, and if it didn't work out, I wouldn't care much, I could always go back to welding or machine work. In contrast, Ryan Dechent had significant military role models: one of his grandfathers was a B-24 "Liberator" bomber commander for a pair of tours in the Pacific theater during World War II and stayed in long enough to fly a C-119 "Boxcar" in Korea. His other grandfather served in the Navy. He had a granduncle who was a B-17 "Flying Fortress" captain in World War II who stayed in long enough to fly in Korea *and* Vietnam, and his father was involved with military aviation as a C-130 "Hercules" maintenance officer. His father also created perhaps the most tangible aviation reference in Ryan's life by flying as a private pilot. You could almost sense that tradition in Ryan. He was ahead of me in his career and in his duties, but essentially we were two pilots flying the same mission with different aircraft and enjoyed an easy rapport. Still, talking with Ryan had the potential of making me feel a little bit like a rottweiler talking to a border collie. Not from anything he said or did, but from the simple dynamic that my presence in Afghanistan was far less deliberate: Afghanistan was where the Army threw my stick, and I went yapping right after it. Ryan had been more thoughtful, and his career decisions more intentional. I appreciated that.

Back in my quarters, I relaxed into muted privacy and went to bed, letting my skull sink into the cool pillow. I sent the crash conversation to the folder of my mind marked *futility*, and fell asleep.

CHAPTER 9
SMOKELESS POWDER

Day 40. After a somewhat fitful night's sleep I woke up, sometime in the middle of the day, to virtual silence. My room was dark, except for the one sliver of light that sliced in through the plywood window shutter. Peace and calm, cozy warmth, and almost total silence. I lay happily in my custom cocoon, pondering what to do with the few hours I had off before my next shift. At least one of those hours would be in the gym, and probably a half hour in the DFAC and another half hour in the routine of showering and suiting up for the day. I decided to throw on my PTs and my stupid bright-yellow reflective belt and go to the local market. PTs were the only authorized casual uniform. The only way to wear actual civilian clothes would be inside the confines of my tiny room, or on R&R.

Incidentally, "local" meant *on* base. There was a time in the Iraq and Afghanistan wars when the troops could mingle outside the wire with the local population, but that time had come and gone. Security concerns and suicide bombers had ended it. I understood that when it used to be allowed, mingling and dining with the Afghans was a wonderful, wholesome experience. That time was no more, though. We were inside the wire to stay, and the only way out for me was on a helicopter.

Either way, I wouldn't be walking off the base. I went to the bazaar, which comprised several small local businesses, some of which may have been indigenous to Afghanistan, but many of which likely gravitated toward military bases all over the Eastern Hemisphere. A lot of the vendors were Indian, and there were a lot of imported items: many from Asia and, ironically, even some from America. There was a rug shop, a suit shop, plenty of jewelry shops, and my favorite, some junk shops. Even Burger King and Pizza Hut had been brought to the base, in little trailers with big American posters, and tasted *almost* like fast food from home. Good enough to keep everyone reminded.

In the junk store, hundreds of items were woven into the fabric of the place, ranging from junk brought from outside Afghanistan to local handmade items, jewelry, jewelry boxes, baskets, knives, smoking accessories, stylish clothing accessories, even rudimentary tools. The smell in the junk store was exotic: different oils and scents from all over the world, the smells of different animal products like stale old leather, various critters' hides, Middle Eastern perfumes, and even actual snake oil. It was a good smell if you didn't live in it every day, one that triggered scenes from *Indiana Jones*; my eyes washed over pans full of fake gems with a snake charmer's gourd flute creeping into my mind. Was there a cobra uncoiling from a basket somewhere in the store?

I found a collection of metallic turtles made of sterling silver, each with various colorful gems soldered onto their shells. I liked these but continued my slow scan of the store. There was an expensive-looking scope in light green with Russian lettering, probably the sight from an artillery piece, quite intriguing. I imagined the item sitting at home on my coffee table as a conversation piece. Then again, for $200 I wouldn't be able to have much of a conversation about it, except to say that I found it in Afghanistan *on the battlefield*—a bit of a stretch.

Then my eye was caught by a collection of long guns leaning in a corner. *Whoa, rifles for sale?* I wondered if they were in serviceable condition. It was maybe twelve or thirteen guns, various old models, some with slings, some with bayonets, some with magazines, some without. Four of them were similar, and for some reason those four looked the best to me. I picked one up, and right away I thought it seemed heavy, which in my mind equaled authenticity. Bolt action, nicely made pieces, greasy wood. *What was this thing?* I didn't know, but I felt a protected attraction to it. I didn't want to buy anything on a whim, but I decided to go back to my room and research this little treasure without telling anyone else about it. I left the bazaar and the tiny shop of aromas with childish intrigue.

Deciding to ponder the weapon over dinner, I went to the DFAC. The lines were never too bad because the dinner service was three hours long. The ritual was to stand in line, listen to deployed-type conversations, and scan your ID card. The conversations in line were sometimes related to a recent operation, how the convoy had gone, who was acting like a dumbass, or complaints about someone's decisions. But it was never about a gunfight or anything entertaining. You want to hear someone say, "Oh man, they opened fire on us, so I pulled the pins on all my grenades and chucked 'em to the left and right and then ran screaming right down the middle and killed three of them with my M9!" But you never heard that; it was always something more mundane. "Did you see they replaced some of the wooden slats in the third shower stall? That's the one I'm usin' from now on." Or "Are you going to be on *World of Warcraft* tonight?"

Two or three times a day I would wait in this line, all year. Listening to the same shit, looking at the same cracks in the sidewalk, flinching at the same little screech the door made every time someone opened it. After a while I figured out how to get there late so there was no line, but I certainly spent enough time in the line to know it as part of the routine.

Just inside, I noticed the woman scanning the ID cards look at me twice out of the corner of her eye, the second time with a discernible smile. There was something different about the DFAC though: behind her, in the typical line of glossy eight-by-ten photos that represent the chain of command, I noticed that the picture of President George W. Bush had been replaced with a new picture of President Barack Obama. Other than that, not much had changed. As I got up to the little scanner, I held my ID card under the red beams until I got the little beep. Eye to eye, she smiled again and looked away shyly. The name tag on her uniform said THATCHER; I smiled back and moved on down the line . . . surf and turf night apparently. The meals congeal into one after a while; same trays, same routine, same dull atmosphere, same napkin dispenser, same chairs rumbling in and out, same trash can by the door. Imagine eating at the same restaurant three times a day for a year . . . The folks who ran the DFAC knew this, however, and tried hard to change it up once in a while. A careless person could easily fall prey to the comforts the DFAC had to offer.

There seemed to be two sorts of people within the military ranks: those who used the deployed opportunity away from the various distracters of life to get in shape, eat and sleep healthfully, exercise regularly, and come home looking like a million bucks, and those who seemed to go the opposite direction. Units typically do not conduct organized physical training while deployed, at least aviation units don't, so folks are welcome to shrink or expand to their hearts content. Without that in mind, I enjoyed a small scoop of cookies and cream, then departed past the same napkin dispenser, same chair rumbling back, same trash can. I went home and jotted down a simple note to leave on my computer, RESEARCH GUN. It had to wait as I left for my shift.

CHAPTER 10
GRIFFIN'S REACTIVE ARMOR

Day 41. Out of time somehow, I showered and got changed for my shift. As soon as I walked into the CP, platoon leader Ronnie Allen informed me the QRF would be picking up a convoy security flight, on the basis of the Apaches having some overwhelming maintenance issues.

"OK, when do we go?" I asked.

"About 2200."

"Then they'll be picking it back up?"

"Depends on how they do with their broke shit," he replied. *Right*. That pretty much meant we'd have it all night.

Convoy security could be fun, basically flying around a convoy, down low with some guns sticking out the back, hoping to scare anyone trying to fuck with the convoy. We'd fly up and down a road, as low to the ground as we wanted, as fast as we wanted, with rollercoaster turns at each end. That's fun for a few minutes, because of how sweetly the Blackhawk is engineered; with a slow-moving convoy, though, it could get tedious quick. But that was our job, and the fellas in the convoy appreciated it because any amount of extra team on hand was comforting, and any amount of extra security was welcome.

The first part of the shift went slow until we launched, only a brief discussion of the recent Chinook crash punctuating the time. Apparently on a typical resupply mission, the huge craft had been hit in one of the fuel tanks with an RPG,[1] became engulfed in flames, and made a hasty landing onto the top of a stump, which caused it to roll over. One person had been killed during the crash, which happened in the Pech River valley. The Pech mission kept getting mentioned. I hadn't flown it yet, but it was quite the hotspot.

Pondering helicopter crashes is something we all did over there. The conversation was unavoidable when it happened multiple times in the same geographical area we serviced. I knew I wasn't the only one with absent friends; a good buddy of mine from flight school named Kyle Jackson had been killed when we were in Iraq and his helicopter got shot down, and it seemed surreal. There is the immediate frustration that comes with losing someone, but somehow there is also the impervious feeling *it won't happen to me*. I don't know how to explain it, other than to say it didn't make me fly any differently on my next flight. I do think that after enough exposure to the various dangers, we slowly learn to avoid certain things, certain flight profiles, and certain combinations, but there is also a component of luck involved. Kyle probably felt lucky too.

Capt. Allen ended up being my stick buddy for the night. We were chalk two behind Peter Griffin and Sammy Park. We all launched and flew an uneventful flight of about forty-five minutes to reach the convoy, just as the last of their other air support was leaving station south of Ghazni. They had been covered until then by the 58s, who could no longer cover them, so we took over, doubting the eventual attendance of any Apaches. A battle captain at one of the TOCs had been orchestrating this concert, as well as coordinating assets TOC to TOC for us to weave in. No matter to me; the QRF did as it was told. My only hope was that they wouldn't leave us out there all night.

We started in. Griffin and Park took one side of the road and we took the other, up and down, back and forth. It was like watching a parade to look down at the troops, the HMMWVs, the LMTVs, and the HEMMTs[2] all creeping along, with dismounted troops out front looking for IEDs. I imagined what it would be like to be one of those troops, how it would be arduous, how my knees and feet hurt just looking at them trudging along with all that gear, in heavy boots, on a gravel road, carrying a rifle. I was thankful to be floating aloft in my spaceship, but I still found room in my mind to be miserable somehow. I mean, it was cool what we were doing, and there were probably guys down there wishing they were up where we were, but it was still monotonous work. We were responsible for the parameters and safety of flying, and sitting there with these miserable night vision goggles connected to our helmets. That's extra weight, front and back, and extra eyestrain for hours on end, sitting in a seat that historically gave pilots a lifetime of post-career neck and back trouble. Sometimes I think about how distracted we got. At times we flew a four-or-five-hour mission and it just flew by, because we stayed so busy and had so many things to keep track of. Then other times, on less captivating missions, it couldn't seem to get over fast enough. Just imagine driving somewhere in a car and not getting out of the seat for six or seven hours, the paralysis that goes along with it, and the monotony. It's that same feeling, but at a much more exhausting stress level.

In the helicopter, there was always a lot to be monitored: where we were, how much fuel we had, where the customers were, would we get there on time, was there threat, was there dust, power management, maintenance issues, crew issues, making the required radio calls, etc. etc. Don't forget safely handling the aircraft, over the same duration of that long, boring car ride. As a result, the physical toll was greater, because mental stress accumulates physically. Not to mention the fact that we strapped on 25 extra pounds of crap just to be sitting there, with body armor, survival vest, survival radio, M9 pistol,[3] and a bunch of extra bullets. The obnoxious NVGs clamped onto our heads (about the weight of a Campbell's soup can duct-taped to your eyebrows) were thoughtfully counterbalanced with weights Velcro'd to the back of the helmet, something like having your kid sister trying to do a pull-up on your mullet. No big deal, really; we did it every night. Sometimes I looked down at that guy walking, and I wished I could just walk with him, even though he was wearing all the same shit and then some. I could tell that I would survive being in the infantry, and that I'd find a way to love and dread just as much of it. I wondered if he at least had good coffee. I asked Ronnie to take the controls, then reached down into the door pocket for my thermos. A friend had sent me the perfect little copper thermos, which remarkably kept its contents hot for eight hours.

The life of an assault pilot has a degree of excitement but is mostly many romantic hours of sitting in the dark, feeling for switches and knobs, making unconscious minor adjustments to various things, accounting system parameters, and discounting most of them again, perpetually. The Blackhawk is so well made, it feels like an extension of the body, responding with Olympic agility to even the slightest of control inputs. It is a wonderfully designed machine. It was good on the drawing board when it was conceived, forty years ago, and has only been proven and made better in every version since. Every switch and knob is thoughtful of the pilot, and a pilot who lives in the cockpit gets acquainted with it intimately. Mostly, it's pilots like me, melded into their machine, comfortable as one, minds free to wander. You can tell who the great ones are in casual conversation; you can tell by their posture, by how few questions they ask, and by how few accessories they mount to their rifles. You can tell by how many playful insults they absorb with a smile on their face without trying to parry. You can sense the comfort level.

Unfortunately, the opposite exists as well; people who sit there nervously, clumsily groping for things, adjusting things to worse settings than they already were, needing to turn on a flashlight for everything, displaying a level of ignorance bordering on negligent, trying desperately for punch lines worn out weeks earlier, and oblivious to the operational efficiency they pollute. Compensating for this sort of person made me wonder how the system allowed them into the cockpit at all. It was like Disney took a french fry from under someone's car seat and found a way to animate it into a grotesque facsimile of an early primate. This greasy, potato-based gorilla brings a machine gun with so many flashlights, laser sights, pistol grips, and extra magazines attached to it you would guess they were expecting to fight in a zombie apocalypse instead of demonstrating the finesse required to navigate a craft through space, but perhaps you'd be wrong; their side of the cockpit seems like a fight after all. Fortunately, they were not the majority.

In the privacy of darkness, I reached down to the door pocket, pulled up my thermos, and unscrewed the top. I held the little cup up to the light of the displays in front of me, and by a simple glance below the night vision goggles (which are suspended about an inch in front of the eyes), I could see the silhouette of the cup and thermos, backlit by a moving map of Afghanistan. I poured a perfectly brewed cup, and my eyes went back out front, looking through the goggles again, everything green. My hands worked automatically in the dark, the thermos going back down to the door pocket, the cup coming up for a sip. It's the romantic moment—I pulled the microphone boom out of my way, pondering the perfect flavor for a few moments, in my own little world. The thermos flew on every mission, and the coffee was always brewed in a manner considerate for its important role. It could be a commercial: *Folgers . . . Liquid tactical enlightenment for your toughest missions.* It was Starbucks, but whatever.

We floated along, I sipped the coffee and scanned the instruments a little, but mostly I couldn't help thinking this mission had reached the boring point. The convoy was just crawling through an area of no threat, nothing suspicious, just slow, plodding progress. *Damn.* We would most likely be there through shift change.

The morning ticked on and we went for refuel twice, which, including the tank of gas we started with, meant six hours of continuous convoy security. In theater, the goggle limit is six hours. This prompted a discussion over the internal radio between me and Griffin, who was notoriously inconsiderate of anyone else's thoughts. True to form, Griffin wanted to remain on station as long as possible, not only despite the regulation, but despite the fact that both crews were exhausted. We still had an hour to fly home. A brief discussion ensued about how important it was to the troops for us to provide top cover and *blah, blah, blah.* If it was so important, the TOC would have sent a replacement before we expired. In fact, they had no intention of replacing us, and neither did the Apaches or the 58s. The convoy simply wasn't in enough threat to justify an overwatch element. It's also a mathematical certainty that some portion of the troops would have enjoyed a quieter walk over one with screaming turbine engines keeping their anxiety amped up.

Peter Griffin was an unremarkable pilot who thought highly of his tactical poise, though no one concurred with him. His sense of aviation wasn't founded on a love for the art of flying so much as an addendum to his ego. He began his Army career on the ground, fourteen years and 40 pounds earlier as a ranger, and carried a lot of unfulfilled tactical want in the cockpit with him. One example was a few years earlier, to the amusement of most of the pilots in the company, in Kuwait: We had staged in Kuwait for our deployment into Iraq in '05, and during the two-week acclimatization, in between mouthfuls of Oreo cookies, Griffin pondered what his response would be if he was ever to be shot down or get in a gunfight with his heavily accessorized M-4 rifle. In Griffin's Styrofoam psyche, the thing that pleased him most seemed to be his dream of getting pinned down in a huge firefight. The longer this scenario played out in his mind, the more and more bullets he was going to need. It didn't take much romanticizing before he recommended to the company commander that each pilot be required to wear a special bandolier of eight additional M-4 magazines on their chest, in addition to the required two in the vest! This seemed ludicrous to everyone, but somehow Griffin had found a military paraphernalia supplier that shipped to an APO address and was already wearing the ridiculous thing! It was about the size of two bricks and appeared to make everything else on his vest uncomfortable. Within minutes someone dubbed it "Griffin's Reactive Armor," and he pushed the command to make wearing the ridiculous ensemble a universal requirement. Fortunately, it never caught on. Eventually, even Griffin found the 130-degree Iraqi summer too hot to sport this dream accessory and just lugged it around with his gear, leaving it on the cockpit floor if he flew.

With everyone on this morning's flight yawning through mistakes, I eventually told Griffin we were leaving, on the basis of the risk of one of us having an incident due to fatigue becoming higher and higher by the minute. If he wanted to stay in a formation at all, he would be following us home. Of course, the ex-Ranger in him wanted to stay with the ground pounders, trying to live his paunchy life vicariously through their mission. I wasn't pleased, and neither was anyone else on the flight, but that was the perpetual risk of working with Peter Griffin.

We parted company with the convoy then, flew north into the morning, took the goggles off en route at sunrise, past Ghazni again, past Airborne (a small FOB in the pass), and sleepily descended back into the Bowl. Nine hours. Back on the ground, Griffin had a look like he wanted to talk to me, which I answered with a *talk to the hand* gesture and kept walking. To the DFAC then, door screech, Thatcher smirk, french toast, chair rumble, trash can, sandbags, gravel, plywood quarters, shower, and crash.

CHAPTER 11

WE ARE BUDWEISER

Day 42. We learned in flight school about circadian rhythm and its importance. It was a weird shift to Afghanistan in the first place, at 10½ time zones from where we departed in Ft. Campbell, but to shift over to the night quick-reaction force was another transition to living on the wrong side of light. The body objects noticeably for three or four difficult days, and there is a longing for diurnal normalcy, even after a few weeks of stability on the night shift. Most of us went to bed right after breakfast, around 7:00 a.m. Arabian Standard Time +30. Seven or eight hours later would be 2:00 or 3:00 in the afternoon, leaving three or four hours to burn before the shift started again at 6:00 p.m., or 1800 military time. But it's a brutal twelve-hour shift, 6:00 p.m. to 6:00 a.m., and the body knows it's wrong. If we did launch, the elevated responsibility of flying and the cold night air could help with maintaining a higher level of consciousness. If the QRF did *not* launch, by the final third of the graveyard shift our bodies craved sleep, even after a few weeks of being "reversed out."

Some would nap a little, uncomfortable in some sticky chair, and wake up greasy, achy, and waffle faced, while others would fight sleep with perpetual Rip-its[1] or Red Bulls. Very few of us found real production at that time of day, but we were supposedly ready to leap out into the night if something happened. Lots of times it didn't, but when it did we were thankful to have the shift go by. Either way, our bodies did not wake well in the dark of night or sleep well in the light of day.

I started on my shift the next evening, having been further thrown off my circadian rhythm by Griffin's quest for action the previous night, which in reality was just hours and hours of pointless circling. After a while you end up hoping something *will* happen, and you run scenarios to pass the time. By the time you run any given scenario in your head five or six times, your own actions become so smooth and remarkable that you start figuring there could be movies made capturing your tactical brilliance. But then you come out of the dream and there's nothing happening, the engine oil temperature is still "in the green," there is still enough gas in the tank, rotor rpm is still at 100 percent, and the steady hum of the main rotor against a faint backdrop of high-frequency white noise in the intercom system hypnotizes your mind back into the trance again.

After having gone to bed late, I woke up on time, with deep fatigue saturating my skin. No amount of hot shower on the slimy slats would wash it off, and no coffee would be strong enough to amplify my diminished humanness. *Ugh.* Nothing is right when you're tired to the bone. You don't think as well, you can't be efficient or productive, and your muscles are weak. You can go through the motions, but for a pilot these decisions can be dangerous. I slugged through the motions of my spare time, moping to the gym, doing less, moping to the shower, lingering longer under the hot water, moping to the DFAC, eating junkier food. By the time I scuffed my way to the CP for work, all I could do was hope for a quiet night.

In the CP, Todd "The Duke" Wolfe was making preparations for his pilot-in-command check ride with Griffin, who looked just as tired as I did from the previous night. While Griffin and I still found no energy to review the previous night's events, the Duke seemed confident and relaxed, and I was pretty sure even Griffin would sign him off. The Duke had a good bit of previous flying experience, as well as a pilot's license on the civilian side, to include a floatplane rating. Usually, the real aviation enthusiasts in a company land the pilot-in-command slots the fastest, having spent years building model airplanes, reading magazines, and flying whatever they could get their hands on. It would be great to have another pilot-in-command in the company, and I figured that was exactly what Griffin had in mind, even as he seemed to be absorbing the CP atmosphere from a chair in the corner, one Oreo cookie after another sieving its way through the light-brown baleen plates of his pie hole.

For a while our quiet evening was going great, and I had started to research the secret stash of old rifles at the junk store, but just before mid-rats[2] the phone rang and it was the TOC. We had a mission to run down to Ghazni, Goode, and FOB Shank, to pick up R&R pax for tomorrow night's fixed-wing flight out of Bagram. Why they couldn't jump on a ring-route the next day frustrated me, but someone at least one level above my own TOC decided this one, so there would be no point in arguing.

That night I was battle-rostered with Jake Cassadonte, a great pilot who had a lot of time in the unit and was classically even keeled. We got the weather and threat updates, grabbed whatever found-around grub we could find, rounded up the crew chiefs, mounted up the guns, saddled up, and launched. It was a sleeper mission, and I was sleepy. Unfortunately, there was just no way to responsibly take a nap as the pilot in command. I could have been asleep by that point if we hadn't launched, but we had. We were flying a warship 141 times the value of my annual salary, plus four crew members, through the mountains, at night, with artificial night vision clamped onto our heads. I had to tap into the rote vigilance embedded in my persona during years of standing watch on a submarine: DEMONSTRATE DISCIPLINE BASED ON PRESENTED REQUIREMENTS. No problem.

From the time I entered boot camp at seventeen years old, until I left the Navy in 2000, I had absorbed, robotically executed, and responded well to the brainwashing the Navy ran on, which suggested a level of discipline and obedience only an introverted country kid would comply with. Within days of being assigned to my first boat, I had been told I would go topside in the middle of the night, and in the middle of winter, in an exposure suit, and stand watch with a 12-gauge shotgun for six hours, in Korean War–era boots, standing on a steel hull. I said OK with no further thought or complaint. This wasn't hazing; putting a gun on the youngest crew member and having them guard the ship, alone, through a winter night, was the standard operating procedure. Years of situations like that truly harden an individual. Discussions of comfort or convenience scarcely enter the mind. That's your duty. Embrace the suck.

That programming was in my character, but I fought with my exhausted physical component.

Flying across Afghanistan was generally quiet and peaceful. In the daytime, the Hindu Kush Mountains were grand and majestic, the sky was huge, and in certain areas the terrain adjacent to the rivers was terraced, lush, and spectacular in shades of green. It looked almost Irish, a stripe down the middle of so much light-brown desert, and it was beautiful. At night it was harder to get that sense of things; I could still see the silhouettes of the mountains, but they were fuzzy and dark green. Looking straight down, I could see the houses and yards clearly. Almost every house had a high wall of mud block built around it for the summer winds. During the so-called *120 days of wind*, the wind at ground level sustained 10 to 20 mph on some days, and on the ground, in the dusty areas, it could feel like walking through some hot form of sleet. Most of the stops we made had high walls or Hesco barriers around them, and the helicopter-landing areas were covered with gravel, pavement, or "Elephant Snot," an Army technique sort of like varnishing dirt. I had no idea what was in the stuff, but I'm sure it was just as environmentally considerate as everything else we did.

Within the tall mud fences of an Afghan home, typically there was a garden, a clothesline, maybe a vehicle, and sometimes vegetables curing on the roof. In the case of hot summer nights, sometimes people slept on the roof. That was common in Iraq as well, but Iraq had a much-lower elevation and was quite a bit warmer.

The country houses were typically conservative, almost always squares or rectangles, but in some cases featuring a nice courtyard or a pair of opposed dwellings. The limited number of black highways in the country led me to believe these places must be very quiet most of the time, something that had appeal to me. I could sense that being an Afghan wasn't the misery Western media tended to highlight. It seemed obvious that there were wonderful people living a pure and respectable life out in the country.

With each house we flew over, the only things available with which to imagine their lives was the appearance of their yard and how quiet our flight was. Another tall mud fence, another square house, another sip of coffee, mind wandering. Jake was quiet as a clam, sitting over there in the darkness, oil temp in the green, 100 percent rotor, another fence, another cube. . . . Only a third of the way to Ghazni so far. *Damn*. I was going to get out of the helicopter at Ghazni and do some jumping jacks or something.

Quietly we droned on, eventually made our stops, refueled, and headed north again, a long and tranquil flight. Floating down into the Bagram Bowl, I was thankful I had stayed awake somehow, the flight was quiet, we could shut down, and I could take an uncomfortable, drooling nap in one of the greasy vinyl chairs. As we came dragging in from the ramp, one of the TOC personnel came out before we were 50 feet from the helicopter and said they were going to need us to launch again for a last-minute Pech resupply. The Chinooks had already left, and after hot refuel, we were to depart for the mission. *Immediately*.

Good Lord. Nothing was further from a nap. Rote discipline or not, I lived in a human body suffering from acute fatigue. The Pech was the helicopter shoot-down capital of the world. In a narrow valley with high terrain and high threat, a helicopter maneuvering slowly in the low ground would be extremely vulnerable. It was historically volatile due to its proximity to the Pakistan border, and the worse it got, the more troops we sent to stabilize it. The more troops, the more resupply missions. What choice did we have? None, really. Soldier up. Our mission wasn't the actual resupply anyway; the Chinooks would handle the moving of troops and supplies, make the approaches, and conduct the ground coordination. Our portion of this mission was to fly a pair of Blackhawks in a high orbit with ten Pathfinders in the back of each, ready to deploy if we had an evolving situation or helicopter crash.[3] We would then fly into the same threat that brought an aircraft down, land, insert the Pathfinders for crash site security, and depart again, waiting for the EXFIL[4] call. In assault terms, actually, it was an easy mission. We'd flown this mission before, though it had never played out beyond the point of spending hours in the high ROZ.[5]

A quick pit stop, then I topped off my copper thermos at the Lighthouse, grabbed a few Powerbars for dinner, and told Jake and the gunners to spool it back up. A chorus of groans carried us back into our seats. We fired up the huge General Electric turbines again and sat waiting for the Pathfinders to come out, as our new composite rotor blades spun back up.

For the pilots, any pax in the back can be a mysterious thing. Very often on the milk runs and ring routes, stop by stop, the pax come and go without the pilots ever making eye contact. Sometimes they were just an anonymous name on the manifest, and sometimes they were not even manifested, just space-A pax. We didn't necessarily even know the members of our own battalion all that well, if that's who just got into the back, but in a unit with 760 people it's impossible to know everyone.

Eventually, this band of death dealers came walking out, from where I don't know, dressed to kill (literally), rifles in hand, and mysteriously climbed into the back without a briefing, without code words, and without any expectations of the crew, beyond the fact that if we dropped them off somewhere it meant their ass. The Pathfinders were not up on ICS[6] with us, they had no intel, and because we always did this mission at night, they would most likely sit in the back asleep for three hours. If we got the call, the crew chief would shout something like "We're going in!" or "Rise and shine, motherfuckers!" And without further ado, they would goggle up, feel the aircraft land, open the door, get out, and respond to . . . *something*. What a fucked-up mission.

After repositioning to hot refuel, I transmitted REDCON ONE to our sister ship, and off we went. Going to the Pech directly would be around forty-five minutes, but we diverted somewhat due to terrain, staying just north of Jalalabad, and went up the Kunar River valley to head north. This would make the trip to the mouth of the Pech around an hour and ten minutes, to say nothing of station time in the ROZ and the return trip. We were facing at least four more hours. Additionally, the flight to JBAD[7] was mostly over barren desert, which in my fatigued condition presented a challenge.

As soon as we were away from the bright lights of the Bowl, I began struggling with my eyelids. I knew it was happening, and I was on the controls, but I didn't say anything to Jake. It seemed logical to me at the time that if I fell just three-quarters of the way asleep I would still be one-quarter awake while simultaneously taking three-quarters of a nap. After all, we were out in the middle of nowhere. Now, this isn't as bad as it might seem. The new Blackhawks had a pretty good autopilot, which I was using. That means it was accurately flying a predetermined route. I was also flying the lead ship in the formation, which meant there was no danger of crashing into the guy in front of me. While the Blackhawk had an autopilot, it would latch on to only one altitude. That meant if I was trying to stay 1,000 feet above ground over mountainous terrain, it couldn't do it. I did select "altitude capture," which meant I could let go of the controls and make altitude adjustments with a small switch on the side of the collective. Astutely using my remaining quarter consciousness to control altitude, I eased into a three-quarter nap, which almost immediately got away from me.

As we approached the lights of JBAD, or the suburbs of JBAD, I was in and out. I don't think Jake noticed, but every time I would wake up with a start, looking through those God-forsaken goggles, it took my eyes too long to focus, and a diagonal array of lights on the ground looked like the attitude indicator in a heads-up display, which I wasn't wearing. HUD is a debatable device for helicopter pilots in the first place, and even though I stopped using HUD a few years previous, I had used it enough to respond immediately to the bright-green symbology. One of the problems with HUD is that the symbols go through the same amplification and phosphor screen as everything else the eye sees, so the HUD symbology is the same color as lights on the ground, stars in the sky, bright-white snow, or moonlight reflecting off a body of water: Green. All green. I wasn't *wearing* a HUD, but my sleepy mind remembered, and those four or five lights in a row on the ground looked just like a HUD artificial horizon, which, in my shocked slumber, told me we were rolling to the right. After a minor freak-out moment, either some amount of discipline kicked in, or I hesitated to fix the problem until I could sort it out. Eventually, the adrenaline rush forced my eyes to check the actual aircraft instruments, which were perfectly steady. *Damn, must have dosed off. I should really tell Jake to take the controls.* The problem was that an adrenaline rush doesn't last that long, and afterward exhaustion is magnified. I dozed off again within minutes, waking up again to the same illusion. The only thing that fixed the illusion was falling asleep again. Through all of this, I was the pilot on the controls, but if I knew Jake as well as I think I did, he *knew* I was falling asleep and was amused by it. There was only a small chance that he was also asleep, which simply meant we were down to only two layers of redundancy, the crew chiefs in the back. With that many layers of redundancy, I think we stood a good chance of completing the mission without incident. A sobering radio call helped me regain full awareness: we had arrived at the entrance to the Pech River valley.

That particular junction of the Pech River and Kunar River valleys established the position of Asadabad, as well as a small coalition base. Pech resupply missions would frequently refuel there at the two pads for hot refuel. ABAD also had one of the few JLENS[8] balloons in the country, a large, tethered blimp that was an expensive component of another Army defense system. It was cool to see the blimps, but the tether could be hazardous to a helicopter, or you might say a helicopter could be hazardous to the tether—a few of the JLENS balloons had been set free by unsuspecting helicopter pilots, only to be hunted and shot down by the Air Force to recover the special-equipment suite, much of which naturally would get destroyed upon impact. Flying near ABAD at night required special vigilance not to cut the tether; I really needed to wake up.

All right, snap out of it. It was one of those moments where I had to turn on everything I had, be on my A game, and stay focused on the scenario. I was right in the middle of doing a back stretch to wake up when I heard another call over the radio: "GUN 1, this is BIGTIME 56; we are BUDWEISER."

I recognized the voice of Chinook pilot Ryan Dechent talking to the Apache pilots on the radio and thought, *You have got to be kidding me.* "Budweiser" is the assault-lingo code word that means the final load had been picked up from the PZ.[9] The mission was over.

I had a mini conniption fit that brought me as close to being awake as I had been in two days, and verified this outrage in plain language over the radio.

"Ryan, are you serious? You guys are done?"

The straight-talkin' heavy-cargo hauler replied with no inquiry as to whom he was speaking with: "Yup."

"Dammit, the fuckin' TOC sent us out here for last-minute Pathfinder support. We just got here!"

Dechent deadpanned back that we were welcome to stay if we wanted, but they were heading home.

We immediately turned back to begin the hour-long flight it would take to get home, being silently disgusted with a thoughtless battle captain who didn't have enough mental connectivity to verify the status of one mission before dispatching another. We flew back with an unusual combination of annoyance and relief. It's a good mission when you're well rested, but I wasn't. By the time we crested the rim of the Bagram Bowl, I was exhausted and thankful to see the brilliant stadium lighting surrounding the airfield. I finally told Jake how tired I was, and to pay attention until we got the blades stopped.

After two days of air assets being mismanaged, I finally went into the operations center to find the ops officer himself, the very reserved Major Malmgren. Giving him a truncated explanation of events over the course of the last two days, with tense-enough language that he shifted his physical stance as if he was waiting for the whistle in a jujitsu match, I made the point that I would have appreciated more thoughtfulness on the part of his battle captains. With expressive eyebrows, he seemed surprised to be hearing from me at all and acknowledged with only a series of slight nods, and the nasal tension that comes with trying to smell something without actually inhaling. I realized he simply wasn't going to put up a fight, and it became apparent the speaking portion of this confrontation was over. I returned a gesture that was part smirk and part snort and shook my head during a long wink to let him know his operations center had just about killed me. Twisting his mouth over to one side with sympathetic eyes to acknowledge, he went back to whatever he was doing, having never said a fuckin' word.

CHAPTER 12
FAINTLY SCREAMING

Day 65. I woke up on Valentine's Day after a mummifying eleven hours of sleep, feeling like I had clamped my face in a waffle maker. I was rested. My room was remarkably quiet, in the middle of the day, on the busiest airbase in the country. A quick trip to the blue canoe brought me face to face with the latest in trending Chuck Norris banners: "CHUCK NORRIS DOESN'T DO PUSH-UPS. HE DOES EARTH-DOWNS." This, like all thoughtful inscriptions of the war, brought a smile to my face.

On the way back to my room I happened past a glum-looking Todd Wolfe sitting outside on a homemade plywood bench, and twisting my head like a curious dog, asked, "Sup?"

"Hey," he flatly responded.

He didn't seem much like holding up half of a conversation, so I pried, "How'd your ride go last night?"

"Like crap, apparently."

"Oh no," I said, trying to interlace just the right undertone of laughter so he wouldn't worry about me judging him. "What happened?"

"Fuckin' Griffin wants shit his way, even though what I was doing met all the standards, was a good plan, and ended up being a good flight, but he would have done it differently. It's just bullshit."

"Ah."

There wasn't much point in cracking open the transcript of what happened; everyone knew Griffin had a reputation of getting bogged down with trivial shit that wasn't even worth noting, let alone giving someone demerits for. He was one of those guys who must have struggled to get somewhere, but once he got some status he made sure everyone else had to pay the same dues he did whether they deserved to or not.

"Well, I wouldn't lose much sleep over it. Nobody gives a fuck about his dumb agendas anyway. You'll just take another ride with someone else. Fuck it."

"Yeah, I know; it's just fucked up though." The Duke was going to simmer in this stew for a while. "The shit he wanted to make issue of is just his own stupid shit. And Bill doesn't even care what Griffin does or doesn't check. I had that shit wired tight."

"Everyone knows you're fine, and everyone knows Griffin's a fucktard, and Bill knows he can't fix him either. That's about all there is to the whole thing. You're going to have to brush it off. In two more weeks you'll take another ride with another pilot and that'll be the end of it."

"Spoze."

"I'll catch you later, man. Shake it off."

We traded up-nods and I went back to my room for a lazy day off, made a pot of coffee, and decided to check my email before watching *First Blood* for the day.

My note reminded me to research the rifle I had found in the junk store, and within the hour I was able to identify the mysterious weapon: a model 1886 French Lebel from the late nineteenth century! I made a few mental notes: what the bolt looked like, the caliber, how many rounds, what style of sights, and certain markings.

I went back to the bazaar to look again, walking past Burger King and through the small collection of shops and textile and knickknack stores, winding up back in the junk store that smelled like Indiana Jones just shot the Cairo Swordsman. The guns in the corner were a dead ringer. *Are these junk, or in working order?* I wondered. I looked around the store, then cycled the bolt on one; it felt and sounded right. It was heavy, definitely not a prop or a fake. I smelled the chamber, which smelled like more decades of dust than gunpowder but had a hint of the sweet smell of machine oil, which was a good sign. I took a closer look at the combination of woodwork and metalwork, then closed my eyes. Nineteen years earlier, I had worked in a machine shop near my hometown for a man named Vladimir Krusic; he ran the machine shop and was also the local gunsmith. He was a larger-than-life personality, with a big, deep voice, and when I was a teenager, he had been a great mentor to me. He was also ex-military, and a family man, and a great teacher. He had given me a wonderful perspective on machine work but also taught me a little about gunsmithing. I remembered the conversations. I remembered the things he taught me to look at. I opened my eyes again, and hearing his voice in my head, took one more look. The thing was legit.

Taking the best-looking one up to the counter, I asked the owner how much, and he told me $300 American. "Thank you," I said, excited that it was so obtainable. At that moment my romance with the Lebel began. I would have that gun and find some way to get it home with or without customs. Certainly there was a way, and if the junk store in the soldier's bazaar sold them, other people were finding a way to get them home.

Back in my room, I began a lengthy research of the Lebel over a fresh pot of coffee. Almost three million of them had been made, between 1887 and about 1940, so it wasn't all that valuable or rare, but it was a cool item. With 8 mm ammo, bolt action, a ten-round forestock magazine, and a bayonet, the Lebel outranged any previous weapon of the time by being the first weapon to use smokeless-powder cartridges. This thing had its own small place in history! For the mechanical sort like myself, it was fun to find local battlefield junk, whether it had fought there or not. Any rifle of that era produced in such numbers was likely used in one war or another. There would be no way to answer the grisly question of whether or not this particular weapon had put anyone's lights out, but it was certainly an authentic instrument of death.

Later in the morning, I strolled down to the post office to see about mailing the Lebel home and found they would mail anything customs would sign off. Farther down the desk I found the customs people who had dealt with this before, and they had a complete photo spread under the glass for every weapon they would sign off as an outgoing mail parcel. Mailing rifles was permissible as long as the weapon was made before 1898 and did not have a clip or magazine, whether it was in working order or not! Delightful. I could gift the Lebel to my uncle who was a gunsmith, he would enjoy it, and then I could fire it the next time I went to visit Raton, New Mexico.

What else would make a nice present? I wondered. Imagine if I could send him some bullets too . . . what fun. A quick search of the internet revealed that indeed I could buy the tapered 8 mm rounds. I bought the gun and mailed it to my uncle and had the internet purchase of ammo shipped directly to his address. Somewhat obsessively, I found online that the rifle was originally issued with an operator's manual of sorts: the French *mouchoirs d'instruction militaire* (military instruction handkerchiefs), perhaps more interesting than the weapon itself: a 30-inch-wide cotton square, mechanical details of the Lebel on one side, and tactical strategies on the other. These instructional handkerchiefs were issued along with the weapon, at a time when many of the soldiers receiving them may have been illiterate, and eventually became collectors' items referencing not only the Lebel, but all sorts of other war-related topics. I acquired one from eBay and had it shipped to Afghanistan to enjoy for a few days before personally sending it to my uncle. Within three weeks, the package arrived. Remarkably, you can get almost anything shipped to an APO address. The sender had been thoughtful with various levels of packaging, so the item was protected by tissue paper, cardboard, and a ziplock bag. It reminded me I was receiving something authentic, as did the musty smell. This fascinating historical item was so intense, I had to set it down to regard it. Not only was I reverent of its legitimate relevance to World War I but I also needed a translator—all of the writing was in French. I took the *mouchoir* to the task force "S-2," the battalion-level intelligence officer, Lieutenant Gilley, who could speak and read French at a conversational level. We were intrigued by the tactical information this artifact had to offer, from 130 years earlier.

The illustrated battles and the smell and stains of the eerie relic created a vague portal, faintly screaming a bloody account of wars past.

CHAPTER 13
PURPLE HEART

Day 94. In the middle of winter, there were occasional days of fog or rainy mornings, which left the helicopters grounded. When the weather was good, there were a lot of quick trips down to Kabul or JBAD, moving people back and forth. So it went; days and nights went by, more of the same, often just the daily routine with no significant activity to speak of. The quietness seemed to report that there were no benchmarks to hit, and no tactical goals, only a requirement for basic sustainment. There was no advertised measure of progress, only the abstract requirement to be there until we were supposed to leave. Very often the missions we flew were milk runs, just moving people, normal commerce. On at least one such flight, a moment of levity ensued that would be repeated time and time again for much-needed comic value: Large white Russian Mi-8 helicopters with the NATO reporting name of "Hip" had several missions in Afghanistan. I don't know if it was mostly cargo or people, but they flew often, huge white orbs in the sky, with Russian pilots. They spoke with a heavy accent, and their call sign was Vodka. The way it came across in deep, broken English, was *oo-odd-kah*. "Kabool Towah, zees eez Wodka. Pay-mishy-own to lond on vunway." Then the tower would clear them to land on runway 29. You could never miss them, neither the accent on the radio nor the blatant white beast, guzzling barrels of kerosene to lumber across the sky. For the tower controllers, they would have been unmistakable. No other helicopter was that visible, practically a mechanical cloud floating by.

Despite the irony that Russia had its own long and bloody affair with Afghanistan throughout most of the 1980s, we were then decades removed; Russia manned at least one proper hospital in Kabul and a field hospital outside the city in support of the coalition effort, as well as providing limited generic logistical support. The Russian pilots were very friendly, of course. At combined stops, once everyone was shut down, they were just as eager to host a tour of these magnificent, tanklike machines as they were to sit in the cockpit of the Blackhawk. The cockpit of the Hip was extremely roomy, the gauges were easy to read, and classic Cold War–era faded green paint was a pleasant background color on the dashboard.

Blackhawk assault pilot Pete Latham was especially amused by the Russian aircraft. On descent into Bagram one day, he decided to play a joke on the tower. Achieving a masterful, heavy Russian accent, he called in with a comically loud voice, "BAGUDUM TOWAH! ZEES EEZ WODKA! LONDING VUNWAY TAH-DEE!!" The tower controller, looking toward the end of runway 3, didn't see any massive white helicopters, just a pair of Blackhawks coming up from the south.

"Uuuh, Roger, Vodka; say again your position?"

With something surely premeditated, and to the delight of every pilot listening to the frequency, Pete came back on the radio and famously replied, "Bagudum Towah, zees eez Wodka . . . ZOOPRISE!!! I AM IN BLACKHAWK!!" Pete would forever be endeared in my heart for this level of wartime bravery. It became instant radio folklore, with enough copycat Vodkas calling international control towers with worse and worse accents that within days the joke grew tedious. That first one was magical, though.

Early March finally brought some variety to the daily grind. FOB Shank was being developed 100 miles to the south, and they needed pilots to be assigned there on one-week medevac standby shifts. Each pilot would eventually fall into the rotation for this abstract duty away from the command post, but a handful of us were in group number 1. I packed a bag, enjoyed the last private moments of my plywood stateroom, and went to the flight line to deploy.

Anytime the Army decides to set up a new base, living conditions evolve at a predictable rate. If the encampment is truly out in the middle of nowhere, as FOB Shank was, it can start with a simple squad-sized element, a tent, some water, and a few cases of MREs.[1] That would get you only a few days of employment before the usual problems began to arise. Troops would develop backaches from the cots, some would get sick, and others would get athlete's foot from no laundry and no showers. Army guys can be some of the best campers ever, and also some of the most resourceful. It doesn't take long for the refinement of living conditions to take place, because on deployment there is plenty of downtime to address creature comfort and luxury. In the woods, a squad of Army guys would use the terrain, dig encampments, use the trees and branches, make fire and furniture, find running water to conduct personal hygiene, and do laundry. There were all sorts of ways to be comfortable and happy in the woods. In the desert, the challenge is different.

Over the first nine years of the US Army being deployed to Afghanistan, there had grown an undeniable perpetuity of plywood, lumber, basic hardware, and DeWalt cordless tools. There wasn't a camp where these items weren't being continuously utilized. Adding tools and materials to a bunch of resourceful soldiers with time on their hands equals structure and organization spreading like a virus. The Army Corps of Engineers comes in to help with the broad strokes, such as drainage, roads, and runways, but soldiers themselves built the structures at the FOBs and COPs, and they were happy for the opportunity to build and complete anything during what could be many long hours of ambiguous time.

By the time I got there, FOB Shank already had several months of development, which meant over a hundred different structures. It was kind of a nice little village, complete with boardwalks, plywood bathrooms, plywood showers, and a plywood dining facility. I had to wonder if this was instinct for the basic need for shelter, or if there was just so much extra time that soldiers naturally gravitated toward construction.

We were allotted a small patch of the FOB, big enough to easily land two Blackhawks outside the plywood hospital and plywood bunkhouse. Some ambitious pilots or crew chiefs had already built a nice porch on the front of the crew quarters, along with a somewhat utilitarian pergola for shade, and a dusty old cargo net slung over the whole thing for looks. Not bad! I slung my duffel bag up onto a bunk away from the doorway and settled in.

Army structures in the desert are usually raw lumber. Any sort of paint, varnish, or other finishes were rare, because (a) there usually wasn't any available, (b) nobody cared because everyone was transient, and (c) if something got rained or snowed on, the next day it dried in the sunshine. The most-resourceful builders found rolled tar paper or other roofing to keep stuff from leaking, but it was common to find the walls and floors, inside and out, completely unfinished. Such was the texture of FOB Shank—a lot of dry, raw, dusty plywood and two-by-fours in every direction. I certainly wasn't about to go scuffing around in bare feet in this den of slivers, but it was a fine structure to live in with flip-flops. With the exception of modern vehicles, the whole camp provided a frontier-town level of luxury.

We toured the TOC, a simple room with a few pieces of communication equipment, a few phones, a few maps, a Blue Force Tracker jumbotron up on the wall, and the typical coffeepot. Shortly thereafter, boredom fell upon us, and I realized we were indeed sitting in the middle of the desert watching the dust blow. Where I sat was not very comfortable, and I was soon pondering the construction of a new Adirondack chair.

After a very brief search for materials, I found the necessary wood and a few power tools. I decided to spend the rest of the day designing and to begin construction after breakfast the following morning. Just as I brought pencil to paper, though, one of our walkie-talkies chirped, and I looked up to listen: "Dustoff 42, report to the TOC." So much for the boredom.

As we walked into the TOC, the attendant specialist looked up without greeting and conveyed an urgent medevac over to Catamount for a gunshot wound to an American soldier. *That's the real thing*, I thought to myself, and without exchanging any further pleasantries I ran out to the helicopter, shouting for the gunners to join me.

On a serious medevac standby mission, the helicopter is ready. There are no tie-downs, no cowl plugs, and no pitot tube covers. Our ALSE[2] vests were ready, the key was in the ignition, and the guns were already mounted. The standard was three minutes, and we could meet that easily, even in the fancy computerized M-model Blackhawk. There were some pilots who would argue that *no*, the gyros alone took four minutes to spin up, and that it wouldn't be prudent to launch prior to that; those pilots had more limitations than just being slow. It's a constant in our dynamic business that some types of pilots just don't end up on some types of missions, because they aren't savvy enough to work around minor details. Any grassroots pilot would be comfortable letting the gyros align in flight, and that was our standard for this mission. One of our own had a gunshot wound, probably being held together with field dressing and a bunch of excited combat medics, wishing he was on his way to a proper hospital. Our tires left the dirt after two minutes and twenty seconds. The actual medevac aircraft, which had the additional equipment and medical personnel on board, beat our takeoff time by ten seconds.

We took off rapidly for what would be an eight-minute flight over to Catamount CP. We headed southwest, the gyros aligned, and we refined our course and sped up to top speed. This was going to be as fast as we could sustain without overheating anything, which based on the current environmental conditions worked out to be 147 knots, or 169 mph. It felt like a snail's pace when we knew someone was on the ground with a gunshot wound. We didn't have any details on how it happened; maybe a squad on routine patrol of a local village, and someone spooked a local who had a gun in the closet? There was no way to know. Once in a great while we would hear about an organized attack on coalition forces, or an ambush, but usually it was just potshots. Sometimes the medevac guys got the details, sometimes not.

After what seemed like an eternity, we finally started our approach into Catamount. From 300 feet, it wasn't exactly clear where we should land, because there were two distinct groups of people clustered about. Then an individual broke from one of the groups and popped a violet smoke grenade for us. It's always nice when you get smoke on the LZ, because it not only shows exactly where to land but is also a great indicator of the wind. I felt annoyed for a second at the color of the smoke; it wasn't rational, but it flashed across my mind that out in the desert, during a year of tans and grays, the color of purple was gorgeous, and no one should be enjoying a gorgeous color splash like that when one of us was dying. After that moment it didn't bother me again. We landed, and within a few minutes the Dustoff bird had the patient, and we took off again to race back to the hospital at FOB Shank for immediate surgery.

As it turned out, that poor soldier wasn't on a patrol at all. Another soldier was standing watch from a guard tower and decided to balance his SAW³ machine gun on the railing for a second so he could tend to something else. The SAW fell, of course, went off, and a round flew across camp, hitting a fellow soldier in the waist.

This may have been the most frustrating moment of the deployment for me.

After we got hot gas and shut down, I staged my gear for the next launch and strolled over to the hospital to see what the status was. He was still in surgery. I asked the medics if I could stick my nose into the operating room, which they allowed as long as I didn't get my unsterilized self too close to the action. "What's up, Doc," I asked, getting only a half-second glance from the surgeon before his eyes went back down to his work.

"Who are you?" he calmly asked, perfectly justified. The soldier's feet were sticking out from under a heavy green wool blanket, and his midsection was behind a short, paper curtain, with quite a bit of activity going on.

"Just a pilot. We brought this guy in a few minutes ago. Just wondering how he looks."

The surgeon softened to my presence in the OR and said, "Not good. Bullet destroyed one of his kidneys on its way to his spine. Most likely he's paralyzed from the waist down. He's going home."

My stomach turned. I left the operating room and found a seat outside. I can imagine the guy who dropped his gun wishing he could go back in time for a second chance. The fantastic amount of trouble he's in won't matter at all when he finds out his brother-in-arm's life was just altered in one of the worst ways. One bullet altered two lives, in a moment from which neither will ever be free. It was a terribly inglorious way to go home for the victim. I sat there pondering it all and suddenly despised the operating room and the surgeon. *Another irrational thought*, I noted, but it seemed like removing a simple chunk of lead and sewing a few things up shouldn't be a problem. But the violent projectile had plowed through soft tissues that weren't coming back, severed the nervous cord, and lodged into bone. The young captain would get the lead out, all right, but that was it.

I walked back to the shack, put the pad of paper on the floor, and lay down to stare at the ceiling. *Totally pointless.* I felt bad for the battalion commander who was going to have to make the phone call to the family. There would also be no gain from the loss. We won't eventually say we fixed a problem in the world. He won't spend the rest of his life in a wheelchair for a good cause. If he gets the Purple Heart, he might not even want to talk about it.

CHAPTER 14

BREACHING ROUND

Day 95. The next morning brought sunshine. I woke up to the same unremarkable plywood shack, noting a slipshod level of construction in the rafters. I thought back to the previous day with frustration and had no interest in going to visit the kid. There was nothing to say. He'd have to fight through it on his own, and it just sucked. I had my own defense mechanism about this sort of thing, which was not to think about it. Within a day I moved on like nothing had happened, and so did everyone around me. I threw on some PTs and strolled to breakfast.

Breakfast was always a good time for me, being a morning person, but also just for loving breakfast food. In my opinion, the Army had breakfast figured out. They had a short-order grill for eggs and omelets, a nice selection of freshly chopped-up ham, peppers, tomatoes, mushrooms, and onions. They had sides of shredded cheddar cheese, salsa, and sour cream. They had the usual things in the big stainless-steel serving line, such as hash browns or home fries, bacon, sausage, pancakes, and french toast sticks. They had a cereal bar, an oatmeal station, and a waffle maker. They had things to toast. They had a decorative glass refrigerator full of various yogurts and cottage cheese. They had fresh fruit. There was a great wealth of food at every meal, but I enjoyed breakfast the most. I had the patience to order up a special omelet and got a side of coffee cake, a side of yogurt, a big bowl of oatmeal with raisins and brown sugar, and some hot black coffee.

On deployments, some people count down the meals. It's almost always the same scene in the DFAC, except for holidays, so it was déjà vu three times a day. It's not like you can go out to dinner at a different place every week. Some people every meal as "another one down." It was easy to get into that mental rut, but I made a conscious choice to enjoy my breakfast for what it was, and to do some people-watching in a DFAC, which had begun to display the decorations of St. Patrick's Day.

A wide variety of people accumulate within the various DFACs around the country. Fighting a coalition war makes for a greatly diversified cross section. Americans tend to think they are the center of the universe, but it was very much a conglomeration, and one of the places where that was apparent was the DFAC. That particular morning, two Danish soldiers sat delightfully conversing with one another while enjoying some McDonald's-style hash browns and orange juice. They had no apparent stress. They seemed just as relaxed here as they would be at the beach. I wondered what their unit was assigned to do, and whether they felt like they were accomplishing anything, and how long their deployments were. One of them glanced over at me, catching me analyzing them, and nodded politely. I smiled in return with an expression to convey good will, and felt excused. I could've greeted them, asked them their deal, but I anticipated them saying the same thing I would've said: *I'm just here supporting the coalition effort, whatever that may be . . .*

"Whatever that may be" was a good question. An abstract question that sometimes surfaces with the troops is how we would feel if this was our home turf, and some foreign military was occupying. It's hard to imagine the *Red Dawn* scenario. Japan occupied part of the Aleutians briefly during World War II, and Guam, but those are pretty fuzzy examples. Imagine one of the other superpowers occupying the Lower 48 . . . How would Americans act, for example, if China were suddenly to attack, achieve a position of superiority, and then occupy Pennsylvania? South Dakota? Texas? Forget it. Any *good ol' boy* from any state would be fighting with every chance they had. Plenty of red-blooded Americans with the right to bear arms would grab their rifle every time a Chinese military aircraft was flying over, and take a shot at it. That scenario is a dysfunctional example, though, because the coalition was never trying to attack Afghanistan. We were just supposed to be getting rid of an infestation.

It's not hard to understand how some of the people responded to us being there. We were in someone else's country, and a portion of them didn't want us there. I wondered how the two Danish soldiers felt about this, but didn't think the resulting conversation was something I wanted to have. A complete summary, which may not be possible, would have to include that some of them *did* want us there, because a great deal of decent, wholesome civilians of Afghanistan did not want to be harassed or controlled by the Taliban anymore. Either way, I finished breakfast and left.

I headed back to the ready-launch shack for the medevac crews. I found an uncomfortable chair under the dusty cargo net and positioned it to look out past the helicopters to the east, to enjoy a desert sunrise. It was nice. I felt full, sunshine was starting to warm me up, and the view extended out 100 miles. There were mountains in the distance regardless of which direction one might look in Afghanistan, and they were always beautiful. I found myself with a vacation level of relaxation, feeling happy. There I was relaxing in a blocky wooden lawn chair, in the morning sun, sipping hot black coffee and enjoying life. I found perspective and patience and was content with my assignment. We were about a quarter of the way done with the deployment, and I was in no hurry to get home. I didn't feel like I was missing anything. I was established, confident, and comfortable in my surroundings. Even lucky, really; it would always be a good memory, being able to say I was there, that I *went*, that I had served when I could. There are people in the service who find ways to never deploy, but if they could sit out there for the crisp desert sunrise, they might realize it wasn't all bullets whizzing by or grenades exploding. Any military activity involves a HUGE amount of downtime, and it is a special skill to realize that and enjoy it. I enjoyed the morning, even though there was a paralyzed kid in the recovery room with a pair of IVs running into his arms to boost his remaining kidney.

The morning eventually found me sketching a more comfortable chair. This was an organic moment. I had a lot of sitting around to do, there was lumber, and I was going to make a chair.

I drew the basic Adirondack chair profile, then took it one step further for custom ergonomics and measured my legs from foot to knee and from knee to hip. High school shop class would suggest the next step was a bill of materials, which I achieved instead with an exploded view, then set out to gather materials. I found a skill saw, a saber saw, the ubiquitous yellow DeWalt cordless drill, a few drill bits, a bunch of screws, and a pile of assorted lumber from general stockpile.

In the real sense of working with my hands, the production helped solidify my overall feeling of contentment. The sounds and the smells of woodworking reminded me of my dad, a woodworker, and brought me back to my youth when I would sit in the shop and just watch him work, which was one of the most wholesome things in my life. In the construction of the chair, I enjoyed another mini escape from the unusual experience of being deployed.

I took a few additional measurements, such as how wide to make it and what a good back angle would be. Over the course of the morning, the chair came together and became forevermore a piece of Afghan lawn furniture. It was solid, comfortable, and deserving of a good book to read in it. I put away the tools and swept up the sawdust, carried the incredibly heavy chair up to the porch, and went to shower. The next morning's sunrise was going to be sublime.

The rest of the day and the rest of the week brought little action. Life was calm, the weather stayed good, and I drank a lot of good coffee in the custom chair. Only one other mission was discussed for the week, which was to go salvage a crashed UAV near a mosque, 20 miles west of FOB Shank. While it sounded inviting at first and would have interrupted the boredom, within just a few seconds it seemed like a bad idea. Apparently, the UAV had crashed *into* the mosque and created a great deal of displeasure with the locals. It had been the suggestion of a local captain to use the medevac assets to go recover it, and a bad one. First of all, if it crashed, it's junk anyway. Second, I wasn't about to go hover or land near a mosque full of angry people. That just didn't sit well with me, because Kyle was killed in a similar situation. If the powers that be wanted to get the thing back, they were going to have to suit up with a full-scale operation and go in there with intel and a backup plan, and none of that was happening. The pilot in command of the medevac bird was a guy by the name of Brandon Lynch. He looked at me and said, "Heavy-D is never going to approve that," and he was right. *No one* would have approved it. We exchanged eye rolls and walked away, knowing the agenda would fizzle on its own.

The only other point of notable interest was a visiting Russian Mi-24, or Hind, attack helicopter. This Cold War relic was a sight to behold. As usual, I had no idea where it came from or who was flying it, but it sported a Polish flag and appeared only to be stopping for gas. As a cousin to the Hip, this bizarre, prehistoric-looking variant used the same tank engines and was heavy. There was an attempt to streamline it for speed, but I couldn't see how it was much faster with all the extra junk it carried on stub wings. It seemed to have a tandem cockpit siamesed onto the original Mi-8 fuselage, and a host of different guns bulging out from other points like tumors. I don't know if it was required for the weight, or if the pilot was simply practicing, but after refueling they had decided to do a rolling takeoff. Using what I believe was a UAV landing strip, the Hind began accelerating, apparently by ejecting noise out the back to be propelled forward. Progress seemed slow, and the aerodynamics of this evil creation caused the main landing gear to leave the runway prior to the nosewheel, and they continued down the length of the runway like a wheelbarrow. Eventually the contraption defied gravity, the wheels retracted, and the volume began diminishing. The Hind disappeared into the distance.

As my one-week stint came to an end, the next crew arrived. We gave them a tour of the facilities, shared lunch, high-fived, and departed, another week down. *All quiet on the western front . . .* I never did see the kid who got shot. I didn't think it was appropriate at the time to go find him. I did stay frustrated that so *little* was going on that guys were getting careless or bored.

We experienced the same phenomenon in Iraq a few years prior. Being deployed to either of those countries as a highly trained assault pilot and getting to do fewer than a dozen assaults seemed to indicate there wasn't much of a fight occurring. People felt stagnant, the pace of training slowed down, the hours dragged on. Pilots started asking the battalion commander to come up with actual missions to fly so we could feel justified with being there and have a chance to practice our trade. Assault pilots train in made-up scenarios time and time again to develop the skills necessary to put troops on the objective in a very rapid and precise manner, and then they want to go do it for real to be validated. The problem was, when an assault battalion goes looking for actual work, it means actual troops were going to be delivered to actual targets and some shit was going to go down. That's exactly what we did in Iraq; there weren't enough deliberate missions,[1] so the unit offered services to customers who weren't requesting our help through the normal channels. When those offers made it to commanders of stagnant units who were also wishing for some action, we had a dangerous combination: a bunch of operators out there looking to pick a fight with anyone they could, and an extremely effective way to show up. Units naturally labeled these operations as whatever it took to get approval, and away we went.

Part of this is normal. Unit commanders are supposed to train their units to reach an optimum level of performance, then market their capabilities to any customer who could use them. That's part of normal military synergy. A potential dilemma occurs if every unit in a theater is trained to proficiency, deployed to an area designated as a combat zone, then realizes there is no real war. It causes frustration because people are deployed away from home, away from their families, and there'd better be a reason for it. It doesn't take much for there to suddenly be areas of "potential threat" that "need to be searched," and pretty soon you have a pack of trigger-hopeful troops suiting up to go on a mission. Any unit commander could justify this action with the slightest indication of threat, and depending on how you read the intel, there is always *some* threat. *We're deployed here to provide security, right? Let's provide it* . . . Perhaps that was the nature of the SASO[2] mission; to go snooping. It's not unlike an overambitious police officer looking for trouble. You can shape *probable cause* out of just about anything. The more this happened, the more justified the troops became; if they had been engaged or suffered losses, they could feel vindictive the next time they went out. It perpetuates again, just like the police officer who gets battle-hardened by the deviant behavior of everyday criminals.

Such was the case in Iraq one night, summer of '06. We went on a minor assault with a flight of four Blackhawks to conduct search-and-seizure operations outside Balad Airbase. The intended mission was to find any sort of IED cache or any collection of ingredients that could be used for making bombs or mortars. We were going to do this by landing in people's backyards at two in the morning for a surprise search-and-seizure operation. This flight was less than five minutes outside the wire, to a small village. We were going to insert the troops to four separate LZs and return to Balad to wait for the EXFIL call.

This seemed fine to me as I stood on the ramp at one in the morning, nursing a premission coffee. Then the chaplain came walking out. *Oh shit.* Every time that guy comes out to pray with the troops, everyone gets all serious and nervous. We huddled together, a bunch of badasses, flying multimillion-dollar equipment at a bunch of unsuspecting civilians we outgunned ten to one, and listened to the chaplain praying we made it back unscathed. He had a sobering effect. It was great that he came out and prayed for us, but it sure could make things heavy.

My most vigilant effort was to clean the plastic window of the cockpit door. I knew from studying imagery of the objective that we would be landing right next to a house, and that I would have the best vantage point of that house. In Iraq, the nightly temperature could get so hot that it was not uncommon for people to sleep on their roofs at night. If one of those people felt safer sleeping with an RPG and woke up with a helicopter descending onto his position in the middle of the night, he may just be startled enough to use it. I would need to study the roofline intently, with my left hand under the collective to pull up as I was shouting "GO AROUND" to my copilot. I cleaned the window to the best of my ability for five minutes inside and out, and I felt ready.

With an 0200 H hour,[3] we lined up for a 0155 takeoff time: a short mission. One of the older maintenance pilots joked that we should have just driven the Gators out there, it was so close. In this mission, we took off as a flight of four to a common release point, after which all four ships fanned out to different objectives. All too easy; all I had to do was hit the RP,[4] hang a left, go three drainage culverts, and land in someone's backyard.

The first problem arose when chalk one, which was being piloted by Peter Griffin and Arturo Matos, completely missed their objective and, in circling back around to try again, found themselves facing a head-on collision with my aircraft. Fortunately, everyone was already in a left turn, and we all kept turning left. In my case, the turn just became a lot more aggressive, and I'm sure it did for them too. We were lucky nobody followed the general rule that in a collision situation, everyone should turn right.

Back on approach and having passed one of the drainage culverts, I refocused on the objective, which was by then easily starting to look like the imagery. I shook my head a little about what just happened, made one final scan of the horizon to make sure nobody else was crashing into us, and shifted focus forward and down again to the objective. Past the second drainage culvert then, the house easily in view. I verified that my copilot and I were looking at the same thing by range and clock position, and from then on focused mainly on the roofline, with a few glances at the overall property. I shouted back to the crew chiefs and pax, "ONE MINUTE!," which everyone on board echoed. Oddly, this battle cry happened off ICS, over the noise of the helicopter.

There is an intimate moment in assault operations when I relate to the people whose day we are about to ruin. The radios had now gone quiet; we passed the final ditch and began our short descent into this guy's yard. With the goggles on, you can't see what color anything is; everything appears to be shades of green. If I had remembered we were in Iraq, I suppose I would have imagined everything was a shade of brown. But that's not what came to mind. In the short moments before we came barreling in, for just a glance, I saw a normal-looking farmhouse, a modest house, a fence, livestock in the backyard, and some shrubbery. In the green glow the yard was easy to imagine covered in grass. Maybe it was, even. This looked like any other house I had seen in my life, the house of a simple farmer, nothing threatening, nothing out of place. There could be no way of knowing if the people who lived there were part of the bad guys in their spare time, but at that moment, it felt just a little bit too homey.

During the final approach, I eyed the roofline critically. I asked the left-side door gunner to keep his eyes on the rooftop, but not to shoot unless I verified somebody indeed stood up with a shoulder-fired weapon. Therein lies the trick; the gunners are usually the most junior people in the unit and at times are even borrowed from other job descriptions, so our own crew chiefs can get some rest and keep up with maintenance. If the gunners are trained on a target and someone stands up quickly, there's but a hairsbreadth of safety from a 7.62 round ripping through their chest. But it's not a crime to stand up quickly. In fact, it might just be the normal reaction for someone who was awoken by a helicopter landing in his yard.

Making sure there is real threat is a level of perception for which assault pilots have to mentally condition themselves. Having the element of surprise usually means there isn't much of a fight, but you never know. Sometimes the HUMINT[5] is working both sides, or, for other reasons causing operational security to become compromised, the opposition can figure out your plan and set up an ambush. To me, the greater danger is making a mistake and shooting someone who doesn't deserve to be shot. Most of the population doesn't. How do you know, though? Obviously if they shoot first it's game on, but I wouldn't wait until they fire the first shot if they're holding something on their shoulder that's threatening. If our door gunner was really on his game, already aiming with a round in the chamber and the safety off, he might be able to fire a few rounds and at least get the threat to duck back down. If . . . It's particularly difficult to even see people on the ground from a helicopter, especially through goggles, let alone shoot with any accuracy. The M-240 machine gun is a hand-aimed weapon with iron sights, mounted to a constantly shaking rollercoaster. There's a handful of gunners who are effective in those conditions and get good at walking the tracer rounds toward the target, kind of like filling up the clown's balloon head at the carnival with a water cannon. Regardless of how good your gunner may be, you still have to be willing to absorb that first round anytime you fly into the threat. That's the nature of being an assault pilot; a willingness to show up to the fight. Once someone comes to terms with the possibility of absorbing that first round, they can get accustomed to the job and become combat effective.

Nary a twitch, though; there was no one on the roof. We landed without further incident 25 feet from a cow, deployed our troops, and departed back to the ramp.

Back on the ramp at Balad, we shut down to the APU[6] and continued to monitor the radios while waiting for the extraction call. They weren't very far away, but because we were on the ground, the line-of-sight radio transmissions were broken and scratchy. After some period of time, we heard some fairly excited voices saying something about a gunshot wound, but with only part of a garbled transmission, it was impossible to say who had been shot. The most concerning assumption was that one of our guys had been on the receiving end, but we didn't know. Despite the report, the search and seizure continued with no extraction call, and we simply remained ready for departure. I turned on the key and made sure the fuel valves were lined up, and we had only to push the starter buttons to be on our way.

Eventually we got the call, and it was not expedited, but the gunshot wound had occurred at my LZ. As it turns out, the guy who I had imagined sleeping on his roof with an RPG had been sleeping in his bed with his wife like a normal farmer. He had awoken in the middle of the night, either to the screaming turbines or to the rumbling percussion of the main rotor blades, and got up to see what the fuss was about. He had, unfortunately, walked up to the back door of his house just as the door was being opened with a 12-gauge breaching round, and he took a chestful. By the time we landed, the man was being carried in a makeshift litter out to the helicopter so we could fly him to the hospital. His wife, clearly distraught, stood in a nightgown on the back patio in what could only have been a state of disbelief.

Of the four objectives, only one had any contraband material. That's enough to call the mission a success. Just about anybody involved would say that's exactly why we were there, and we detained a few bad guys and cleaned up another cache. I suppose what happened had been an accident, and that if the Iraqi farmer hadn't been standing behind the door at that particular moment, the mission would have been purely successful without collateral damage. But had someone in the intel chain proceeded on a hunch? Had there been only one suspect house, but we decided to check three other houses because we were going out there anyway? I don't know. But dudes were certainly bored in Iraq in '05 and '06, and happy to be out on a *good ol'* air assault.

I just don't feel like we won any hearts and minds that night. We were there for reasons largely political, and we were looking for trouble anywhere we could find it, and now we were in Afghanistan doing the same thing. After some period of time, we admitted that *no, there weren't any WMDs in Iraq*, and I wondered if after some period of time we would admit that *no, we weren't able to eliminate all of the Taliban or al-Qaeda from Afghanistan*. As long as they can hide in Pakistan, once we leave, they will be back. I don't know why we think we can go over there and resolve anything. Russia tangled with Afghanistan and the Mujahedeen for a similar period of time in the 1980s with no luck, and they had deployed to their own backyard! We were trying it from halfway around the world. I'm sure it's easy to prove we can forward-deploy to anywhere in the world with enough money, but at the very core of the matter, what makes us think we can clean up millions of square miles of overbaked bad guys who have sustained their posture on Paisas for thousands of years, while our own occupation is costing $157 million a day?

There was a sense that we had to respond to the September 11 attacks, but doesn't it seem like occupying the Middle East for a few years would have been substantial? The America who was upset that we were attacked and thousands of people died is no happier that after ten more years all we have is thousands more dead.

There was one theory that our presence was making matters *worse*, because the reason we were attacked in the first place is that we were the bully on the playground, a bully then responding with more bullying.

There was the theory that we were actually *winning* the war on terror, that the most wanted deck of cards didn't have too many face cards left in it.

Of course, there is also the theory of the Hydra.

CHAPTER 15
APRIL FOOL'S DAY

Day 100. Flying home to Bagram from FOB Shank, our forty-five-minute trip north past Alikel, Malikel, and Dimeena, past FOB Airborne, and past Kabul went fine. Once again, we floated down into the Bagram Bowl after a slow week, nearly a vacation. We parked, stepped onto the ramp, and felt immediately saturated in the noise and dust of the major military airbase. *Damn, I'm still deployed*. I walked into the CP to have a brief reunion with friends and check the flight schedule. Bob Massey and Bill Westergaurd were standing there with dry-erase markers, working on balancing the crew mix for each flight for the week.

"Howdy boys," I said, to get them to reveal their masterpiece for a moment.

"Mr. Havill, how was life down south?" Bill asked in his signature drawl.

"Oh fine, I suppose; nothing to it, really," I replied. "Kind of like watching grass grow." This was an extra-qualified response in the middle of a desert.

Bob's face cracked into the usual charming smile for acknowledgment, and they both turned back to their administrative task. From the looks of it, I had the next two days off to reset from my exhaustive schedule and proceeded to the DFAC for lunch before returning to the peace and quiet of my room.

I was back on the gravel street with the sandbag skeletons, mustard-colored haji-wood shacks, Jersey barriers, and John Deere Gators. I crunched and choked my way along through the bustling activity of Bagram until I reached the DFAC, pulled open the door with the screech, and stepped into modern air-conditioning. Alas, there stood Ms. Thatcher.

This time there was no doubt, while having never shared so much as a complete conversation, she gave me the smiling "welcome back" eyes. *I don't suppose a smile will hurt anything.* I smiled back but wasn't collected enough to stop my own eyes from having extra twinkle. That seemed like consent enough to put the attractive attendant at ease with talking to me, during which I noticed she had control neither of her own eyes nor the dimples in her cheeks, which she flashed along with a metallic smile full of braces.

Emily Thatcher seemed to know I was a pilot, and we exchanged pleasantries and greetings as if meeting for the first time, and she mocked my somewhat guarded demeanor with unabashed flirting. I wasn't able to maintain my guard long enough to turn and walk away without her seeing I had smiled again. Halfway down the fast-food line, I figured there were so many people behind me I could safely look back. In one swift movement while reaching in with tongs to grab some fries, I turned my head just enough for my eyes to find her still gazing at me, and was not fast enough to turn back to the fries before she flashed me the braces again. *Trouble.*

I went to the mail room on my way home to find a few letters from family along with a hefty box from a friend back home. That was exciting! I would wait until I got back to my room to open it.

Finally, back in the cool, dark quiet of my room, I shed my raunchy uniform for a shower and some PTs, then opened the box. Most delightfully, my friend Katy had sent from the land of comfort food and alcohol some savory Doritos, a big bag of M&Ms, some oatmeal cookies with jam in the middle, a yo-yo, and a sweet bottle of Knob Creek Bourbon. The package had the desired effect. I locked my door and decided to escape into the coziness of the bourbon and watch *First Blood*. Oatmeal cookies, bourbon, and Will Teasel keeping the streets clean.

The following morning, commotion converged near the runway. I strolled toward the flight line in my pajamas, along with a handful of other gawkers, to see that a C-17 had landed with the gear up. What a sight. Helicopter operations were unaffected, but a massive cargo plane smeared onto the runway stopped the flow of some of the fixed-wing traffic for a few days. Bagram has a huge parallel taxiway that was the main runway before the airfield was upgraded, and this somewhat rough and neglected provision was swept off and provided relief for certain types of fixed-wing traffic until they could get the wreckage cleared off the main runway. It sat there, a massive aluminum whale, dead on the asphalt beach. Eventually, a huge crane and some airbags were used to get the craft's wheels to come down, after which it was towed off the runway. Apparently, the pilots had turned off the low-altitude/landing-gear warning system, and in the commotion of making a nighttime landing with certain elements of the airfield's approach radar inoperative, they forgot to put the gear down. Embarrassing and expensive, but luckily no injuries. Both pilots lost some status over that one.

My two days off went by slowly, after which I found myself back on the daytime QRF schedule. The typical time to leave people on the QRF shift was two weeks, although sometimes people would request either shorter or longer amounts of time. Some people enjoyed the night schedule because it was typically quieter; the day QRF assets tended to get used by the battle captain for any purpose, including running paperwork and people around the battlefield for administrative reasons. This was a poor but justifiable war posture; the QRF assets should always be on standby for the very worst of circumstances, to be employed as a ready-launch asset. However, because there was no actual war going on, if flown by the book the QRF would never launch and therefore not be as proficient at launching rapidly. In that sense it was good to go on a flight now and then, even if it was a minor misuse of a combat provision; Lift-6 could do whatever he wanted with his chess pieces and obviously knew what he was doing.

To me, QRF was the quintessential deployed experience. In all of my deployments, in Iraq and Afghanistan and also in the submarine force in the 1990s, deployment was a time to focus on who you were as an operator. Back home, in what the Army calls *the garrison environment*, there is really a lot of bullshit. Uniforms have to be perfect; haircuts and grooming have to be perfect, and units conduct physical training. Buildings are clean, stuff smells like pine oil, floors get waxed and polished, and vehicles get washed. Dress uniforms get inspected, people conduct drill and ceremony in formations, and operations are conducted to the letter of the law. Any little snag back home regarding any of the hundreds of rules and regulations, and missions ground to a halt. Being deployed could be the opposite.

The main focus is *operating*: whatever it takes to keep up with the pace of operations. Maintenance seems to get done faster, people work with less sleep, haircuts aren't as much of a priority, and everything is dirty. Since there are actual flights going out, actual missions to support, and actual customers to work for, less training happens, and it happens during a mission only when it can be woven in.

Because the sergeant major isn't asking for soldiers to show up for dress formation and inspection, and because troops really aren't doing any cleaning or training, there is a true opportunity for an operator to sit back, reflect, and evolve into the operator they're going to be known as. There is *a lot* of time available. The deployments I went on in the Navy lasted only a handful of months each. In contrast, the Army evolved into a routine of deploying for twelve months, and in some cases fifteen. That's a long time for someone to be away from their family and operating out of a temporary building. In our case it was not terribly busy time. It was merely . . . time.

Although there are many examples of far-longer deployments during World War II, *years*, for example (and the effect was that much worse on families), the world war was a real fight for borders and nationalities, including American territory, and we would kill ourselves to defend it. Comfort and consideration for family stability took a back seat for a *long* time. OIF and OEF were different beasts, lasting much longer in total years. So while the deployments were shorter than during World War II, many units had to rotate in and out to cover it year after year, and twelve months away from your family wasn't exactly something to brush off. I was lucky to go to Iraq once and Afghanistan only once, and lucky to have no children at the time. I knew guys who had deployed away from their families for a year up to seven times. By that measure, some had it worse than World War II.

Some guys like to sit around and read, watch movies, play video games or cards, or just bullshit with each other. It is the sitting around waiting that carries the conversations and the atmosphere of the unit, and the QRF mission was a twelve-hour, structured period of sitting around; the same guys, the same faces, sitting around the same dusty but somehow greasy plywood table every day, or every night, for twelve hours.

Sometimes we would be begging for a flight to go on, but other times the boredom would grab us and we would hope the *bat phone* wouldn't ring so that we wouldn't have to snap out of a twelve-hour trance. This could be the worst during night QRF, if we dozed off and then the TOC called for an urgent medevac. It could be awful to wake up, run to the helicopter, fire it up in the black of night, and launch out still rubbing your eyes. I tried to avoid that with the usual rituals and some discipline, but the sleepy monster was always lurking.

In that regard, daytime QRF could be a relief. It's pretty nice to sit around in the daylight, feel relaxed but ready, and feeling naturally awake. It's a bit of an art form, staying ready to launch at any moment, but also being able to relax and feel casual. It's a compartment of the mind, the piece that stays ready, and a compartment easily accessed. It takes practice to develop it into something invisible. With a few mental rehearsals, you can look into the compartment and see a protocol, or a course of action. *I'll grab the radio and direct my crew to get to the chopper, five seconds. I'll grab my thermos and stop at the Lighthouse to fill it up, forty-five seconds. I'll stop at the TOC to get a synopsis of the mission and a weather update, two minutes. I'll walk directly from there to my aircraft, the closest one parked, copilot already has it ready to start, put on my vest, jump in, and hit the starter buttons for the main engines. While the engines start, I'll put on my seat belt and give the crew a short synopsis.*

I went into this compartment in my mind a few times during the shift, so when the phone rang, not only were my actions cool and collected, I would also be able to reach the point when we proceed into the unknown without having expended any extra adrenaline; the maintenance of mental and physical well-being must include not stealing from one's own reserves. I was a ready element for the twelve-hour duration, mentally and tactically. I saw people around me who were not as ready, but I suppose they didn't need to be. If it turned out that any of them slowed us down, we'd chat. More often, it was the scope of the mission that slowed us down. Since the QRF mission is sometimes diversified to accommodate functions other than emergencies, sometimes the speed at which we responded was altered. If the phone rang and someone said urgent, it was the rehearsed protocol. If they said something starting with "Hey, the battle captain wants to know if you guys can run down to . . . ," then, just as rapidly, the urgency evaporates. It becomes an admin flight. Certain words prompted the real thing. Urgent medevac, troops in contact, or Fallen Angel.[1] Everything else was just a milk run.

Step 1 during the QRF shift was to set up all the pieces for real, so when I went into the mental rehearsal, I could visualize everything and get a good feeling it would work. I went to the TOC for an update brief on anything that had happened overnight. I talked to the staff weather officer for a weather brief. I looked at the assets overview to see who else was working for the day, and who I could call if I needed anything. This ranged from fire support[2] to UAV[3] feed to the Air Force high-element[4] frequency and call sign. If I ended up on the ground outside the wire, I needed to know who to call. I drew a blood chit[5] and radio. My crew assembled at the aircraft for preflight and run-up, so we could be ready for the potential rapid launch. We checked the systems at 100 percent and got a little bit of heat into the engines and gearboxes, which was important for rapid launches during the winter months. Then we'd shut down. I put my gear on the seat where I could get to it quickly, comm-checked with the crew on the handheld, and split up for breakfast. All elements of the QRF shift were expected to carry their handheld radio for the shift and to respond in a timely manner, and for the most part everyone went their separate ways unless the radio chirped.

On days when there was no launch, that might be the last I saw of the crew for the day. The crew chiefs and gunners had a separate hangout from the pilots, mainly because they did more maintenance, and we did more planning. Their plywood hut had tools, oil, rags, and gun-cleaning supplies; ours had planning computers, maps, a briefing table, and a huge plotter for printing maps every day. Both had couches and chairs, large-screen TVs and video games, refrigerators, coffeepots, and posters. Both were equally essential.

Once everything was set, we went to breakfast. That day I walked with my copilot, Sammy Park. Sammy was a ranger who switched over to being a pilot and was a good pilot who spoke with either a moderate Asian accent or a minor speech impediment. Maybe a moderate accent *is* a minor speech impediment, but either way, it was surely due to his company that I got nothing more than a coy smile from Thatcher when we walked into the DFAC, which I responded to with a longer stare than I needed to, none of which Sammy seemed to notice. During breakfast, she walked by our table to make eye contact again without stopping or saying anything, but smiling in such a flirty manner that there was no longer any doubt about what she had in mind. She would have to wait.

Later in the CP, we settled in for a long day of sitting around. A visiting flight surgeon from Task Force Odin, Maj. Joe Puskar (pronounced Püsh´-Kar, with the r being slightly rolled), showed up as well, asking to ride along on any flight that was going out, to which I immediately invited him if we went anywhere. Joe was a seasoned special-forces operator, had deployed many times, and carried a charged-up charisma that suggested he'd be a good guy to have on the ground with us if we went down somewhere. In his go bag he carried an assortment of Afghan garb that would allow him to blend in with a local populace if no one was looking too closely, and seemed to be wearing some sort of moccasin in contrast to the typical desert-tan combat boot. In any contingency-planning discussion as to what our actions would be, were we to land outside the wire, Joe would volunteer the information that he wasn't about to sit around waiting for some "*Air Farce* pussies" to come pick him up, and that he'd happily egress and evade his own way back across the country. He seemed to be the sort who could do it as well.

Air farce. It made me smile that he had a particular angst.

We sat down for some coffee.

This was deployment, as far as my military career had been concerned. I knew people who had gunfights and IEDs going off during convoys and on long foot patrols in dangerous villages, but in my military experience, deployment was a lot of sitting around. That was the way of things in the submarine force as well, at least in the post–World War II naval scenario. There was threat and there was tension. We were there, and we were ready, and sometimes we even found Russian submarines to track, but we never pulled the trigger. There was never a real torpedo evasion; there was never a real torpedo shot. I was on boats with a limited cruise missile capability but never fired them. In the years since my own submarine service, submarines have been used more to attack land-based targets, but I've been lucky enough to never get caught in any real action. While I never went looking for it, and never avoided it, I had never been to a location with enough *real* action for it to find me. Sure, there were little things that happened. On occasion, I saw bullets coming up from the ground in my general direction. With night vision goggles (which amplify any light source thousands of times), it's hard *not* to see tracer rounds, but none of it ever hit me or my helicopter. I went on urgent medevac flights and hauled bloody people to the hospital. I hauled an unfortunate number of people in body bags. All of that is the fringe or the residue of action, though. I've landed on plenty of LZs but never landed on a hot LZ, never had to fire my sidearm, never directed the door gunners to fire on anyone, and essentially never felt threatened. I suppose after a career of this, you get hardened to the things that should be scary, but seriously, I had never been *in the shit*. That was good fortune. I don't fly along thinking it isn't likely; I knew a few people who *had* flown into the shit, so to speak. I just hadn't.

I tried to fly in a manner that was harder to hit, which is a simple matter of flying more unpredictably. Assault pilots are trained to maintain formation discipline: to fly exactly a certain distance from the guy in front of you and stay at a certain angle. If there are multiple ships in the formation, this is important; you have to move like a centipede to stay together like one. But in Iraq and Afghanistan, most of the missions were two-ship missions for the sake of the buddy system; the more elaborate advantages of being in a disciplined formation were irrelevant. There weren't going to be any target handoffs from one ship back to the next, and there weren't really overlapping sectors of fire; one guy wasn't really protecting the other. It was an opportunity for both helicopters to fly randomly, making it harder for our biggest threat to hit us, our biggest threat being small-arms fire and rocket-propelled grenades. For the most part, the obedient mind doesn't proceed beyond practicing the trained discipline; most pilots fly a tight formation. I like to fly like a Formula 1 driver keeping his tires warm, back and forth across chalk one's wake, speeding up, slowing down, climbing, and diving a little, if we were down low. Up high, above 500 feet or so, there isn't much chance of being hit with a hand-sighted weapon, so we just flew straight and level.

How much of a threat was there, really? This was always something to ponder, but in the discussion of small arms, there no doubt were hundreds of thousands of rifles old and new that had completely saturated Afghanistan after an endless history of conflict. Among the AK-47s, PKMs, DShKs, and dozens of foreign-made predecessors and variants, it was possible our opposition had the most impressive and historical collection of machine guns in the world. Whether or not they would be picked up or pointed at us on any given day was unknown, but you had to assume they would be. For RPGs the frequency of threat was lower, but very real. It seemed from most war stories that firing an RPG with any accuracy was difficult; I remember a friend in Iraq who had three of them fired at him on one flight, and even at an altitude of only 200 feet, all three had missed. The problem was, unlike small-arms fire, if one of them *did* hit you, you were fucked. The S-2[6] seemed to be telling us at every morning briefing that the influx of RPGs was alarming, so the potential of RPG fire was always there, but always nebulous. Yes, we're concerned about the unknown. *OK*, now we're concerned about *more* of the unknown.

There are a lot of gung-ho military folks who like to talk about being *in the shit*. They will take that little thing that happened, and tell it and retell it until years later, when they retell it again, and it has grown so much that they get excited and animated telling it, that after a while it evolves into an adjusted truth. You know you are listening to one of these guys when even in casual conversation you realize you are hearing the same war story for the third or fourth time, and it's being told with a lot of vocal inflection. It's easy to do, slipping into perpetuated recollection, and it takes a responsible consciousness to avoid. It's important to avoid, though, unless you're a recruiter, so you don't discredit yourself to people who have been in worse shit than you. Any *real* badass plays things down, not up.

One person who was sometimes considered to be holding himself in higher regard than his peers was Arturo Matos. Art was one of the instructors in the unit and was also the other pilot in command for chalk two of the QRF. He seemed confident, conducted himself in a very professional manner, and was always sharply groomed, punctual, and proficient, but he seemed to know in his mind that nobody else was as proficient as he was at flying the Blackhawk. There were parts of his character I admired in my military mind, and other parts of his character I loved in the brotherly sense, but he had that air about him, and it wouldn't take much for him to see somebody who was deficient in some way, and step right in to tell them. The only problem was they weren't deficient at all; they just weren't doing something *Art's way*. From his point of view he was doing his job and trying to get everyone around him do theirs. He mostly tried to tune up the junior pilots, and anytime he made the mistake of trying to talk down to someone senior, he'd be told to fuck off and would back down. In truth he was a good pilot, but he wasn't special enough for the poise he carried. One point of concern was in defending his own expertise, which included seven years as a Blackhawk crew chief and seven years as a pilot, Art adopted the haughty attitude that he had been "operating" Blackhawks for fourteen years.

That particular day, though, Art had brought an electric remote-controlled helicopter into the CP and was flying it inside, much to the delight of everyone in the room. I enjoyed watching it fly. As he flew somewhat cautiously around, ages of dust floated up and papers blew around, but mostly the flight was uneventful. Jasper Diego joked, "Do a dust landing!," along with his jovial laugh. This entertainment lasted for only one battery pack before we had to settle back down into hours of coffee and repeat trips to the blue canoe.

It seemed like we were going to make the shift without launching when the phone rang. There was an order from the battle captain to launch one Blackhawk for a TIC[7] resupply mission. Art and I still happened to be in the same room and looked at each other. I shrugged and he asked, "Do you want it?" As I was standing up, he had a look like he wouldn't mind not going, so I said I would go and started moving. Not knowing if he was there or not, I shouted for Joe Puskar on my way out the door, without waiting for a response.

CHAPTER 16
FIGHTING AGE

Day 101. This was one of the real ones. Our troops were in a fight somewhere, running out of bullets. In this case, we were going to escort a Chinook out to the grid, they would conduct the resupply, and we would be their escort. First the handheld radio: "Honcho 44 crew, rapid launch for TIC resupply. Acknowledge." Next came the coffee, the TOC, then jogging out to the helicopter. This went fast; everything was in place, and everything happened as a reflex. We got strapped in and fired up faster than the Chinook by almost four minutes. I felt frustration creeping up my neck and considered prompting the Chinook crew but decided to be patient. I knew how easy it was for complications to occur during start-up. It's hard to say what was happening with them, but no point in jumping to conclusions that would annoy someone working through a real problem. I was happy we made it out to the taxiway with no one waiting on us. One distracter occupied our brief delay: I heard one of the cargo doors open, and my crew chief for the shift, the delightful and effective Victoria Burns, told me we had an unexpected passenger. This concerned me, of course, since not only was this pax unmanifested and getting aboard a higher-than-normal-threat-level mission, but whoever it was had run 75 yards across a taxiway, past the tail rotor, and helped themselves right into the back seat of a machine heading into harm's way. I looked back and asked Victoria to hand the stranger an ICS[1] phone, but Joe Puskar plugged in his own headset faster than we could hand him the phone and thanked us for the free entertainment. "Howdy, boys and girls! Y'all mind if I catch a ride?!"

"Hello, Doctor." Joe already knew his attendance was approved.

"Honcho element, this is Bigtime 23 on air battle." I reached down without looking, my hand landing on the transmit selector via muscle memory, clicked it two notches clockwise, and stepped on a small floor mic switch.

"Honcho 44."

"Hey man, sorry about the wait; we dumped an APU.[2] Is that you out on Bravo?"

"Yes sir, and good morning," I replied, recognizing the voice of Chinook pilot Conor Whitehead.

"All right; well, apparently this thing is just over the hill to the south. We're getting it loaded up now, and we'll meet you out on Bravo in about three minutes."

"Rrrroger, Bigtime." Somehow it was important in that moment that my voice stay in the bass-pro-fisherman, don't-scare-the-fish vocal range, but I didn't have much chance to use it.

We monitored ground until Bigtime 23 came thumping out, circling around us in a huge dust cloud. I used the flight controls to lean our relatively small Blackhawk into their downwash; a hovering Chinook can produce 100 mph winds depending on how heavily it's loaded, and we were notably buffeted by its arrival. I saw them all the time; wasn't just gawking like a little kid meeting a superhero at Disney, but I watched their arrival with admiration—the Chinook was an awesome sight. A smile crossed my face to be lucky enough to fly in formation with one. As they touched down, they made one more call over air battle, stating they were REDCON ONE, which I parroted back, simultaneously switching COM 2 to tower.[3] Immediately, I heard their call.

"Bagram tower, Bigtime 23 and flight are on bravo taxiway, ready for departure to the south."

"Bigtime 23, tower, you are cleared for departure via runway 21."

"Cleared for takeoff 21, 23 and flight." Without another word, the huge craft floated up off the ground and began a smooth acceleration up to 110 knots, and I made sure we stayed above their downwash. Chinooks, while slow to accelerate, are the fastest Army helicopters once they get up to speed, due to the fact that they have two main rotors for forward thrust and 10,000 horsepower. Within seconds of departure, I transmitted the Eagle Lift code word to indicate we had fallen into formation with them successfully: "CONVOY."

"Roger, Convoy," acknowledged Conor Whitehead.

We had reached the best part of the job: flying a real mission. We had gotten successfully through the hustling part of the launch, and we were comfortably strapped in. The QRF mission was great because it involved no planning. There wasn't the extended planning cell and briefings and rehearsals of a deliberate assault mission. Don't get me wrong—I love a good planning cell, and I love the strategy of it, and generating the products. . . . There is a real art form to creating a plan from maps and imagery, then organizing it into a mission packet any pilot can use to fly the mission effectively. Sometimes *a deliberate* was a lot more intense and therefore caused folks' performance to be a lot better, or caused folks to be more vigilant, but the planning was a lot of work and time. The QRF didn't have that element. In that regard a QRF mission was like being a medevac pilot: always launching rapidly with no planning involved. This left more room for error, but if you do it enough, you become a pilot who can think on their feet a lot faster. In this particular case, we were going to a fight.

As it turned out, a small squad was on patrol in a village and got too close to someone who wasn't comfortable being inspected. A small gunfight ensued, during which the defending party scurried up into a rock formation.

One consideration for us in Afghanistan was that we usually outgunned the bad guy. Regardless of what kind of homemade shit they had, what kind of Russian shit they had, what kind of Chinese shit they had, or even what kind of black-market shit they could get from Pakistan, we had something bigger and better. But another truth was that not much in our arsenal would go through solid rock. These guys had maneuvered rapidly from a dumpy-looking mud hut, up a goat trail, into what would prove to be an almost impenetrable fortress on the high ground. At the start of the gunfight, our own guys had been able to duck behind an up-armored Humvee, and then to a better area of cover for themselves, but they still did not occupy the high ground. As it was, they volleyed back and forth with little progress until they were running out of ammo. That's not a lot of time, either: ammo is heavy, so it's undesirable to carry enough of it for an extended fight. Gunfights aren't all that common, but the weight of whatever you have to carry for twelve months is a brutal constant.

The troops in this case were not pinned down; they were merely in a standoff. When they were running out of bullets, they could have covered themselves long enough to drive back the other way, but then by anyone's assessment they would have lost the scrimmage. And why had the five amigos fled up the hill in the first place? It seemed suspicious, or at least worth investigating, which is the whole reason our guys were on patrol in the first place. But once the bad guy had the high ground, there could be no further investigating until the threat was subdued.

By the time we got there, Conor and I agreed my ship would stay in orbit while they flew in with the ammo. This was fine with me, because it meant a front-row seat for the show, with nothing to worry about. It's almost impossible for a rifle to hit a circling helicopter at 500 feet, but if they got lucky, we had a layer of armor that worked well from the bottom up. They wouldn't shoot at a tiny little dot up in the sky when they had their hands full on the ground. From our orbit, we could easily see rounds going back and forth, but without the associated Hollywood firebombs and vehicles exploding. I could see why they were running out of ammo: they seemed to be spraying lead up into the rocks at a phenomenal rate. I'm not sure if they were hoping for a ricochet shot or just suppressing the opposition, but for us to see what appeared as an *atmospheric* change between the two sides of the fight from 500 feet up meant an enormous volume of flying lead, tracer rounds, and smoke dominated the scene.

"Yup, they're having a little bit of a party down there," Joe said, most likely still not feeling close enough to the action.

It became apparent to everyone involved that the Air Force had also shown up for the party, with a pair of fighter jets circling above 12,000 feet or so. I don't know what altitude stratum they were assigned to, but it was well above ours, and above the UAS[4] stratum. Their call sign that day was HYPE, and apparently Hype was a gift from the JOC.[5] Our own TOC had no high asset to dispatch but did have "TOC-to-TOC" comms with the JOC. Whether requested or not, Hype had arrived for the same reason anyone else did: they were out and about looking for action. Since neither the Taliban nor al-Qaeda had an air force, our own fighter jets patrolled a pretty boring sky. Once in a great while there was the need to support ground activity, and because they never get to shoot anything in the sky, if there was ground activity they enjoyed showing up.

Then a frustrating thing for the ground forces commander happened. The rules of engagement prevented the Air Force from simply dropping a 500-pound bomb in the notch, because we had shown up offensively and the supposed insurgents had simply fled and began defending themselves. While they were shooting at American troops, they hadn't actually hit any of them. So, the only thing they had really done was get surprised and go to a defensive position.

I have seen missions go wrong before where the collateral damage cost us tremendously in the progress toward stability, even with reparations being paid to the families. So, it wasn't exactly an automatic thing for us to decimate every situation just because we could, even though that might seem like the most appropriate immediate response to the people who were in the fight. These guys had been shooting back and forth for some time, and I'm sure they were excited, focused, and determined to overcome this situation and proceed with the original assignment, which was to investigate something suspicious. Then came the radio call from the ground element asking the TOC to coordinate with Hype for air support.

This was immediately relevant to me because there had been no aerial deconfliction. If they did want to drop the big one on these guys, where did Hype want to come in from, and how could we get out of the way? I could wait until the request was acknowledged to really worry about it, though; the Air Force didn't do anything without permission, and they wouldn't get it immediately.

When the response came back as a *negative* over the SATCOM radio due to rules of engagement, the little gunfight continued as it had prior to the resupply. The troops *were* in contact, but they would have to decide *not* to be and just leave, until we could get organized and come back from a different direction. This was not very well received by the ground forces commander, and he requested again along with his own moral justification for needing to vaporize the opponent: "REQUEST IMMEDIATE AIR SUPPORT! WE'RE UP AGAINST FIVE FIGHTING-AGE INSURGENTS IN A FORTIFIED POSITION ON THE HIGH GROUND," which of course was denied again. They were just going to have to pack up and go home for the day, which was a hard pill to swallow. Whoever was in charge of the ground forces knew they were not pinned down, knew that the intel indicated no high-value targets in that area, and knew that the squad was on a routine patrol in the first place. Adding a massive explosion to the community wasn't going to help with counterinsurgency.

The thought crossed my mind that we could add 1,600 rounds of 7.62 ammo to the equation if I adjusted our flight path down into a low orbit. From that position—for example, 150 feet up—we'd have the high ground and could easily light up the five amigos. After all, they were shooting at our guys. By having the left-side gunner do all the work, I could circle the target counterclockwise and direct Victoria to fire or stop firing while monitoring the action with my own eyes. She knew how to rock the 240. The right-side gunner could bring his ammo cans over and be the belt man for the left gun, and we could wrap this up in about four minutes if the barrel of the 240 didn't melt. We were the legitimate QRF and we had gunship support, even though the gunships were in the wrong stratum to do anything but drop bombs. Tempting . . . I knew Joe would have loved it too, but the ROE[6] just didn't cover it. We hadn't been shot at. If I flew low enough, we might have gotten shot at, but that hadn't happened and wasn't a legitimate loophole. Mainly, the ground element had already requested the pile driver and got denied, so it seemed like the commander's intent here was to walk away from it. If the troops had been pinned down, my plan would have been glorious, but they weren't. Sometimes being senior enough to have tactical discipline could be a bummer.

As Bigtime 23 called back to get my position and reported they were coming out, it occurred to me we had two fighter jets, a Chinook, a Blackhawk, and a bunch of guys and equipment on the ground. That adds up to over $100 million worth of tech and firepower, being held off by five booger-eating morons behind a rock. No wonder the Russians eventually went home.

Was the whole thing a battle? Was it part of a war against the enemy? It's possible the younger people on the ground felt like there was really a war there, since they were in a notable firefight. It was just as dangerous as any other gunfight, but aside from another red thumbtack on the threat map, it wouldn't substantiate a single account of victory or defeat, territory gained or lost, lines shifting forward or back, or any other indicator of progress. It was only another example of having two catalytic elements in the same compound. It was just bad chemistry.

As long as we stayed in Afghanistan, it would happen. Ground patrols don't go into a village with their weapons slung over their backs; no commander would allow that. They proceed *at the ready*, looking cautiously around every corner, trusting no one. They do that for a year and become pollinated with a dormant condition that later blossoms into PTSD, in some cases not being able to walk down the sidewalk for years without considering where best to take cover. And which Afghan local or part-time Taliban fighter with any sort of weapon leaning in the corner could see such a force walking down the road without feeling uneasy? Despite the pace of progress, the amount of potential energy in the equation was something to be weary of.

We flew back to Bagram with a similar feeling to driving home in a quiet car after a loud concert. There was suddenness to the silence of the radios, and immediate dissipation of threat-related stress. No one in the crew felt the need for conversation. It was as sudden as turning off an action movie on the TV and realizing it was eleven at night and everyone else in the house was already sleeping. As soon as we flew away for five seconds, we were out of range of any possible threat from the scuffle and back into friendly blue skies. Heightened senses dulled. One moment our attention was directed at an intense event on the ground, and the next moment we said, *Fuck it; we're outta here.* It created the feeling that everything was *too* quiet. It wasn't though. We just clicked it off.

CHAPTER 17
GUNS AND ALCOHOL

Day 122. The daytime QRF shift ended at 1800 every day, or 6:00 p.m., and most people followed the routine of walking to dinner on the way home from work. The line was short, and I stood outside under the awning for only a few minutes, looking at familiar cracks in the sidewalk, before I went through the screeching front door of the DFAC to swipe my ID card. Immediately inside was Emily Thatcher, and when our eyes met she beamed. This time she had thought it through enough to have a plan.

"How are you?" she said with a pleasant smile.

"Fine, I guess. You?"

"You want to catch a movie sometime?" she said rapidly, trying to finish the conversation before anyone else came in behind me.

My eyebrows went up in surprise at the suggestion of this blatant violation of General Order #1.

"Yeah, that'd be great," I replied, trying to sound like I had no concern for the rules she was asking me to break. I didn't, apparently, though one's mind begins canvassing various thought processes to stay out of trouble.

"Cool!"

"Cool." For another moment neither of us said anything, maybe hoping the other would suggest the next move. My eyes went around the ceiling and back to her, indicating I had no idea.

"My place is probably better."

"Yeah, probably," I said. There was no way in hell I would invite her to my place and risk being seen with a junior soldier from another unit. "Where do you live?"

"Down Disney, past the JOC, then hang a right after the medevac headquarters and it's the third street down on the left, fourth B-hut."

"I see." My eyes went to the door and back. "Sounds good."

"I get off at 1930; want to meet at eight?" she said, her transition from military jargon to normal clock time eluding to formality disappearing after work along with her uniform.

"Sure. See you then." I turned quickly then, already uncomfortable with how long we had been talking. I closed my eyes when I reached the salad bar to imprint a map of what she said in my mind.

My heart rate was noticeable in the fun sort of way. We were not supposed to be fraternizing, but it was a little bit exhilarating to be doing something "wrong." What do they expect, keeping people away from the opposite sex for a whole year? A lot of infractions occur really, all the way up the chain of command, in almost every subparagraph of the general order.

I had already violated at least two subparagraphs of the general order: The consumption of alcohol, and purchasing or possessing a privately owned firearm; namely, the Lebel. I didn't think this additional violation would make me more or less of a saint, and by my account I hadn't done anything immoral. We were both single.

The items listed in General Order#1, in my opinion, are a means to control people who might otherwise make bad decisions. For example, if someone tried to take a souvenir AK-47 home as a war trophy from someone they just shot, that would be inappropriate. Buying an antique rifle permitted by customs and the post office feels different. The other things in G.O.1 are purely a hopeful measure of instilling obedience. If it isn't wrong for me to be drinking or dating at home but it is here, then it's just a local regulation someone created trying to keep the amount of deployment drama down. It does not indicate the moral high ground or the responsible way to think. It's just a set of rules, and for people obedient enough to comply, it probably does reduce the amount of incidents that occur while deployed. Of course, anyone with their own moral compass will do whatever they want, just more secretively.

Anyone who has ever been deployed knows that a road-weary soldier is going to find ways to relax. It would be one thing if we were there for only two weeks. Being deployed for a year is a different story. Every Army deployment I've been on has been dotted with the typical soap-opera-style affairs by one person or another. There were always indicators that at least a few people were using drugs. There was always drinking. There was also the smoking of cigars, and in some cases, hard-to-acquire Cuban cigars. Wouldn't the kind of person willing to acquire such things also like some fine bourbon to go along with it? What better way to relax and unwind than to kick back with a nice stogie and some Maker's Mark? You won't always find proof, because seasoned guys get more and more skillful about it, but the same thing goes on behind closed doors all the way to the top. The number of flag officers who've made headlines for getting in *surprising* levels of trouble is an indicator. That's the way it should be, though; no strait-laced, robotic, strictly disciplined, politically correct individual is freethinking enough to make the most-cunning decisions in real time. Compliant people spend the most time getting approval and therefore become the least effective. They aren't thinking on their feet or taking any risks. I saw it again and again, the ones who bent the most rules also got the job done the best; ergo individual effectiveness is based on having interpretive ability. History is replete with military rule breakers experiencing exponential success, from Henry Lazelle to Jim Gavin. I wasn't totally rogue, but I couldn't sit around for a year demonstrating pure obedience. No one actually wants that, either. *Shit, Hawkeye and Honeycutt had their own still!*

After dinner I went home, showered, shaved, got into PTs, and quietly strolled out into the night. Interpreting what I saw in real time against the somewhat pliable map in my mind, I made my way across the base to a darker street, farther from the flight line, feeling just as amplified and focused as I would on an air assault mission. *I'm not supposed to be using my skills for this*, I thought. I approached the last B-hut in the line and began thinking I didn't have enough intel to go inside and pick a door to knock on, when I saw a silhouetted person smoking on the front stoop. I stopped, cocked my head over, and regarded whoever it was for a moment.

"Nice walk?" I heard Thatcher's voice ask.

"It was," I smiled, uptick in heart rate. "How are you?"

"Good . . ." I could hear the smile in her voice. I knew there would be no discussion of which movie to watch.

I looked up and down the street for some reason, though there was no hope of anything clandestine by that point. My only cover was that I was an anomaly in the neighborhood; most likely no one would recognize me in the darkness if at all, and I moved in to sit on the stoop next to her. She looked over at me, and seeing her face lit up slightly by the cigarette when she took her last drag of it, I saw an expression of pure amusement. It made me smile back. No further words carried us quietly to her room before instinct took over.

CHAPTER 18
LITTLE AMERICA

Day 123. The sun was shining again the next morning. I woke up in my room, feeling amused. Of all the poor bastards stuck out there for a year, I was among the lucky minority enjoying unauthorized stress relief.

There is a great variety of people in the military, but with less diversity across the psychological spectrum than an equivalent civilian body. In a loose interpretation of Jane Loevinger's *Stages of Ego* model, people in everyday life exist somewhere between being a preconformist, a conformist, or a postconformist, with most people settling in the middle. Even within normal civilian life there are fairly persuasive influences to color inside the lines, follow rules, and behave like everyone else. This even hints at the definition of civilization, with penalties for divergence in almost every category, and the rules are written and enforced by the people in the middle: conformists.

A young person yet to conform may rebel against whatever they can, simply for not liking to be told how to think or behave. This is the preconformist. After enough spankings, enough time in detention, enough speeding tickets, or enough exclusion, the general slump of conformity can saturate a persona like molasses, gradually dousing the rebellious spark. For some people it takes a long time, and they never do *quite* conform, or learn the easiest way to live, which is basic compliance.

Most people are conformists. The more conscious an individual is, the sooner he or she learns to conform, in some cases even in the earliest years of development. They develop to get good grades, perform well on teams, and succeed easily in society. They paint their houses before the neighbors start wishing they would, change their car's oil on schedule, and even have a plan for how to pay their taxes every year. While the preconformist may resent the conformist and the postconformist may pity the conformist, the conformist himself feels great security and even pride in how well he is conforming to society.

Finally, the postconformist: people who outgrow the suggested restraints, free thinkers who have already conformed but soon realize there's more to life than obedience. *There must be more to life than vinyl siding or trying to go on a cruise.* The postconformist knows the furthest you can get with conformity is however far the societal average got and decided was adequate. They come up with new ideas, trying them without approval or consent. The postconformist still mostly conforms to avoid hassle but is comfortable making unconventional decisions. While a conformist saves money to go on vacation, the postconformist finds a way to own the airline. The Elon Musks of the world.

The vast majority of military people are conformists. Even at higher levels, many senior leaders begin by asking, *Will this be in compliance with everything?* It starts with basic training, where a young person falls into the mental trap that if you sign that contract and don't follow through with the obligation, an unfavorable discharge will follow you around for the rest of your life. Then the two months of time-proven brainwashing begins, starting with taking off the clothes you showed up with and shaving your head. You're told when to eat, when to sleep, how to stand, how to dress, how to walk, and how to talk, with various coercive measures in between, making compliance the easiest path. It's overt enough that conformity becomes relief. Recruits begin conforming *urgently*. It is a form of psychological reprogramming that if sustained for a great period of time (years, for example) would indeed create a new and very organized, however emotionally dysfunctional, person. Fortunately, years of reprogramming aren't possible. The military needs bodies to work. So the military gets only two months of reshaping an individual before he or she goes on to some other form of specialized training. Individual job-skills training in most cases will also have constraints on behavior, but not with the same intensity as basic training.

Different people retain various amounts of brainwashing from boot camp, in most cases settling back into a more organized or slightly more compliant version of their old self. In today's all-volunteer military, often it is people who were attracted to organization in the first place and were already somewhat organized. For some of these people, rules and regulations become almost a religion. Compliance, even the ability to quote the very regulations they are in compliance with by page and paragraph number, provides a sense of comfort and empowerment. They start thinking they are more efficient than the people around them, who aren't complying as well, and evolve into superconformists. Within the already constrained spectrum of military psyches, some evolve into poster children or even *Compliance Nazis*. Mostly, though, it's just dudes and dudettes, normal people doing a job. Jamie is still a kid who likes engines, and Melissa is still an enthusiastic person who collects unique clocks, and Pete is still a guy who just likes flying, and Stephen is still a guy who likes playing the guitar. They keep doing the same things they liked when they were civilians, just within more structure. Extreme conformists are exceptions; mostly the military is made up of regular people wearing a uniform and trying to follow rules.

Whether my behavior of the previous night had been revolutionary or rebellious, the greater problem of OIF and OEF was that thousands of free-thinking soldiers (or hyperconscious, entitled, sarcastic conformists?) were deployed with the ability to realize the conflicts were both greatly political in nature and ambiguous in effect. Everyone involved realized that within the risk management structure, there was less worth taking a risk for, and the long-term effect may have been a weakening of our own military. There were few situations calling for ingenuity or bravery. There was less drive. There were not the moments undefined by regulation needing decisions in real time. There was not the cultivation of gut instinct that comes with real war. There were no "holy shit" moments causing young, obedient soldiers to be slapped in the face with the bloody reality of the world. What there was a lot of was echelons of leadership making sure no one made any mistakes or took any risks. Compliance. Conformity. The defining goal for senior leadership during the endurance marathon of OEF was to make it through the year with no losses. Be there, but don't break anything. And we *were* there. We had the worst parts of deployment, which are family separation and the compactly stratified problems associated with that, but we didn't have much of the *good* stuff. We didn't have any glorious, clear victories to make the sacrifices feel like our country and our families were protected from something.

Some of it highlighted the phrase "choked with caution" and groomed many a junior lieutenant and captain to spend a career hesitating.

Speaking of free-thinking postconformists, Special Forces doc Joe Puskar was hanging around the CP again, hoping for an adventure during what would turn out to be a slow day for the QRF. Curiosity finally got the better of me, and I asked Joe what all he had in his bag. Whenever he flew with us, besides his unconventional footwear, he had that bulky go-bag, unusual for a passenger but essential to Joe. I had to wonder, since he was obviously an operator, what was important enough for him to carry. The multilingual doc had joined the Special Forces in the early 1980s, at the start of his checkered military career, and had real ground time in Central America, along with the normal tours to Korea, Alaska, and Ft. Bragg, before getting out to go to college and become a doctor. Having missed the action, he came back in after 9/11, this time with the Air Force, as a flight surgeon assigned to a wing of Spectre Gun Ships[1] in the Air Force Special Operations

Command. He was unsatisfied, though, specifically due to the fact that he was too far removed from the action. Sometimes, looking out the window of the Spectre, he would see Army helicopters way down low, proceeding into danger the Air Force covered only from up high. He saw it was closer to the fight and was drawn back to his roots, back to the Army. After some negotiating with a helpful recruiter, Joe was able to transfer back to the Army as a flight surgeon with a lot of special-operations background and eventually found his way into the Army's new counter-IED program: Task Force Odin.

Either through love lost from his own time in the Air Force, or the fact that Task Force Odin was established in the first place because the Air Force was never around when the Army needed them, Joe maintained a healthy disdain for his old branch, a disdain that lay at the very heart of his unique go-bag. Always maintaining (during the crew brief) that he would not allow himself to be rescued by the Air Force if we found ourselves on the ground for some reason, Joe had everything it would take to blend in with his surroundings and evade.

My own collection of essential evasion commodities in a small backpack included only a few magazines of M4 ammo, a few magazines of M9 ammo, a set of thermal underwear, a bunch of Harvest Bars, and one of those small eight-packs of V-8 in metal cans. I figured I just needed to stay warm, have some snacks, and maybe defend myself briefly until I could call for extraction on my survival radio. Joe's bag held so much more: not only did he have extra clothing, but he had culturally appropriate clothing so he could blend in with the populace, to go along with his rather inconspicuous footwear. He was the only one wearing some sort of moccasin every day. He had a Soviet Spetznaz shovel, not only to dig in if he had to hide, but also to go hunting or kill people with. He had tan netting he could camouflage his encampment with for hiding in the day and moving at night. He had some Steiner 7× marine binoculars for pulling security or mapping out an evasion route. Furthermore, he carried a personal GPS receiver with him, which he had populated with his own database by flying around with us and storing memorable landmarks. It was obvious if he ever hit the ground outside the wire, not only would he be fine, he would be feeling the excitement of Christmas morning.

It didn't happen that day, though; our shift never launched.

CHAPTER 19
TIP OF THE SPEAR

Day 150. There is something about being removed from normal life, and isolated in a container of sorts, that can have a magnifying effect on certain things such as news, music, or even simple conversations. I remember being deployed on the boat and, after some number of weeks of isolation, borrowing a Beatles tape from a friend of mine to listen to on my WALKMAN. For whatever reason, the path of my life had kept me from ever hearing the song "Hey Jude" until that moment. Don't get me wrong, it's a hit song no matter how you first hear it, but within the psychological experiment of living aboard a submarine in the middle of the Atlantic Ocean, hearing it for the first time was like hearing music *at all* for the first time, or tasting milk chocolate for the first time. Any level of isolation can cause what remaining stimulus there is to be amplified. I experienced an amplified reaction again to the news that Admiral Mike Boorda had died while we were underway. Things can just hit you harder when you're on deployment. It's similar to the discussion of someone who loses one of their senses experiencing heightened awareness with the other four. Back at home, every member of the unit goes home at the end of the day and occupies himself or herself with an unlimited number of various activities and personal agendas, which tend to have a balancing effect on unit chemistry. Everyone stays grounded by normal life. It also has a diluting effect—the problems of the unit become harder to solve at home, because the members of the unit are greatly distracted, and sometimes even hard to keep track of, but in the sense of emotional balance the personalities of the unit can seem to be very much *on the level* at home. During deployment, every member of the unit shares the same daily problems and is present and available at all times. Considerations or conclusions get circulated rapidly and either amplified or stomped on by the group. We become our best team. Often, team dynamics can rapidly resolve problems, but sometimes within this emotionally unbalanced combustion chamber, conversations explode like objecting chemicals being poured into a laboratory beaker.

One morning found what should have been a lighthearted debate, being somewhat bitterly volleyed back and forth in the CP, stemming from an episode of *MythBusters*: Could an airplane take off from a treadmill? This would prove to be just as ridiculous but somehow more heated than the average deployed debate, primarily because Peter Griffin and Arturo Matos could not get their mind wrapped around the physics of the question. You would think the two flight instructors would be able to comprehend something as basic, but somehow they had mental blocks.

Instructors in the Army don't necessarily have the most experience and aren't necessarily the savviest. Being an instructor simply means someone went to the four-week school to be designated as an instructor. That four-week school covers a little on how to teach, how to explain, and where, in the many regulations and publications, one could find answers to the usual questions. It did not hone one's flying ability or make someone a better pilot. In some cases, it did the opposite, because the aforementioned conformist is then refreshed on the *unbelievable* multitude of rules and regulations, gets encumbered with demonstrating compliance, flies more cautiously, and does more paperwork. It is the incidental castration of instinctive flying.

As this discussion surfaced, for either obstinacy or ignorance, Griffin and Matos each took an immediate position against an airplane being able to accelerate on a treadmill up to takeoff speed. Much to the befuddlement of the junior pilots who disliked Griffin and Matos anyway, their position was especially difficult to understand in light of the fact that Jamie Hyneman and Adam Savage had already busted the myth. Within *MythBusters* lies the truth. Either Griffin and Matos were ignorant, or they were so set in their position that it was too embarrassing to reverse themselves. They certainly weren't teaming up with each other to mess with the company; everyone knew they despised each other. The wheels make the treadmill irrelevant. The airplane is still pulled forward by the propeller, which is still grabbing relatively stationary ambient air. Consistent with their insecurities, Griffin and Matos would defend their position to the point of disintegration, each becoming more and more childlike as this amplified discussion went on. Everyone eventually walked away, perplexed by their stubbornness, but the conversation was reignited the following day, and the following. It was indicative that *this* was what we were spending our time arguing about.

After a few days of this crisis, I decided—despite my own contempt for one of these individuals—that I would try to explain it in easier terms and with diagrams. As one of very few pilots in the company with full immunity from repercussion, I offered that I was willing to explain it sincerely and one step at a time. Matos said he didn't need an explanation and didn't care about airplanes, and he left the room. Griffin was open minded enough to sit and listen as I carefully drew a treadmill with a shopping cart on it, with someone standing on the floor behind the treadmill, holding the cart as the wheels began to turn, etc., etc. But he continued to shake his head that it wouldn't be possible for an airplane.

It would have been funny if it were something that wasn't relevant, but we were pilots! We're supposed to know about air molecules and physics! It ended up being some pretty embarrassing deployed folklore for the two instructors but was also an interesting abstract on the cross section of *our nation's elite*.

There was a pretty substantial advertising campaign crossing America's media landscape at the time, boasting of the precision and power of our military: "The few, the proud," "Army Strong," "Aim High," etc. It's great promotion, as well it should be. Public support for the military (not necessarily the wars) felt like it was at an all-time high, a stark contrast from the obvious low point of the Vietnam War. "Support Our Troops" seemed to be plastered everywhere, and it would be unpopular *not* to support the troops. Getting back to the banners and the promotion and the projected image, naturally, the DOD propaganda machine painted a very rosy picture. In reality, only a select few rise to the tuned discipline of marching in front of the Tomb of the Unknown Soldier, clad in perfect dress, sabers laser-sharpened, boots clicking, or, more importantly, rise to the occasion of conducting a complex, multitiered mission to conquer an objective with singularity of purpose and precision. The majority of service people, while being good people, settle somewhere slightly above the level of performance they had before training. There is no perpetual progress toward being elite. The military as a whole has the same range of personalities and cross section of performance as any other demographic, empowered by different authority and bigger toys. There are *some* who are above average. There's far more who are passionately average, and some who are below average.

One might even conclude that someone in the military could be a citizen with below-average functionality, because they are never burdened with paying for housing, food, medical or dental care and have job security regardless of performance. Unless they do something illegal, service members are unlikely to get kicked out. Regardless of performance, a person who was able to make it through basic training can reasonably expect to stay in the military if they don't get into trouble, with many promotions happening on a schedule rather than being performance based. This is a predictable outcome until the top four or five levels of the pyramid.

In the military, the average person moves every three or four years to a new assignment or duty station. The average *green tabber* (Army lingo for a person in a leadership role) will move to a new job every eighteen to twenty-four months. With this influx and outflux of people, it is hard to establish a trend on someone's job performance, and hard for a leader to develop a very solid course of action through the required steps of counseling. If a problem was identified with an individual, the predefined administrative course of action would take months to inflict: first verbal, then several rounds of written counseling, followed by letter of reprimand, article 15 punishment, nonjudicial punishment, captain's mast, admiral's mast, board of inquiry, or court-martial, with the required periods of time in between, let alone the paperwork required by it. From this comes the expression "You'll spend 90 percent of your time on 10 percent of your people." No new leader (or soon-to-move-on leader) has the time or wants the burden of administering disciplinary action, so mostly it doesn't happen except in the most-severe cases. Many infractions get entirely handled with the easiest level of recourse, which is a single round of verbal counseling; basically, yelling at someone for being a dumbass.

Without committing any horrible crimes, the majority of below-average performers in the military can sulk along without much worry. As such, the average unit has some percentage of these boot scuffers. It's not unlike any other job in the civilian sector. Obviously, there are millions of civilians performing in an excellent manner, but the point is that the military isn't exempt from poor performers. If said performer stays in long enough without incident, they will gradually get promoted on schedule all the way through a thirty-year career, whether they are the best thing for the unit or not. Just like in the civilian world, there are also performers who never miss a beat but, for whatever reason, do *not* get promoted. There is always that occasional ambiguity to ponder.

There is also every unfortunate dynamic all demographics possess: there are womanizers, thieves, sexual abusers, cowards, slackers, malingerers, liars, people of low moral fiber or questionable character, people with poor hygiene, people with evasive attitudes, irresponsible people, cheaters, drug addicts, and alcoholics. Our current battle against cases of sexual harassment and sexual assault in the military is an indicator. There are also geniuses, heroes, patriots, hard workers, defenders of the weak, generous people, valiant people, and daring people. There are as many highs and lows as any other group, with the aggregate mean being only slightly more distinguished (on the basis of each soldier in this all-volunteer army having the initial inclination to serve) than a similar civilian cross section. Typically, a person in the military works less per day than a person in the regular world, whose hours equate directly to pay. Military folks are salaried, but there is no output product. We show up, stand ready, and either do or do not work, depending on what comes up during the day. A watch stander might argue with me, someone who essentially works the same shift every day, but with few exceptions, being in the military isn't as hard as working in a factory for eight hours a day. There is a lot of standing around, a lot of waiting. A lot of time spent on a QRF, for example. A lot of time sitting next to the pier in the submarine, cleaning, painting, or just watching movies. By virtue of being part of an on-call asset, being in the military is based on *always* being ready but seldom getting called. It's a cousin to being a firefighter.

So a transparent report of our unit would account not only for a lack of activity in our particular assignment to Afghanistan, but also a saturation of unremarkable people who fulfilled it. That would be fine if the media, the chain of command, or the individuals themselves labeled it responsibly, but they didn't.

The *media* wouldn't report on a unit with no mission or no goal, because there is nothing to overdramatize about it. They only wanted to hear about anything going wrong and turn it into "violence erupting." The *unit* wouldn't take the position that we weren't doing anything special, because that would cause everyone to let their guard down while simultaneously *destroying* morale; there's nothing more depressing than being isolated from family for no reason. Besides, every leader from the division commander down to the company commanders reminded us frequently that we had a rendezvous with destiny, ever since Gen. William Lee said it in the first place, during the activation ceremony of the 101st Airborne Division in 1942. No command element was about to walk out and say, "OK, guys, this whole deployment is stupid, so don't be too intense about anything." That just wouldn't happen, regardless of any private feelings the commanders may have had. Because SECDEF and the commander in chief said to go over there and endure displacement from families, the fantastic expense, the horrific injuries, and thousands of resulting deaths, the deployment had to be painted from the top down as a gallant and necessary event, destined to shape the world for the better. No other version of things would dare be disseminated, and certain levels of command even evolved into pathological optimists.

Finally, certain personalities chose to misrepresent themselves in the same manner, absorbed into the perpetual exaggeration of circumstances and burdens, until not only did they convince the younger people in the unit of their capabilities and expertise, in time they even started believing themselves that they were the charismatic element around which the unit pivoted. It was like a symphony of misplaced chest pounding, cascading from the Pentagon all the way down into the egos of operators, that could incubate unusable aggressiveness during a conflict requiring restraint.

Such as it was then, the aforementioned conformist boot scuffer, having merely stayed in longer than anyone else in the unit, rose with unremarkable ability to a senior position, considered himself to be the tip of the spear, demanded respect in situations requiring no leadership at all, couldn't understand the simple physics of an airplane taking off, and looked around the room with pity at intelligent people who knew the correct answer but didn't feel like wasting their breath schooling the stupid motherfucker. With such a person in the unit reminding everyone they're not good enough for the mission we didn't actually have, it's no wonder morale sagged. It sagged all year for some people, especially the ones whose sense of spirit was tied to the company.

Two such people were Sammy Park and Jasper Diego. Sammy was a good pilot who, for whatever reason, continued to be misunderstood by three or four arrogant senior pilots. Even though he had almost seven hundred hours, he couldn't convince enough people in the unit that he was a good-enough decision maker to be signed off as a pilot in command. Jasper was in a similar boat; he came into the Army as a commercial fixed-wing pilot and FAA-certified flight instructor. For some reason the senior warrant officers looked down on his jovial, lighthearted personality as somehow not being "military" enough, and he wound up in poor favor during the monthly discussion as to who should be signed off as a pilot in command and who shouldn't. Providing no guidance to either of these individuals, only the verdict that *they hadn't been recommended* was a recurring and disheartening theme for the year.

Cinco de Mayo had come and gone, it was mid-May, and as the day unfolded without needing to launch anywhere, it became apparent that a pirated copy of J. J. Abrams's new interpretation of *Star Trek* was available, which was nice because we were all missing the new release in theaters back home. We were about to watch it when news of remarkably deviant behavior reached the CP. Apparently, a deployed soldier in another unit at Bagram was arrested for posting on a social media site that he would pay $2,000 to anyone who was willing to ejaculate on his face. While it didn't seem enticing to anyone present, it got a lot of crinkled-up faces, and even mock acceptance from Bill Westergaurd, who exclaimed with amplified expressions in his typical drawl, "Uh, uh, ah'm not gay or anythang, but for two thousand dollars, . . . ah'm probably gonna bust a nut on yer face!" A cackle of awkward laughter disapproved the conclusion.

How someone had gotten to that point was hard to imagine, but to be stupid enough to advertise such promiscuity was asking for trouble, which the individual apparently found. We would have thought that was going to be the big headline for the day, but unfortunately, it wasn't.

Later in the shift, we were further shocked and disappointed to hear that one of the junior enlisted personnel in our task force had accidentally killed himself while huffing whippets in his room. He hadn't shown up for work, and the rumor mill informed us he was found in his room with the symptoms of asphyxia and several expended containers of canned air. As the day unfolded, anonymous sources whispered of contraband drugs, either shipped in or acquired from local nationals working on base.

I was friends with the commander of the kid's unit and asked how she was doing with it all. At the time, she was flipping through his Facebook page, shaking her head and saying she couldn't believe it, but she was going to have to call the kid's parents and explain to them he had accidentally killed himself somehow with recreational behavior.

This was another unfortunate sample of our experience. The kid was a fobbit[1] in the first place; his deployment would consist of living on the base for a year, fortified and covered, never leaving the wire, and never supposing to. He was a cook, and one assigned to the interior of Bagram. Out of boredom he had looked for an escape and had either overdone it or gotten his hands on something that wasn't as refined as he was expecting. He'd be shipped home in a flag-draped coffin, processed at Dover, and received by family members standing in complete dismay. There would be no justification; he didn't die winning a war. No rationalization: he probably wouldn't have died otherwise, because he didn't go out on missions. There would be only disbelief and frustration. He should have been fine but made choices that ruined a family.

CHAPTER 20
BLIND SALVO

Day 166. On the morning of Memorial Day, I had a mission up to Bamiyan to pick up eight Norwegian commandos and fly them down to Kabul. While my crew and I briefed the mission and headed to the ramp for departure, the only other notable activity seemed to be a private flight briefing taking place on the side table, almost at a whisper, between Arturo Matos and Todd Wolfe. The Duke had finally been able to reschedule his pilot-in-command evaluation, almost six weeks after the last unsuccessful attempt with Griffin. Certainly, Art knew Todd was good to go, and this ride would just be a formality. I wished him luck without actually saying it as I headed out the door.

Going to Bamiyan was one of the scenic flights we could take out of the Bowl, different from the normal ring route flights to JBAD, Kabul, Airborne, Goode, or Ghazni. Bamiyan was 100 miles southwest and was 3,500 feet higher than Bagram, with an 8,400-foot elevation. That meant it was cooler, and for some reason people just seemed nicer out there. The accumulation of red thumbtacks on the threat map was certainly sparse around Bamiyan.

Bamiyan was a forty-minute flight up a very scenic valley, most of which drained down into the Bagram Bowl. There was no real sense of *threat* flying out there, few FOBs, and few troops moving around. There was a coalition presence, but it was hard to say how much of it was defensive posturing and how much of it was developmental. In parts of the country, the coalition had made productive efforts to improve roads and schools and helped with energy management by installing orchards of windmills. On that flight, as in much of the country on most days, everything felt quiet and peaceful.

Bamiyan was home to an upsetting historical site: a pair of holes in the mountainside. Up until 2001, there had been a pair of giant buddhas carved from the sandstone in the face of a tall cliff on the north side of Bamiyan, both of which had been over 100 feet tall. The sixth-century statues were recently destroyed by the Taliban, though, who had declared they were religious idols that had to go. It must have been a sad day in Bamiyan when the sandstone exploded out of the mountain in a huge dust cloud, leaving two vaguely human-shaped recesses in the rock. Flying by the cliff face and observing the result was disheartening.

We landed and picked up the pax, eight extremely heavy-duty-looking Norwegian brutes. I'm sure not all Scandinavians looked like this, but Norway's elite forces accumulated the toughest of them. Not one of them was under 250 pounds, and each was stacked with special equipment. They looked like they could handle just about anything. I'm not sure what their mission had been or was about to be, since this was merely an administrative flight down to Kabul with no action on either end.

We lifted off with our heavy load and cruised back down the long valley, turning south of Bagram, en route to downtown Kabul.

Flying in Kabul could be fascinating for a variety of reasons. A flat city surrounded by magnificent mountains, it was reminiscent of flying over Phoenix in the topographical sense, though 4,000 feet higher. The international airport on the north side of town was busy, and while international control towers all spoke English on the radio, some of the traffic coming and going was hard to understand and hard to tell from which direction they were coming. Electrical distribution had found a different course than it had in Iraq, so at least the city wasn't strung up with massive super towers and high-tension power lines like in Baghdad. Kabul did have its own indigenous problem for helicopters, however: dozens of kites flying high, every day.

You might not think a kite would be a big problem for a 20,000-pound helicopter, but the kites flew in our altitude stratum and represented a windshield and engine hazard. They could be hard to see, and dodging them always happened at the last second, which was never desirable in formation. It wasn't uncommon for the first helicopter to shout "KITE" over the radio and duck in one direction while chalk two would dodge in the opposite. If chalk two had been in a close formation at that moment, on the side chalk one was swerving toward, it could cause chalk two to decelerate suddenly and split up the formation for ten or fifteen seconds. Finally, if some kid wanted to fly a kite, it didn't send a very good cultural message if we came along and chopped it to pieces. Unfortunately, there were several occasions during the year when I would land and have to unwind kite string from the tail rotor.

I read Khaled Hosseini's wonderful book *The Kite Runner* prior to going to Afghanistan, and every time I saw a kite, I would look down to see if there was a pack of excited children at the bottom of it. Sometimes there was, which was wonderful, but sometimes the kites had simply been flown up to remarkable altitudes and tethered.

Between the international traffic coming and going from the airport and the kites, birds, and other helicopter traffic such as the massive Vodka Hips floating around, the sky over Kabul was a busy place. More fascinating was the amazing swarm of activity in the streets of a Middle Eastern capital city.

If Kabul had three million people living in it, it could look as if every one of them was standing out in the street. In every visible corner of the city, folks were moving from one spot to the next, nearly climbing over each other, all within seconds of getting run over by one of the thousands of cars and trucks chugging through the city. There were neighborhoods that seemed to have buildings built on buildings, stacked-up dilapidated shacks existing in unbelievably desperate states of poverty, apparently cemented onto the backs of more-modern buildings providing structural integrity. Like any city, there were mosques and mausoleums, car dealerships, markets, banks, schools, universities, sports arenas, parks, hotels, and hospitals. The Kabul River ran through the city, with traffic jammed up at each bridge. There were Afghan military troops and police cars. There was a huge, abandoned palace. There was a 300-foot-tall replica of the Eiffel Tower down the street from a rainbow-colored shopping mall. On the outskirts, houses seemed to taper off structurally as well as economically; downtown displayed three-story houses of concrete and glass, with fancy paint schemes and private driveways, while on the fringes and smeared up into the foothills were thousands of mud huts and goat trails. The place was intense.

There were many locations from which we typically dropped people off and picked them up, some secure and some not. It was always entertaining getting to these places while looking down into the streets of Kabul, dividing our attention between fascination and the forward-facing dangers of flying. We dropped off the Huge Norwegians at their base and departed to the north again, weaving between birds and kite string, climbing out over the last of the mud huts and under the heavy traffic of the international airport, then across the open desert between Kabul and Bagram. Easy mission.

After a very truncated debrief, Sammy Park caught my attention and quietly told me that Todd had failed another pilot-in-command check ride and had gone back to his hooch. Apparently, Arturo wasn't even sure of the result himself but, after a quick consult with Griffin, informed the Duke he was a no-go again. After Sammy and I shared a round of disbelieving expressions and head shaking with each other, I strolled off to ponder. Sammy must have known the feeling, having failed multiple pilot-in-command check rides himself, but he probably took it as validation that the current system was biased. I thought about asking Art what happened, but I really didn't want to hear his answer. Not only would I have guessed he would do the opposite of Griffin and give Todd a satisfactory evaluation, but to hear they had actually conferred with each other to make sure it was okay to keep him under their thumbs was disgusting. I couldn't fix it, except to invite someone from outside the company to give Todd an unbiased evaluation.

I had a moment of clarity then; the Duke was a threat to these two instructors, one self-centered and clumsy and the other an emotional lightweight. Not a threat to their flying ability—everyone pretty much controlled the machine in the prescribed manner. Somehow, he was a threat to their egos or their self-esteem. He had reached their level of expertise far too easily, and maybe it was unsettling to them. They were obviously going to prove they could hold him to every standard in the book by their own nearsighted interpretation. That could only be depressing to Todd, and as word of the evaluation spread through the ranks of the copilots, all were shown our company had embedded oppressors in the instructor ranks. The situation would eventually resolve itself, but only through the dissolution of the company.

There were days when time went by quickly, days when there was a mission or a lot of activity. There were also days that dragged on. Sometimes we'd fly a fun or a busy mission, get tired, stroll to the DFAC after work for a casual dinner, walk home, settle in for a movie, and fall asleep. Those were good days, when we didn't have time to realize a year of our lives was slipping by. Those were days I could purely enjoy, feeling like I had commanded my small piece of the battlefield, achieved my mission, and celebrated with some decent bourbon. On the active days I felt content, and it was a good life experience.

There were other times when days dragged on with no action, no mission, and no accomplishments, and boredom eroded unit morale at a rate similar to Alka-Seltzer dissolving. This could have a catalytic effect on the occasional tendency for people to misbehave. For my own account, having been fairly content after a flight to Bamiyan, I settled happily down to sleep after a busy scene of Will Teasle calling for the dogs and the helicopter. Others in the B-hut apparently had sustained enough boredom to slip further into oblivion than intended, and the sleepy quiet of the hallway was interrupted.

Pete "Surprise, I am in Blackhawk" Latham had so much to drink and had been surrounded by so rowdy a crowd that he thought it necessary to put hallway neighbor Matt Decker out with a fire extinguisher, even though Matt wasn't actually on fire. In response, my other neighbor, Chris Randle, got up and commenced to beating the shit out of Max, neither one possessing the coordination or energy to inflict harm, nevertheless spoiling the mood. By the time I awoke to the commotion, everyone in the hallway had devolved into swearing drunks, scurrying around in the dust cloud to find a broom and dustpan to sweep up the dry-chem extinguishing agent, with Chris's residual anger being centered on the notion that such behavior would draw attention to the gallons of alcohol collectively stashed. A valid point.

Realizing the midnight commotion was likely over, I settled back down to sleep, smiling that this would easily turn into a lighthearted "war story" within a few days.

Some number of hours later, I was awoken by a dull percussive event, which, in the fog of initially waking, sounded like a shipping container being dropped by a forklift. It was a deep, resonant *boom* that shook the ground slightly, which seemed to fit; I lived only 15 yards from container row. Not pondering the odds of someone moving containers around at three in the morning, I closed my eyes to fall back asleep at the exact moment of the sound repeating. That time I heard it with a conscious mind. Having already cataloged the sound, hearing it consciously caused my eyes to open again in note. *That was no container.* Looking around my room provided no answers. Further listening collected no additional report.

I got out of bed, slipped my toes into flip-flops, and quietly went outside, three or four steps, stopped, and listened. Stepping out of my insulated B-hut into central Bagram Airbase could be like coming up out of water, from muted tranquility to sudden atmospheric noise, but I didn't hear anything out of the ordinary. I walked farther toward the flight line, saw no unusual activity, no people scurrying, no shouting, and no forklifts. Looking down container row also revealed no activity, so *what was that?* On top of the HHC headquarters just outside the runway and ramp perimeter, someone had built a deck, complete with Frankenstein lawn chairs and picnic tables. I ventured up the wretched-looking steps of the structure for a higher vantage point.

Most things in my neighborhood at Bagram were one vehicle, one container, or one B-hut high. There were only a few improved structures that rose to a second story, so from the rooftop deck I could see most of the base. Two nearby black smoke clouds suggested that we had just been mortared, about 250 yards from my B-hut. *Huh.* I stood still a few seconds, forcing myself to look and listen more carefully in that direction to get a sense of the damage and the response, and noticed plenty of people already dressed and responding. Flashing lights of some sort were moving down Disney Drive toward the commotion. It would have taken me at least three or four minutes to run down there, by which time the designated responders would be in place, so I stood.

I continued reflecting in the quiet night about what it was and how concerned to be, but I was not alarmed. It was intense and interesting, but it was just another potshot. Another two mortar rounds fired locally from just outside the wire; any random target will do. This happened from time to time, once every few weeks maybe. I immediately knew I had no interest in getting into one of the bunkers. There were small concrete bunkers randomly placed around the base, enough so anyone desiring a bunker could find one within a minute, but they had a 4-foot-high ceiling and a gravel floor with no seating. They were basically huge, inverted concrete troughs with no ergonomic consideration whatsoever. To kneel or sit in one of the cobweb-filled cells would mean immediate discomfort, and I really wasn't worried about another mortar round. I had that impervious attitude, no fear a mortar round would hit my B-hut or myself, despite the fact that I was looking at two smoking holes in the ground. If mortars had been landing every few seconds with no predictable ending, I may have been inclined to seek cover, but all was quiet. The potshots were always like this, one or two salvos then nothing.

I went back to bed and fell asleep easily.

CHAPTER 21
HEAT ROUND

Day 172. I may have been mostly oblivious, noting mortar rounds to occur about monthly; Milton Duran, the commander of the reconnaissance and attack company F 3/101, flew a mission profile driven by mortar rounds falling on the base at least twice a week in the winter, and almost daily in the summer. Kiowa Warrior and Apache aircraft were assigned the task of patrolling the perimeter of the airbase at night, flying low-altitude recon missions in a search-and-destroy mission profile called CM2RI, which is easier to say than Counter-Mortar-MANPAD-Rocket-Interdiction. The design and effectiveness of this security mission evolved during the year into hunter-killer teams referred to as "pink teams," meaning one asset from the Attack community, whose flag is black and white, and one asset from the Reconnaissance community, whose flag is red and white. One of several mission profiles that worked well was to leave the Apache up high, in the 5,000-to-8,000-foot altitude stratum, and have the Kiowa working down low, in the NOE[1] altitude range. Expert at reconnaissance, the Kiowa could identify a pair of unsuspecting villains setting up a mortar tube, and either destroy them immediately with guns or rockets or call the high element and sit back to enjoy the show. The Apache could set up an approach path with the chain gun that would be indefensible. This focused security effort rounded up a half-dozen confirmed kills during the year, but that's only the ones the insurgency wasn't able to drag away before the ground element arrived; at any grid the Kiowa identified, an infantry squad was dispatched out to secure the site and make sure any remaining explosive paraphernalia did not find its way back to a cache.

The frequency and smallness of mortar attacks represented another dynamic, which the airbase commander eventually realized—*the insurgency was annoying us for their amusement.* Obviously, two idiots with a mortar tube attacking a massive airbase was pointless, unless they hit the main reactor, which of course could start a chain reaction and blow up the entire station. Except Bagram didn't have a reactor. What we did have, and used during every mortar attack, was an extremely effective air-raid siren, straight out of Pearl Harbor. Hearing it brought a smile to my face, which I realize may have been inappropriate. It was possible, however, while speculating on the imminent obliteration of my body, to also admire a thing. Many times, I enjoyed the initial growl of the horn, gaining decibels through its baritone ramp-up before reaching an undeniable stentorian tenor that *howled* throughout the valley and reflected back from the mountains to boot. The creators of this system must have been amused with themselves indeed, obviously nourished by an unlimited budget to achieve so freakish a volume. From outside the wire, launching mortar rounds must have been more fun than a carnival game. *Send whatever you got over the fence and see if you win the prize!*

The airbase commander discontinued responding with the siren.

While mortar fire felt like a minor threat during the deployment, small-arms fire and RPGs were a persistent point of concern during missions. In flight, small-arms fire was a much more common and daily threat than RPG fire, but *risk mitigation* made it bearable. Risk mitigation in this case could be summed up with "BAPS" and flight profile. BAPS[2] was a fairly recent development in the long-standing quest to add armor to a helicopter without adding too much weight. Helicopters are almost universally a thin sheet metal shell with accessories bolted on, and therefore not at all resistant to bullets. A series of custom-shaped armor plates that lined the floor of the Blackhawk, BAPS gave the crew and passengers notable protection against the most common Middle Eastern round (the 7.62 mm of a Kalashnikov), as long as that round hit the BAPS; there were plenty of flight profiles that could render the BAPS ineffective, such as being low enough that enemy fire came in through the side of the aircraft instead of the bottom. Back to defensive driving, the best thing was to take off with as much speed as you could get before crossing the wire outbound, then keep as much altitude as possible for the duration of the mission. A moving target above 500 feet would be difficult to hit with a rifle.

While we flew with confidence in the typical threat of small-arms fire, any pilot becoming aware of an active RPG threat would be maneuvering indeed; while spotting someone with a shoulder-fired weapon from a moving helicopter is difficult, if the crew becomes aware they may be in the sights of an RPG, it becomes the number one priority to be flying away from it, not only to open the distance but also to reduce the size of the target. If we are broadside to the threat, while our apparent speed may be higher and the door gunners have a chance to be effective, we would still be a big target at a constant range; if we put the threat behind the tail, our apparent lateral speed drops off, but we are a much-smaller target with an increasing range. This tactic is not universally proven for all shoulder-fired weapons, though; if the enemy has MANPADS,[3] or any heat-seeking missile capability, it may be inadvisable to point the exhaust system at the threat, whether there is a countermeasure or not. We did have an elegant missile detection system with automatic flare dispensers, but thanks to the intelligence team, we knew we didn't have to worry about MANPADS in the theater. That's a real luxury for a helicopter crew, because there isn't much time after the crew chief spots someone hoisting something atrocious up to their shoulder to figure out whether it looked like an RPG or a heat-seeking missile.

In this sense, the information provided by the S-2 staff was invaluable. They provided a daily brief, as well as a threat map. The threat map provided a visual reference to areas historically saturated with small-arms fire, and could help us be in the right frame of mind if we flew toward those areas. It was important not to make absolute conclusions based on the threat map about where the next RPG might be, though, because RPGs were a much more precious commodity saved for special occasions. You could never know where one might turn up, and yet it was still important to be particularly concerned when flying past an area where one had been; someone who owned the launcher would certainly be trying to acquire another round to shoot from it. In addition to looking at the threat map, listening to the daily threat brief had to be a practiced discipline but was tricky because it also sounded like a broken record; we heard every day that there were more RPGs being smuggled in, but seldom heard of one being used. One might interpret that as danger becoming greater and greater, but in the common optimistic mind, if you never hear of something bad happening, then it's probably not going to happen today, either. This half of the equation summarizes whether the *potential* of an RPG gets any elbow room within your paradigm. The other half of the equation, if you consciously acknowledge that RPGs *are* there, is the question of whether you feel lucky.

Whether or not one may succumb to an RPG or mortar round could be debated differently by every person on the deployment. One notable difference between the two is that mortar rounds are almost totally random—they do get pointed in a certain direction, but hitting anything with accuracy is unlikely after the round goes up and over the arc. In that sense, considering one's fate vs. mortar fire is a philosophical question; when your number is up, that's it, but with so few and so random attacks, mortar rounds hardly shaped anyone's behavior at all. It's true, small bombs fell on the base frequently, but no one ran cautiously from bunker to bunker every day on their way to lunch. RPGs, on the other hand, while also not an extremely accurate weapon, were different in the sense that someone could be aiming it *directly* at you. That factor alone made it more than just something to ponder. The potential of being inside the effective range of an RPG should change your behavior.

Comparable in usage to a bazooka, RPGs have been much more prolific and evolving since World War II. RPG actually stands for *ruchnoy protivotankoviy granatomyot*, which in Russian translates to "handheld antitank grenade launcher." The *rocket-propelled grenade* backronym prevails in English (vs. HAGL), since the weapon is in fact rocket-propelled, making this translation logical enough to stick. But to accept that it's a grenade flying through the air understates the predominant configuration slightly, since the typical warhead is actually a shaped-charge HEAT round,[4] although thermobaric and fragmentation variants do exist if the primary target is flesh.

The launcher is basically a steel tube inside wooden cases, and in contrast to a breech-loaded bazooka, the RPG is muzzle loaded. Once the operator finds a target, either through a basic scope or iron sights, squeezing the trigger ignites the gunpowder of an ejecting charge via the typical hammer-to-primer initiator. Once out of the tube, after a few milliseconds and several meters from the operator's face, the sustainer motor (rocket) ignites, accelerating the warhead up to several hundred miles per hour, depending on how long it gets to fly. The entire device is really quite clever. So, this thing ends up being extremely deadly in the right hands, as long as the target is close—outside about 200 yards, the chances of hitting a selected target fall dramatically, with total uselessness beyond 400 yards. In aviation tactics, any portion of our flight profile below about 500 feet should start to feel uncomfortable.

While the ubiquitous Russian RPG-7 was the most common variant used in Afghanistan, it was in limited supply compared to small-arms fire; RPGs were saved for special occasions. They weren't used for celebratory fire like rifles and machine guns, and the owner of an RPG wouldn't take potshots at an aircraft 1,000 feet up. Aircraft down low, especially those proceeding along smoothly and slowly, presented the most fruitful target. Or hovering, as we suffered in Mogadishu. How do we proceed, then, if portions of every mission require us to be in these flight profiles?

The first part of the answer lies simply with acceptance of risk; flying in combat means you might get your ass handed to you. There isn't much to contradict this basic fact. It's kind of like driving a car; it is dangerous because you might be in an accident. Still, you find techniques and thought processes to reduce the threat to a manageable level in your mind. Beyond the basic defensive posture and combat tactics that pilots use to be a harder target, Army aviation also runs on a decision-making tool known as *composite risk management*.

Starting with *risk assessment*, we arrive at how dangerous a mission is, on the basis of all potential variables as they relate to what we would consider optimum; how many hours does the pilot have vs. the optimum level of experience? Having a thousand hours is a comfortable benchmark, for example, but the pilot in command could have as few as three hundred. What is the weather compared to a sunny day? What is the expected threat level compared to flying high and fast across open desert? What ASE[5] do we have vs. a specific, known threat? And so on. Once the risk level is determined (expressed as low, medium, or high, and needing to be approved by the company commander, battalion commander, or brigade commander, respectively), then composite risk management, or balancing all factors, begins: If bad weather bumped the mission from low up to medium risk, but the pilot in command has only six hundred hours, let's make sure he doesn't have a brand-new copilot. If our route has us flying through a hornet's nest of small-arms fire, let's adjust altitude for that portion of the mission to be out of the effective range. If we can't stay out of the effective range, let's fly the mission at night so we will be harder to see, or let's send in the Apaches first to clean it up, or let's coordinate with ISR platforms[6] or fighter jets to be on station. You realize you're still driving your car where it's dangerous, but you have a seat belt on. You're further comforted knowing that if you crash hard enough, the airbags will deploy, and you'll never feel alone if OnStar calls the EMTs for you.

Pretty soon the thing feels safe enough. Ironically, the defense mechanisms needed to continue operating effectively in a threat environment caused a refraction in the feedback loop between the pilots and the intelligence staff. The more comfortable the pilots seemed, the more the intelligence staff became concerned that the daily threat brief wasn't being received with the appropriate level of alarm. There is a spectrum of premission observable emotions, some of which are worn on the sleeve, others of which get muted by ego; if it was a line graph with threat/fear increasing up the left side, and ego increasing along the bottom, a fairly linear illustration of projected emotional responses could be plotted. Starting in the upper left with a very secure and humble pilot responding openly and proportionately to the threat, the line would plot diagonally down to the lower right, landing on the typical, type A, insecure, arrogant combat pilot pretending nothing is going to scare him. Somewhere off the chart lies the adrenaline junkie, with increased risk somehow equaling a perverse form of joy. Whatever the case, with many pilots focused on projecting intrepidity, the S-2 staff could get the sense that pilots didn't give a shit. Maybe it was a language barrier; many intermilitary communities have their own lingo and their own set of stressors on which to focus. Maybe it was a perception problem; often the realities of a mission look very different in real time than they appear in the planning cell. Or maybe it *was* complacency, which accumulates easily midway through a deployment. Whatever it was, the S-2 couldn't get over a nagging feeling that the information provided daily by the intelligence staff wasn't being taken to heart.

Success for the battalion intelligence staff, led by twenty-four-year-old Lt. Gilley, could be defined as effectively providing information to the unit, thereby preventing any mission from being compromised by pop-up threats, ambushes, or unexpected enemy advantage. If lackadaisical pilots had yet to be challenged by the insurgency, any one of them could fly into a threat, blundering along on complacency, and complete the equation of tragedy; the enemy loves low-hanging fruit. Even though the S-2 staff provided the warnings every day, meeting the initial responsibility wouldn't provide much comfort if someone got shot down. Predominance for the S-2 was a level of connectivity, such that each pilot had the best intel *and* effectively used it to succeed at the mission and return home at the end of the year. The young lieutenant became determined to resolve the language barrier, figure out what format of information would be best for the pilots, and double down on providing it with a level of vigilance commensurate with the alarming indicators trickling down from the intelligence network.

It seemed reasonable that riding along on a few missions might close the gap, to understand how the pilots communicated, what they saw, and what sort of information would be usable in real time; if the S-2 saw the battlespace firsthand, the entire S-2 staff could potentially be empowered to convey information to the pilots in a more usable format. It turned out that Heavy D valued his executive staff, though. Gilley's request for unnecessary attendance into the threat was denied.

CHAPTER 22

ECHO CHAMBER

Day 182. One morning in mid-June, I stepped outside to have a look at the day and quickly bumped into senior assault pilot Gene Decrisci. Gene was a great guy, a great family man, and someone who had developed an excellent knack for gourmet cooking back home. He was one of the guys you could count on to maintain a grounded composure regardless of the scenario, and that particular morning he was reclining in a homemade Adirondack chair with his feet up in the grass, reading the *New York Times*.

You may note there isn't much grass in Bagram; Gene had a yard though. It seemed appropriate that an organic chef of Gene's nature would have come up with it, too. On deployment Gene brought a 13-inch baking pan, some potting soil, and some grass seed with him and for the summer had faithfully watered it. Weekly then, he mowed his little lawn with scissors and, on the weekends and days off, enjoyed a chance to kick back with his bare feet up in good ol' Kentucky bluegrass. The sight of it brought a smile to my face. Gene was in touch with goodness.

"Good morning, Gene."

"Good morning," he replied with a welcome smile.

"Did you hear those mortar rounds last night?"

"Yeah, two people bit it. I'm not sure which unit. Allen came by to tell us 'comms blackout' for 2 days." Anytime a soldier is killed, there is a communication blackout, which is generally honored to prevent social media and emails from reaching families before the proper channels have a chance to get a casualty notification officer and a chaplain to their doorstep. The whole thing was a pointless tragedy, though—someone's son or daughter was just destroyed for no reason.

"What'cha got there, the *Times*?" I asked.

"Yeah, there's an article in here about McChrystal being the new ISAF commander. It's interesting to hear what he thinks about whether or not we're gettin' it done."

"Are we?"

"I'm not." Gene replied with a smile, comfortable in his decision to be relaxing for the morning. "We also might not be able to buy GM cars anymore."

"Why's that?" I asked.

"Apparently they're bankrupt."

"No way."

"Way."

"Wow." A moment of silent contemplation concluded the subject for both of us. "Well, enjoy your yard." I smiled as we exchanged up-nods.

Even that little conversation with Gene gave me the giggles. I realized I wanted to read that article when he got done with it; the top general of ISAF must have a plan for the theater, which had certainly been diluted and misconstrued all the way down to the lowliest private.

It's common for each successive level of leadership to add additional constraints to guidance received from the higher chain of command, such that whatever order is conveyed gets carried out within the comfort zone of each successive officer. It can be the case, then, that by the time a foot soldier gets his marching orders, they are substantially more restrictive than the commanding general intended, and as such, less effective. I wondered in so ambiguous and moldering a war zone, what kind of reports the top guy was getting.

I don't remember observing the same problem on a submarine, and I imagine many Navy ships to be similar: the captain is present all the time, and every subordinate level is almost immediately and locally evaluated on whether or not they are causing the captain's wishes to be carried out effectively. Contrasted by the Army, an order can be issued by a theater, regional, divisional, or brigade-level commander hundreds of miles away who expects that order to happen effectively, despite the interpretation of multiple layers of subordinate commanders, and the dilution across thousands of square miles of desert. Reports of completion or progress return through the same dusty echo chamber, and the process of communicating any status to SECDEF or the commander in chief gets further garnished with political parsley.

The middlemen between the working end of the Army and the secretary of defense must be masters of interpretation; it is debatable that a general officer can receive a negative report from anyone with boots on the ground,[1] if that report gets conveyed through the chain of command. If a soldier on the ground could speak to the general directly, yes. Creating this scenario was something McChrystal, unique in his style, was known for. But the typical unit commander finds himself in a conundrum to report failure up the chain of command, however, because even though the scenario may be a losing proposition, maybe it's losing only because he's not tenacious enough. It's almost like saying, *I can't provide enough leadership to conquer this scenario*. Few leaders, especially the career minded, are likely to provide the unvarnished report that we're losing the fight, we can't get it done the way we're going about it, or *this is fuckin' stupid, sir*. Additionally, any ground force commander would have to pass that message up through several levels, each having their own chance to object and shut it down, or to further dilute it before forwarding. From that perspective the ISAF commander had a psychological riddle to solve in addition to the tactical scenario.

Until this point of the deployment, I hadn't given any thought to who the top guy even was, since my basic function was unchanged by anyone more than one or two levels of command above me, and this guy was six levels above me. Regardless of who commanded the coalition, tactics, or political intent, my job was the same: move people from A to B; I hadn't noticed who the big boss was.

I strolled along to breakfast and saw Emily at the DFAC, though our relationship quickly came to an end. We had fun and got the shot of anarchy we must have needed, but the last time I saw her she was sitting on her back porch smoking pot. I asked where she got it, and she said right from Amazon, that one of the products listed under "potpourri" was actually marijuana that could be shipped to APO addresses. I was annoyed. Not being a pot smoker, I was generally turned off by the idea but also feared that being around it put me at risk of failing the random urinalysis. Our relationship had been based on the thrill of misbehaving, which we had. Slowly but surely, we lost interest and shifted back to twinkly eyes in the DFAC.

A group of B-huts, surrounded by heavily sand-bagged concrete bunkers. *Courtesy of Pete Latham*

Sunrise over the TOC, as seen from the roof of the Lighthouse. *Courtesy of Pete Latham*

A flight from Kabul, heading north toward Bagram. *Courtesy of Pete Latham*

Door guns at the ready as we descend into Bagram. *Courtesy of Pete Latham*

An unusual flight of three in the Bowl. *Courtesy of Pete Latham*

Pete Latham and company commander Bob Massey. *Courtesy of Pete Latham*

A colorful portion of the city. *Courtesy of Pete Latham*

Afghan homes surrounding Kabul. *Courtesy of Pete Latham*

A common hazy day near the city. *Courtesy of Pete Latham*

Flying over the tightly packed mud brick houses of suburban Kabul. *Courtesy of Joshua Havill*

An amusing sight in the bazaar. *Courtesy of Todd Wolfe*

Col. Rob Dickerson with fellow pilot J. D. Campbell. *Courtesy of Rob Dickerson*

The villages surrounding Ghazni. *Courtesy of Pete Latham*

Flying north toward Panjshir valley. *Courtesy of Joshua Havill*

The entrance to Panjshir River valley. *Courtesy of Joshua Havill*

A small village in the Panjshir valley. *Courtesy of Joshua Havill*

Small farm plots near the Panjshir River, many miles north of Bagram. *Courtesy of Pete Latham*

Todd Wolfe running missions from inside the CP.
Courtesy of Todd Wolfe

Landing at a very small outpost in Nuristan Province.
Courtesy of Robert Massey

A brightly adorned member of the local workforce. *Courtesy of Pete Latham*

The "Afghanistan Airbnb" near Bamiyan. *Courtesy of Pete Latham*

A typical summertime landscape. *Courtesy of Pete Latham*

Over the lakes near Bamiyan.
Courtesy of Pete Latham

More gorgeous landscapes of Afghanistan. *Courtesy of Pete Latham*

Missing Buddha number 1. *Courtesy of Pete Latham*

Beautiful scenery west of Bagram. *Courtesy of Pete Latham*

Missing Buddha number 2. *Courtesy of Pete Latham*

Landing in light dust at FOB Shank. *Courtesy of Pete Latham*

A scenic but risky daytime flight in one of the valleys near the Kunar River. *Courtesy of Pete Latham*

Todd Wolfe holding up a Blackhawk on top of some Hesco barriers. *Courtesy of Todd Wolfe*

A close-up of rugged terrain east of Bagram. *Courtesy of Pete Latham*

The charismatic Bradley Cooper during a visit to the troops. *Courtesy of Pete Latham*

Bob Massey and Pete Whitley playing golf on top of the pinnacle landing site as Darren Ohmstede maintains security. *Courtesy of Robert Massey*

Playing in the snow. *Courtesy of Mark Robinson*

Pete Latham trying unsuccessfully to get home. *Courtesy of Pete Latham*

A Blackhawk flying through one of the passes east of Kabul. *Courtesy of Pete Latham*

The author looking annoyed at something during a walk-around inspection before a night flight. *Courtesy of Pete Latham*

A flight of two proceeding north near Kalagush to get to the search area for Red-Handed 56. *Courtesy of Robert Massey*

Bob Massey (*in the left seat*) flying a high-altitude mission based on the nasal cannula oxygen supply system. The glass cockpit of the M-model Blackhawk can be seen, with "moving map" displayed. *Courtesy of Robert Massey*

Honcho 062 in the rocks. Notice the sheared-off landing gear and broken skylight above the pilot's head. *Courtesy of Mark Robinson*

The mighty Chinook with a ramp gunner who knows he's too high to be within small-arms range of anything. *Courtesy of Pete Latham*

Doc Puskar at the crash site in the days following the initial accident. *Courtesy of Robert Massey*

An "F"-model Chinook sitting on the mountain during day 1 of the Honcho 062 recovery effort. *Courtesy of Ryan Dechent*

CHAPTER 23
THE MAIN EFFORT

Day 196. By the end of June, we would have guessed that nothing happening in the war zone could be more interesting than the news stories from home. As the scenario with GM continued evolving, NASDAQ chairman Bernie Madoff was sentenced to 150 years for his record-setting Ponzi scheme, and the World Health Organization declared the H1N1 virus a global pandemic. Almost simultaneously, news of Michael Jackson's death could have been the icing on the news cake, but even that was diminished by the most perplexing historical event of our time in Afghanistan. For reasons unknown and presented with a great deal of ambiguity through the normal channels, a twenty-three-year-old private first class by the name of Bowe Bergdahl exited the perimeter of his camp and walked into history.

As is common with any new event refracted through the usual muck of gossip, reports varied. But in the unbelievable version we were provided with, Bowe had too much to drink and decided he was tired of being cooped up in a small outpost named Camp Clark. He supposedly walked off the camp and wandered into a local market, where he appeared out of place and disoriented and was almost immediately scooped up by the bad guys. Gossip continued telling several versions of what happened, but as word of the situation climbed up the chain of command, normal operations ground to a halt and almost all assets were redirected into search-and-rescue mode, to no avail.

There is a term shared by commanders in cases like these that require the vast majority of military assets available for a single purpose, and that term is "the Main Effort." In my line of work the most common reference is when a helicopter goes down for whatever reason, and the crew is on the ground with no cover, and all assets will immediately converge on the scene to get them off the ground and back to the safety of being aloft. In that sense, you never want to become the main effort. It is only a bad thing.

Bowe became the main effort. Everything that had previously been happening on schedule ground to a halt, and all available resources went to Bowe. Our sister company farther to the south at FOB Salerno launched many flights in the following days to look for the missing PFC, but eventually it became apparent the Taliban or a group associated with the Taliban had captured him. He soon thereafter became a bargaining chip for the Taliban, since they provided proof that they had him and began making offers to trade him in return for a certain number of their own interests who had been captured and detained by the coalition over the years. He would prove to be a low-value bargaining chip.

For reasons known only to him, Bowe left the relative security of his camp and got captured by the Taliban. Why would he walk off his camp?

Several years earlier, before deploying to Iraq, I remember my unit having battalion-level training about not getting captured. It came down to one thing: Don't get captured. Don't get your head cut off.

There seemed to be a real propensity for the bad guys to be cutting people's heads off on camera around that time. The footage is available online after even a casual search, and two of the officers of our battalion came up with the idea to train the battalion by playing three different videos of real, living people getting their heads cut off. The footage is grizzly and shocking, and in one of the videos the victim's throat was being cut from front to back with a slow slicing motion. The victim screamed and struggled. The farther back they sliced, the more the screams turned into tortured howls as the air began escaping directly from the trachea. This continued with the ghastliest howls of absolute panic emanating directly from the torso until they made it to the spinal cord, at which time he finally went limp and silent. As is common for such propaganda footage, the lifeless head then is held up by the hair for the camera, any audience meeting a dull expression. Two or three people had to get up and leave the room, one of them vomiting. Others chuckled nervously, and many looked away to exchange scrunched-up faces with each other as we sat there in total comfort and safety, watching what surely must be one of the worst ways to go.

The training was a success. Most people left the room realizing the enemy was serious, and having a reinforced thought that getting captured was undesirable. Do not get captured. Do not get your head cut off.

So why had Bowe walked off his camp? Maybe he didn't get the training. Maybe getting captured wasn't noted in his mind as the most undesirable fate ever. Only Bowe knows.

After only a handful of days, Bowe wasn't the most recent news anymore. As Gary Larson might note, he had walked out of his camp and into Taliban folklore forever. Slowly but surely, the constants of deployment demanded assets back: resupply missions, moving people from here to there, normal commerce. Our sister company down in Salerno flew a fair number of search-and-rescue missions looking for him, and we used a few assets even as far north as Bagram, distributing flyers and dropping leaflets from helicopters requesting information leading to the recovery of Bowe. These hopeful activities soon tapered off to nothing, being superseded by more-tangible requirements.

CHAPTER 24
MILDEW COLONIZING

Day 201. I started looking forward to R&R three days before it happened. The futility of being deployed with no real battle left me craving stimulus, and being in the land of dust and plywood had me looking forward to real culture. I decided to go to Japan to visit friends. When I deployed to Iraq, I had R&R in Italy, looking for dramatic cultural changes from the deployed scene. Most people go back to the States to visit family or just be home, but I preferred to stay on the same side of the globe and have adventure. Another Army buddy of mine and his family who were close friends were stationed in Okinawa, and visiting them would give me equal feelings of being home and touring.

The Army got R&R right, paying for the tickets to anywhere in the world along with two weeks of leave. Getting out of the country was a test of patience, but most people were happy to be going through the experience even if it didn't run very smoothly. In this case, we would take Military Air to Udairi, Kuwait, then bus to Kuwait International Airport in Kuwait City for a flight leaving the Middle East.

The three days went by slowly; normal missions flew, but neither the QRF nor the medevac chase aircraft launched on any flights. All was quiet. Major Puskar had been hanging around the CP, hoping for some action, but found none. It reminded me of the week I had spent at FOB Shank on medevac chase with only one flight launching during the whole week.

The day before I was scheduled for R&R, I relaxed and watched *First Blood* one more time, saying Will Teasle's lines with him but not being able to match facial expressions or tension with Brian Dennehy. It was funny to be mentally transported out of Bagram with just a movie and some headphones, but the following morning I would be transported out for real and be able to let go of the place for a few weeks.

The pax terminal at Bagram was run with no urgency whatsoever by a handful of disgruntled people. Extreme even by military standards, R&R pax were required to show up at 0600 for the 2300 flight out of Bagram, to be accounted for and listen to all of the usual briefings about process and security. We had to have body armor with us, which was always miserable, but luckily we were allowed to travel without a sidearm. There would be a storage facility to store the body armor at Kuwait, so at least I didn't have to drag it on R&R, but we were still technically going to be flying over a war zone, and the plane could crash, in which case our dead bodies should be wearing body armor. The seating in the pax terminal was cramped and uncomfortable enough to make the folks around me talk about canceling R&R, which obviously nobody did.

An incredibly bossy young sergeant shouted orders at the lot of us, everyone ranging from a private up to a light colonel. Apparently, they had handled many a disgruntled crowd and no longer cared who they were talking to. None of us cared either, realizing it wasn't personal. Everyone knew we had to comply, even the lieutenant colonel. Positional authority supersedes rank; if he wanted to use their service to *get out of Dodge*, he knew he had to obey the little fucker: We had to group up a certain way. We had to sound off a certain way for roll call. We had to walk in a single-file line to the plane, following the bossy sergeant. Finally, we got on the plane and waited, eventually being relieved to hear the growling noise of starter motors spinning up the huge turbines. When the parking brake was released and the first subtle movement could be felt, tension began to dissipate with the same effect as a first sip of beer. When the huge craft finally lifted off the runway, the cabin erupted in cheers, and there was a real sense of being saved somehow. The buzz washed over everyone.

We had hours of flying over some of the scariest-sounding countries on our way to Kuwait, offset by the simple feeling of sitting in a huge jet up in the pleasant sky. I just imagined a flight attendant: *We have coffee or soda. Would you care for a snack to go with your beverage?* Balanced between the thought of traveling on a commercial flight to Pleasantville and the reality of being strapped into the cargo bay of a military transport plane, we flew over five countries that cable news had described as terrorist hives during the last two decades of sensationalistic reporting, and miraculously crossed safely into Kuwait. Certainly, Kuwait was safe for us, ever since HW and Gen. Schwarzkopf shooed Saddam back home.

The process in Udairi ended up being fairly painless, with only a one-day turnaround. It was hot for sure; Kuwait's elevation is quite a bit lower than Afghanistan's, and it was also desert. We checked our body armor and made the liberating shift into civilian clothing. In this part of the world, it is better not to draw attention to one's self by wearing a military uniform, especially as a lone ranger. I had strategically stopped getting my haircut a month prior, so at least I had a little blending ability and wouldn't be such an obvious military traveler. I got on the bus to Kuwait International. The moment I stepped into the terminal, I employed proven reconnaissance techniques to find the nearest cold draft beer, to no avail. I soon remembered from being there in 2006 that Kuwait was a dry country. *Damn.*

In Tokyo my real rest and relaxation began, and the sense that I was in the middle of a deployment seemed like a funny dream. To look around the streets of one of the world's busiest cities, you would never know that a few time zones away there was a struggle taking place, an unresolved tension. Maybe Japan was oblivious to Afghanistan, but having just been time-warped in, it felt ironic. Like being in a cheerful bar enjoying delightful company, not knowing that someone is getting the shit beat out of them out back in the alley. Or maybe being the one beating the shit out of that guy, then going inside for a drink afterward and not quite being able to relax. It was surreal. Speaking of being in a bar, I found the cold beer I was after. It was just as amazing as I had imagined, and the flash buzz that came with slamming the first third of it only magnified the sense of irony. It felt like nobody in the world cared about what we were trying to do in Afghanistan. It wasn't like the world wars, where it may have been headline news every day. The world's economy wasn't hinged on it. People weren't hoping we'd win. It was just this political thing. It felt like we were trying to find a way to leave and say we accomplished something or reach some benchmark of progress, so we didn't have to tell the world it was pointless to be there in the first place.

I was out of the country, though, and supposed to be relaxing and finding peace. I had no traumatic stress to speak of. We were warned that everybody left with at least a little, but the only thing I could identify was a sustained habit of not picking anything up from the side of the road, and not stepping *off* the road. When you hear again and again that everything is an IED and there are unexploded mines in the country, it does stick with you and is something that has to be consciously turned off. I didn't have any of the horror, though, any of the fear. I hadn't seen much blood, not the way some people saw it, and I hadn't heard any screams.

I soon became amused over the great and wonderful differences between Japan and the United States and became disconnected from the burden of being deployed. I was with friends, enjoying culture and relaxing. One revelation I experienced occurred on the Fourth of July—I guess I simply never had to contemplate it before, but in Japan there were no fireworks to celebrate American Independence Day. Go figure.

One of the more humorous differences between Afghanistan and Japan was the toilets. Not every toilet, but a few of them, especially in the nicer hotels in the city, had certain . . . features. Japanese innovation has made it possible to use the bathroom without needing to wipe. They have basically combined a toilet and a bidet. There were several versions of this deluxe bathroom appliance, ranging from very simple to very elaborate, having electronic controls on a keypad. Basically, a controllable jet of water does the cleaning, and then a controllable blast of air does the drying, if you are patient enough. The fancy ones had multiple options such as water temperature and pressure, even water jet angle. This thing could bring peace and tranquility to the Middle East!

I rested and relaxed for two weeks and did a lot of sightseeing but eventually said goodbye to friends and began making my way back to Afghanistan. In the last major airport where it was available, I drank as much beer as possible on general principle. I still had a few months left in the deployment, and this would be the last cold beer I would get until I went home. Eventually, I was on a flight heading for Udairi, and as the day progressed, I found myself clinging to thoughts of Japan and happiness. I had no anxiety about going back to Afghanistan; it was just a dormant area in my thoughts. Japan was bright and busy and recent, and Afghanistan remained dim in my mind. There was no resistance. I wasn't trying not to think about it; I just didn't.

Finally arriving in Camp Buehring, Udairi, I learned that the trip back to Afghanistan wouldn't happen for another three days. This was a source of frustration, since I would gladly have stayed in Japan, but I eventually became convinced that the deciders of this logistical post had correctly manipulated traffic coming and going in favor of those going out, that it was a higher priority to get someone *out* of the war zone than it was to put them back in. I decided to spend my three days accepting the boredom and being patient. After all, those three days would still put me three days closer to going home, and reading a book or watching movies for this time in the air-conditioning was no big deal.

I eventually drew my body armor from storage, put my uniform back on, and was herded back onto a military transport headed for Bagram. During the many droning hours of that relatively uncomfortable flight, the futility of Operation Enduring Freedom slowly began seeping into the delicate structure of happiness I enjoyed during R&R. I was a sponge to any culture I got swiped through: I soaked up the amazing experience of Japan as an open-minded traveler and had been feeling alive and free. Unfortunately for this sponge, beneath the quickly evaporating nectar of R&R the mildew of deployment lurked. By the time my boots hit the dirt in Bagram, dried-up angst from weeks earlier was rewetted and colonizing.

Making my way from the pax terminal back to my B-hut solidified the transition, with turbine engine whine from something nearby stinging my eardrums. Dulling monoxide drifted along with the smoke of chugging vehicles. A helicopter somewhere provided the percussive *whup whup whup*. Heavy dust was everywhere as my boots crunched along in the gravel, through Jersey barriers and sandbags and plywood shacks wrapped in CAT-5 cable. R&R was over.

I made it to my room, pulled my key out of the crack in the ceiling where I had left it, and went in. My room was pleasantly dark and cool, and the bed was made just the way I left it. I threw my body armor and duffel bag down and, for just a moment, longed for that last cold beer again. I went to the shower to freshen up after a day of traveling, shifted into PTs and comfortable sneakers, and went to the CP to greet friends and check the board.

CHAPTER 25
MAGIC CARPET

Day 226. My company was not a permanent company in the Army, but part of a temporary task force; within the assets of a brigade, various battalion- and company-level assets were assembled in a piecemeal collage to fit different logistical demands. Not everyone had operated together before, but we had all known each other from around base and from down the hallway of our common battalion buildings, and we were all operators. We had been relabeled as a new company, but when the deployment was over, we would revert to the original structure.

I don't think that factor is what caused the rift, specifically, but our company was somewhat dysfunctional and of low morale. It didn't matter how much you walked around trying to tell jokes and compliment people, the unit just wouldn't jell. There could be a somberness from being deployed and away from families, plus the *sentence* that whether things were good or bad, a year of your life would be spent on this ambiguous deployment. Unfortunately, there were also members of the company who made an art form out of being insufferable. By his own account, Bob Massey's greatest struggle of the year was managing the scabbed-together assortment of personalities in the G Company "Reapers."

When the brigade decided we would use a task force organization to distribute assets throughout the theater instead of keeping units organic, the Reapers were created—and doomed; the decision to form one additional company by skimming from the existing three meant all three original flight-line company commanders of 4th Battalion had to decide who to get rid of and who to keep. If those flight-line commanders were looking forward to a year of combat operations, who would they keep?

Their best, of course.

Who would they get rid of?

The men who became the Reapers. It wasn't too long before Bobby was referred to as Pappy Boyington, but managing the spume of the battalion, myself included, was a source of exasperation even the most intrepid of leaders may have flinched from. Had there been an objective, for example the classic pillbox a commander might need to throw bodies at, this situation could have proven uniquely advantageous. As it was however, our mission was to sustain a particularly low-impact presence for a defined period of time; we weren't even afforded the luxury of an objective with which to define our term. No matter what happened, we'd be there for a year.

In the great collection of personalities, there are those who can mind their own business and be happy. To a much-greater extent in the military, the web of rank structure and positional authority causes a lot more judging and criticism to take place. There were some pilots in "the Reapers" who thought they were great Blackhawk pilots, and they bore the additional self-imposed burden of having to make sure everyone else was operating efficiently. They couldn't just live and let live.

Many people who fly a Blackhawk get this feeling because of its wonderful design. It was a great design decades ago at its time of conception, and across various revisions and improvements over the years it had become the finest vehicle on the battlefield. It has all the tricky helicopter idiosyncrasies engineered right out of it. Everything people talk about, whether or not you can be a helicopter pilot depending on whether or not you can chew gum while balancing on a basketball and all that, is irrelevant in the Blackhawk. Basic control of the machine can be effectively taught to the average kid with no flight experience of any kind within about thirty minutes. Of the seven different types of helicopters I have flown, as well as flying thirty different types of airplanes and operating hundreds of cars and motorcycles, metal lathes and milling machines, farm and heavy equipment, and even two classes of submarines, the Blackhawk is easily the most elegantly engineered machine I ever got my hands on.

Some people get in and feel how well it flies and their egos become inflated by how smoothly they seem to be handling the craft. Without the perspective of having flown many and varied aircraft, aircraft with less power and elegance, crudely scabbed-together aircraft that don't belong in the sky, or even embarrassingly utilitarian home-builts, they reach the conscious stage of being "an aviator" in a Blackhawk and begin thinking erroneously they are *God's gift* to the Blackhawk, or even to all of aviation. The opposite is true: the Blackhawk is *Sikorsky's* gift to aviation, and over the years, hundreds of Sikorsky engineers and machinists have created and refined a truly ingenious machine, with thousands of meticulously crafted components working smoothly and dependably in concert, creating a sensation indistinguishable from floating on a magic carpet.

In conversing with the helicopter industry, someone who has flown only a Blackhawk in life may be a weak pilot; that individual may lack the skill to fly either as a single pilot (because the Blackhawk requires two pilots) or as the pilot in command of a single-*engine* aircraft flying with limited power. In my experience flying single-pilot, single-engine helicopters, I can state assuredly that, flight by flight, I am merely another person who got lucky enough to find the ground again, hitting it first with the skids instead of the rotor blades. A real helicopter pilot is in fact thankful for his life, or even the opportunity to fly again, that no one noticed his calamity of mistakes and nearsighted decisions, and that by the very fortune of luck and tensile strength the contraption didn't fly apart around him 300 feet above the ground.

Now, when a person of limited skill or fragile ego gets into the Blackhawk and becomes comfortable, it is typical for that person's confidence to begin increasing, in some cases unduly manifesting as superiority or arrogance. Predictably, two of the individuals succumbing to this illusion were Griffin and Matos.

Naturally despising each other, neither would support the other, either rolling their eyes or contradicting the other behind his back. If either one of them was among pilots without the other, he considered himself the authority in the room and would freely admit to being a pretty substantial Blackhawk pilot. Each had their own way of talking down to the junior pilots, creating unnecessary constraints, or generally making people feel bad for the sake of their own sense of importance. This pair of average pilots affected company morale like news of a death.

Some members of the company were strong enough either to ignore them or argue back, but in the military structure of things, many felt as if they weren't in a position to do so and just took their lumps. The problem was, they would get different lumps from either instructor. This dynamic was especially stressful for a copilot trying to impress everyone around him enough to be signed off as a pilot in command. Arturo Matos would come in and say things had to be a certain way; they had to print products a certain way, operate the cockpit a certain way, or give a briefing a certain way, and the pilots would respond. The very next day, Peter Griffin would come in and tell the same group of ambitious young pilots they were doing everything wrong, and to redo it his way. The same scenario would be played out for any young pilot who flew with them in the cockpit. It was a very depressing dynamic throughout the year for anyone who wasn't already established as a pilot in command.

There is a system in place to control this, though. In Army aviation, that system pivots on a person referred to as the standardization pilot or SP. If there are any arguments about how to operate, the SP simply considers each side and makes a decision. All parties then comply with the guidance of the SP, feeling harmonious that there is a decision on how to operate as a team. Unfortunately for those younger pilots, the personality of our SP wasn't one of enforcement as much as it was one of facilitation. Bill Westergaurd, with the heavy accent, would have been a great SP in a company without a pair of self-centered pussies rethinking his every decision. Such as it was, the average pilot felt as if there were three SPs; Bill would make a good decision about how the company should operate, but Art and Peter would passive-aggressively disagree, resulting in three different ways of doing business. It's not that Bill couldn't hold his own in an argument; he certainly could. He just didn't have obedience from the two most self-infatuated pilots in the company, who also happened to be the other two instructors. He was also not in a position to take them off the schedule or otherwise remove them from the equation, since that would have tripled his own workload. Nor could he bear down on them with the wrath of God, because the lot of them, me and three or four others included, were all within months of being in the same year group. Bill wasn't even so much senior; in fact, he wore the same rank. He had simply been promoted a few months prior to the rest of us. My saving grace from being in this mix was that I had not yet gone through the course to be burdened as an instructor, so I enjoyed the full line-pilot privileges without any of the paperwork an instructor endures.

All this, one might observe, sounds more like a personnel issue than an operational problem and, as such, could be solved by the chain of command rather than the standardization officer. An unusual dynamic in Army aviation, however, different from any other branch of the Army, is that the leadership has less experience than the operators.

Due to the injection of "aviation" into the normal rank and status structure of the Army, with *aviation* in this discussion being the delicate chemistry of leaving the ground to operate in the ambiguous medium of the atmosphere, an inexperienced officer can find himself or herself commanding personnel before he or she is ever allowed to be the pilot in command of an aircraft. It is, by this measure, less than optimum for a leadership scenario, unless the individual was of such skill and character as to learn how to fly quickly and be signed off by his or her peers.

More often, a branch officer is encumbered more with the paperwork of command, and the tedious day-to-day requirements of leading the troops, than of learning the finer points of aviating. I have seen several cases where an officer even makes it to the level of being the company commander, "leading" a group of pilots, when he is not a pilot in command himself. It is a poor dynamic that leaves the commander almost powerless, since inevitably he is still trying to be signed off as a pilot in command to have the respect and status required to be effective. But who signs off a pilot in command? The senior warrant officers.

The warrant officers in Army aviation have the absolute ability to blackball a branch officer with the stroke of a pen, specifically in the branch officer's flight records. If a company commander takes command of a company and is not a pilot in command (PC), they have 180 days to achieve the status. This fact alone can have them second-guessing their every statement or command, judging whether or not the warrant officers would agree.

Adding to the ambiguity of this dynamic, unfortunately there are occasions where a senior warrant officer is not a great soldier in the first place and draws the attention of the commander. Let's take the easy example of physical training: if the commander has a PT program and wants everyone to show up at 0630 each day to conduct PT, and an out-of-shape, disinterested senior warrant officer decides not to show up, the commander would feel disrespected and seek to correct this obvious breach of the authority/obedience protocol established hundreds of years ago in the Army, or thousands of years ago in any army. In justifiably counseling the senior warrant officer about his deficient behavior, the senior warrant officer nine times out of ten would respond with a black-and-white attitude (OK, *everything by the book then*) and become maliciously obedient. On the company commander's very next flight, the senior warrant officer would need only to compare the commander's actual performance with the aircrew training manual to note a deficiency in any of the hundreds of evaluated categories, and it would be all over but the shouting. The commander in question may never reach the coveted status of being a pilot in command and, without that qualifying designation, also may never be able to hold higher and higher command positions within the executive hierarchy.

With this unusual dynamic, where the company commander isn't necessarily the ultimate authority in the unit, there can be power struggles and manipulation, through which only an officer of intrepid character, and at least a little bit of actual flying ability, could rise to a point of effective command. In many cases to the contrary, individuals will find themselves in command of a unit only in the administrative sense: facilitating leave, being accountable for property, filling out annual evaluation forms, and conducting PT tests, but being contradicted on every direct operational decision by the warrant officers, with no recourse. In more than one case, warrant officers have directly briefed the battalion commander on a plan for battalion effectiveness, eclipsing the less developed ideas of the company commander, and the company commander finds himself or herself totally impotent. It can be very difficult for a young officer in his or her twenties with only a few hundred hours of flying experience to have any authority over a group of seasoned warrant officers in their thirties or forties, each having thousands of hours and many deployments under their belt, banding together to do whatever the fuck they want.

In our temporary company, the youthful, skinny, blond-haired company commander, Bob Massey, *was* a pilot in command, having obtained several hundred hours of flight time before he ever got to flight school in Ft. Rucker. As such, he was able to demonstrate enough air sense and situational awareness to the world around him to be signed off as a Blackhawk pilot in command. He was a sound operator and remained enthusiastic about operations. Abstracting his optimistic demeanor, though, in the subtle discussion of how to cure an ill family environment, even the charismatic Bob Massey couldn't outmaneuver wet blankets within the company.

Across the relatively young and constantly changing spectrum of Army leadership, officers in leadership roles range anywhere from completely worthless lightweights to granite monuments of propriety and orchestration, with the average aviation officer falling left of center. The younger an officer is, the less likely he or she is to have either the poise or the confidence to stand his or her ground on anything, let alone give commands or order someone to do something. In Army aviation, contrary to how the infantry operates, it is hard for a branch officer to have any real command authority, until the level of battalion command. At the company level, commanders are basically repeating stations for the battalion commander, and every arrogant pilot knows it.

A young branch officer trying to prove they are "senior" to an older warrant officer on the rank structure diagram will quickly be proven powerless by the "warrant officer mafia." This is a known fact, and a point that is the subject of formal training among warrant officers and branch officers alike, with the only saving point of respect being that the young officer whom the warrant officers are manipulating may one day be their battalion commander, if they ever steel themselves to the ambiguous dynamic of commanding people with more status and experience than they.

Bob, in the particular evolution of his own skill set and personality traits, had successfully navigated this quagmire and arrived at a level of respect from the other operators in the company, but in no way could he have achieved pure obedience from egotistical pilots with seven or eight more years of military flying experience than he had. He worked to create and maintain good morale, but if two or three gung-ho has-beens wanted to maintain a lugubrious level of condescension over the junior operators, they'd be able to, and did.

As a result, in our patchwork company, no one could fix this subtle social dynamic for the duration of the deployment. Operations were not affected; we did the same job we otherwise would have done, and everyone carried out the missions they were individually assigned with an appropriate sense of responsibility and duty, but everyone remained resigned to the fact that for some of our team members, our temporary company was *less than nurturing*.

In a last-ditch effort to rectify the situation for the benefit of the junior pilots and for the atmosphere of the company itself, I wrote a letter to Griffin, the most oblivious of the offenders, in an attempt to open his eyes to the possibility that he was coming up short as a team player or mentor. He was my peer and probably realized I didn't give a fuck about how highly he thought of himself, so I was in a position to communicate with him, whereas the suffering junior pilots had to anticipate any criticism of Griffin affecting their status or limiting which missions they'd be allowed to fly. After a few days, I picked up on a discussion among the pilots that he wasn't being himself, seemed to be minding his own business, and wasn't riding anyone's ass about anything. I had a moment of contemplative satisfaction, but it would become apparent within just a few days that ego is a hard thing to groom.

CHAPTER 26
BATTERING RAM

Day 233. The next shift I ended up on was the nighttime QRF, so I reversed out again, staying up as long as possible and sleeping in as long as possible until my circadian rhythm flipped to nocturnal. It takes more than a week to reverse out, but in the deployed world you get two days. This constraint means that for the first three or four shifts of working from 6:00 p.m. until 6:00 a.m., the body continues craving sleep around one or two in the morning. After about a week or so, one can feel comfortably reversed out and start enjoying the relative peace of the night shift.

On my third night of QRF, I was amused to find myself on the same crew as Bill Westergaurd. It's unusual for two senior pilots to get to fly together, unless they arrange it, or for random reasons such as people taking leave or needing a reset. If a pilot hits a certain benchmark of hours, they incur a mandatory day off, to help prevent pilots from having chronic fatigue.

We went through the normal routine of loading our gear into the helicopter and going to dinner before settling into a quiet evening of playing video games and watching movies. Around 9:00 p.m. the phone rang, and the battle captain wanted to talk to us about a mission.

The first easy assumption was that someone wanted an admin run of some sort, needing to be picked up or dropped off for R&R, or maybe we had a tail-to-tail medevac to conduct. After crossing the street to the TOC, though, the battle captain asked if we could support the Norwegians in a few hours, who would be conducting a hasty assault. Hell yeah! A chance for some real action! We were briefed by the S-2, who would also require a formal debrief based on the unusual circumstance of intending to land in the courtyard of the enemy.

This was the thing we trained the most to do, and always hoped to do, while otherwise being saturated with mindless flights to and fro. Assault operations, meaning the insertion of combat fighters into a known fight, came in a few different forms. The most common two forms were "deliberate" and "hasty." *Deliberate* assault operations could be fun because the two or three days of planning created many chances for excellence and efficiency in rehearsal and execution and allowed for the development of much more elaborate tactics. Deliberates could also be a drag sometimes because it meant tedious days of planning. In the *hasty* assault scenario, there was the same action, threat, imminent danger, and exhilaration of doing real business, without as much of the tedium. It could lack the elegance, often limiting us to just shoving troops into someone's backyard and hoping for the best. Either way, in the earlier hours of the shift, this was a welcome way to pass the time.

In this scenario, we would fly down to Kabul to the Norwegians' command post, get briefed by the Norwegian ground forces commander, and fly a small contingent of operators to a grid south of Kabul to nab a midlevel target. He wasn't extremely high on the insurgent food chain, but not a weekend warrior either. This particular individual had the special identifying feature of being one-legged. This seemed unusual to me, but I soon learned that many of the fighting Taliban had similar significant injuries, from years of organized fighting in war-torn Afghanistan or from stepping on Soviet land mines.

The commander of the Norwegian forces was a very relaxed but confident man with an easy sense of humor, who was able to convey a sense of permissible annoyance that his evening was being burdened with going out to bag some Taliban lieutenant. We had shut down and walked into their dank facility, no doubt inherited from a long line of disgruntled transients, and sat in some cold metal chairs on some dirty blue carpet to listen to the brief. Unlike in the 101st Airborne Division, where assault planning and briefing standards are carefully structured and rehearsed, and the format is the same every time, this even-keeled commando gave us the down and dirty with no extra dressing: *Here is who we were after, here is the location of the house, and here is what time we want to arrive.* That was pretty straightforward. We shrugged our shoulders and said *OK*, then spent the next ten minutes or so looking at a possible route and coordinating with the Apache pilots for gun support.

We ended up finalizing the game plan with all players an hour before we would have to launch. I poured myself a cup of Norwegian Blend and sat with the map, studying the route and imagining possible scenarios.

The bad guy's compound was deep down in a valley, and the final approach from the release point to the objective would be like going over Niagara Falls in a barrel. Furthermore, the actual touchdown point was in a yard surrounded by several intricate rock walls. Determining any of this from a satellite image was an art form, but also something that got easier with experience. The rock walls shouldn't be a problem, as long as we don't land on them with our delicate aluminum helicopter, but being that far down in a crevasse with a flight of four helicopters would leave no room for mistakes to the left or right, and the only opportunity for escape would be forward or up. If things got dicey for some reason, and the four of us went blasting through the valley at two in the morning and decided not to stop and get the bad guy, there's a good chance he wouldn't be there the next day or ever again. Consequently, the Geronimo approach would be a critical scenario. We decided to leave the Apaches up high in the valley, so there would be only two of us down in the trench. That would make negotiating the available space easier, even though it might add ten or fifteen seconds to the response time if we needed fire support. Usually with two-in-the-morning surprise assaults, unless it's an ambush, everyone is asleep and there isn't much of a response.

The time came to suit up, and the same band of heavy hitters I had hauled down there from Bamiyan walked out from the building next door. These guys were brutish looking but jovial and laughed and scuffed their way out to the helicopters like a bunch of pals about to get into a boat to go fishing. They reminded me of characters from a Monty Python movie, killing and plundering their way across ungoverned territory. It seemed that no one going on this assault was all too concerned, and I guess I wasn't either; my piece was pretty simple as long as nothing went wrong. I liked working with these guys because their obvious comfort level was a clear indicator—they knew how to control a situation.

For this flight, Bill would be on the controls, and I would be navigating. One minute prior to our own departure, we dispatched the slower-flying Apaches down the route. Fifty-five seconds later, Bill announced to the formation, "Pitch pull in five," and began affecting the controls such that the four composite blades of the Blackhawk simultaneously went from the "flat pitch" position to a biting angle, generating an almost unbelievable downward force of wind that caused our 20,000-pound vehicle to start floating.

After the wheels broke ground, we began a smooth acceleration, and a moment after I said, *Accelerate to 110 ground*, chalk two in the formation transmitted *convoy* over the internal radio. We were en route.

The fifteen-minute flight was easy; good weather, fair illume, and quiet radios. This was the most romantic flight regime of my Army flying career; only on your way to the violent unknown do you get a true chance to ponder mortality. I knew I might be flying into it, and I knew someone who had. One second, I might be just a pilot, calculating the position of a vehicle in space; the next I could be screaming and clawing for my tourniquet, slipping into the cozy embrace of shock, and seeing less and less as the last amplified green photon pierced through the constricting tunnel of blackout. It could be a little exhilarating. It ranks right up there with the first time you ever got to experience a lover disrobing, or the first time you ever dared to open the throttle on a motorcycle to see just how fast it would go. Not the flight, not the assault; just the possibility that someone was going to come out shooting, and you were about to absorb it. You have to imagine what you'll do when the first window shatters or when you see the first tracer whip past the door. After a while of imagining the correct tactical response for a variety of scenarios, you start to add the humor back in and become thankful you were in danger in the first place; this is one of the rare scenarios we need to help season the new guys . . . only if we got shot at could I come over the radio with some variety of flat sarcasm, such as "*These guys don't seem very friendly.*"

At the thirteen-minute point in the flight, we passed the Apaches. There are a few different ways to use gunship support: The Apaches can be deployed ahead of the lift assets by a few minutes to provide a threat report of the objective, known as a "cherry/ice" call, meaning either hot or cold for threat. In that scenario, if the objective *is* hot, it was good the guns went in first to clean it up a little. In other cases, the cherry/ice tactic could ruin the element of surprise, since the enemy is alerted to the lift asset's approach, doesn't respond to the gun presence, but postures for three minutes before sending out a welcome mat of flying lead to any assaulting force, which is not optimum. A lot of how to do it depends on the time of day and the intel.

In this case, the S-2 predicted that the most likely response was going to be *no response*. It was, after all, the middle of the night. I was happy to be the first one landing, because even though the Blackhawks were a tremendous noise generator, we'd drop off the Scandinavian giants and be gone down the valley before Haji could rub the sleep from his eyes. As we went over the falls, one Apache indicated he was going up to the top ridgeline of the valley to look for anyone in an elevated position overlooking the objective. The other seemed to be staying relatively low and behind us, more available for a quick response if we needed it. The two gunship pilots must have worked out the common high-guy/low-guy plan.

After the plummet, we arrived quickly over a maze of rock walls, and on short final our door gunner shouted, "HOLD YOUR HOVER!," indicating he thought we were about to hit something. Bill made a quick stop at 10 feet by yanking up on the collective, which, via rapid-acting hydraulic servos, simultaneously increased the pitch of all four main rotor blades and commanded our digital fuel control to pump in the required amount of pressurized fuel for the General Electric turbines to create a 4,000-horsepower pulse of air pressure beneath us, stopping our descent. The gunner (who was leaning out the window, looking aft, against a body harness on a retractable reel) gave him some quick commands to shift position and come down between two rock walls. He did well; sometimes the gunners aren't trained to provide aircraft-handling recommendations because they are taken from other jobs to free up the actual crew chiefs for maintenance. The gunners can be converted cooks or refuelers, for example, and would not have had the progressive training to be part of a flight crew. He did it though. He saved us from "balling one up" during the most intense phase of flight—*arriving on the objective*. Assault landings can be pretty hard and fast depending on the tactical interpretation of the pilots.

After we landed, the Norwegians deployed rapidly and we immediately departed, having not been on the ground for more than fifteen seconds. That was it. That was the nature of assault operations most of the time. It was still just a flight from A to B with passengers, but it occurred on a precise timeline and flew into kinetic threat, whereas most missions only flew into potential threat.

The art form of assaulting carries with it a lot of formality and parameters, because it had traditionally been a bigger thing; the timeline was precise because, historically, thirty seconds before the helicopters landed, big bombs were dropped along the route to obliterate any possible threat. If you showed up early, you were dead. Larger-scale operations also included many more ships, all landing at different locations but all needing to land at the exact same moment; a staple of the division's success was based on amassing combat power: having hundreds of troops show up at the same moment. That's a lot more significant for an opposing force than having eight or ten troops show up every few minutes. Assault operations evolved into a precise machine.

Even today if we fly a two-ship mission with no further coordination, we land down to the second, within a certain limited distance from the grid,[1] and within a certain tolerance of heading, so the assaulting forces know which way they are heading from the second they step out the door. For any assault pilot who cares about being proficient, this skill set is one that takes dedicated practice and a very attentive flying style. Pilots who don't practice usually don't end up on air assaults.

After we dropped off the package, we flew to a nearby staging area in accordance with our hasty brief; we would wait for the EXFIL call, fly the route in reverse, and take the operators and the potential detainees back to Kabul. We ended up waiting forty-five minutes, coffee in hand, listening to the radios. Another intensely enjoyable period, similar to the few seconds between when you light a huge firework and when it actually explodes . . . you know something unstoppable is happening, but aren't 100 percent sure exactly how or when it's going to resolve. We sat there in the darkness, idling in our Cadillac, sipping Starbucks. It's the best drive-in movie ever.

After the initial surprise and suppression, the commandos had the upper hand and began security sweeps of the compound before hauling the bad guys out. The high-value target was there; he was still in a sleepy daze by the time his bedroom door exploded open, the lead commando using his huge boot instead of the doorknob. He came out without a fight, which was pretty much his only option at the time. *All right.*

We got the call for extraction, flew back in, negotiated the same rock wall, and picked everyone up. Our helicopter would be used to haul in the HVT,[2] and as we sat there on the objective, I looked over with my night vision goggles and saw him being escorted in classic military fashion: binders on his wrists and a bag over his head. That was pretty normal looking despite the artificial leg, but what didn't look right was one of the huge Norwegian commandos limping along clutching and exercising his shoulder. I wondered if he got scuffed up a little but didn't have time to find out before they were strapped in and it was time to fly back.

With a few signals over the internal radio, everyone was ready to proceed back to the Norwegian base, and we flew back without incident. The gunships had the good grace to be the final helicopters to leave the objective, although we did not expect any cheap shots after having neutralized the scene. After shutdown, we were invited back on to the blue carpet and the uncomfortable chairs for debrief, which we cordially accepted to compare tactical notes and see if the customer was happy. We were always anxious to see if there were ways to improve or learn any other perspective, but when the commander came in, he gave us a hearty thanks and said, "That was great; thanks for coming down," with a bright-eyed smile. They certainly didn't muck anything up with monotonous review.

Bill and I looked at each other like, "Okey-dokey then! I guess we'll be leaving," when the big lug with the sore shoulder came limping in, just as jolly with his injuries as he had been without.

"What's happened to you?" his commander asked. With gregarious humility, he began describing the assault; his task had been to secure the building adjacent to the objective with a small team. As the front man in the team, he was responsible for opening the door and clearing the first room, but he didn't have any sort of battering ram. It's hard to tell certain details from a satellite photo recon, but this was the door he had chosen to be the most likely point of entry, and he decided to do whatever it took to get it open. After finding the door locked, he gave it a short burst with his assault rifle, and it didn't open. After a huge boot to the latch didn't work, he had decided with an escalating sense of tactical urgency to barge through with his shoulder, feeling like this delay threatened the timing of the whole operation. On the third painful tackle, the door finally fractured open and revealed that the building was in fact no longer whole; the entire sidewall had previously been blasted out. If he would have walked around the corner, he could have seen the whole structure was open to the weather and empty. *Fuck!*

We all got a chuckle out of that, parted company, and flew home. By the time we landed back in Bagram, it was almost five in the morning, and there was no way our shift would launch again, so we began the postmission process, including debriefing the S-2. While we had little to report, since what we had encountered was exactly what the S-2 had predicted, Lt. Gilley was keenly receptive for any detail that may have been higher-octane intel than the S-2 shop would normally handle. Ever refining the process for how information was provided to pilots, Gilley was still determined to make it out on a mission at some point. This particular debrief, however, ended without being particularly captivating.

By 0600 our reliefs had arrived, and we packed up and went home.

It had been a rare, great night on QRF. No *BS*, no dozing off into a puddle of drool, no admin runs, just a hasty air assault with a bunch of great operators. I could have stayed charged up if things like that happened more often, and if we could have woven a greater cross section of the company into real combat operations so our team could have jelled. I enjoyed the satisfaction of the shift and treated myself to some french toast and ice cream at the DFAC.

Anyone wanting more action is partially a product of the age of action movies, but when we get to enjoy our doctrinal function, we also get to realize it's extremely intense, and having the ability to operate effectively at that intensity level is very rewarding. *Of course we want more action!* We love the threat, we love the danger, and we love shooting things and being shot at. *We're adrenaline junkies!* I didn't know at the time why we couldn't fly more air assault missions and nab more bad guys, but Col. Dickerson eventually helped me see the light: At some of the locations where the intel led us, the elevation was so high and the helicopters were already so heavy because of the BAPS that the Blackhawk simply couldn't carry as many bodies as the mighty Chinook. At thin-air elevations, physics ran the fight, and simple math pointed to the answer—at certain density altitudes, the horsepower of the Blackhawk could carry only four bodies in addition to the crew complement, while the Chinook could carry fifteen or sixteen more. If there was an objective we wanted to *own*, we could deliver the assault package with eight Blackhawks, along with the coordination and landing space that that requires, or two Chinooks. What's easier? *Conservation of power* answers this question easily.

Not only did a two-Chinook and two-Apache assault package become the preferred method of delivering combatant troops to a mountain objective during our deployment, it caught on and became a typical formation for mountain warfare. Lift 6 knew what he was doing.

I enjoyed my low-elevation assault though. Not only was it low elevation, it was a small assaulting force; the Norwegians needed only twelve bodies to get the job done, and at that lower elevation we could carry six each. Two Blackhawks was a great answer in this case.

After the sicky sweet french toast, I took a shower, shifted into PTs, went back to my quarters, and locked the door. A celebratory bourbon was enough to feel content with no additional media.

CHAPTER 27
LION OF PANJSHIR

Day 241. Our mission one night was a short run to Panjshir and back. In the normal grind of missions we flew, some were monotonous and nothing more than part of the usual routine, while others could be quite charming, such as the scenic, low-threat flights to Bamiyan. Another good one was the occasional flight north into the restricted Panjshir valley.

From the Bagram Bowl we could fly in any direction, but the time it took to climb up to altitude steered us toward breaks in the terrain and various mountain passes. Geographically, the Bowl was 10 or 12 miles in diameter, or in Blackhawk terms about five minutes across, so it took only a few minutes to reach one of the passes. The main directions were Kabul to the south (the easiest and wide open), JBAD to the southeast (very scenic until you get past the Naghlo Dam on the Kabul River), and Bamiyan to the west. The final common direction out of the Bowl was due north, to Panjshir.

Within the Bowl itself, and on either side of the Panjshir River trickling down from the mountains, was a green patch of farmland and many mud brick houses up the hillside. Following the river north led to the most dramatic pass out of the Bowl, a sheer rock face cleaved by the river over the last five million years, making for a narrow pass with high winds. The resulting Venturi effect caused us to maintain total focus when flying through it, lest our dainty aluminum aircraft be smitten by strong wind currents and stone. After just a few seconds through the pass, the valley opened up enough for a two-ship formation to proceed in a relaxed manner.

We flew to several locations in the Panjshir River valley during the year, always landing on unimproved helicopter landing sites, essentially just picking an easy spot on the gravel banks along the river to land on. There was also a soccer field where we would land on occasion, not a green grassy one, but a dirt rectangle with goal posts on either end. This sort of off-airport work was common practice in a country without a significant amount of development and was one of the great advantages of using helicopters in the first place.

Nothing was too unusual about the pax in Panjshir, many of whom were connected in some way to the myriad coalition efforts that dotted the country. Panjshir valley seemed peaceful and optimistic, like Bamiyan. Panjshir valley, and all of Panjshir Province for that matter, had more recent popular history than Bamiyan, for with its steep walls it had been a military stronghold on several occasions, most recently against the Taliban and previously against the Russians. In the latter part of the twentieth century, this interesting topography had long been held by the "Lion of Panjshir"—Tajik commander Ahmad Shah Massoud. Massoud created such a signature on the fighting history of the area and as a cultural leader that he was recognized as a hero by President Karzai prior to Massoud's eventual assassination on September 9, 2001. During 2009, a very impressive monument was being built for him in the valley.

There was also a relatively new wind farm in Panjshir, along with notable construction on the main road, and an effort to improve the small schools, all of which created a feeling of prosperity and relief from the unremarkable outlook of coalition efforts in other parts of the country.

I felt like it was worth being in Afghanistan when I focused on Panjshir, and it was fun to fly up there. I wonder if the history of failed offenses within the steep rock prevented further violence, or if people in the area generally wanted to honor Massoud with peacefulness. Either was possible, but most likely the area was so rugged that any insurgent would be too lazy to conquer the intimidating terrain for the sake of controlling such a relatively unpopulated area. Only great historical entities of centuries past had ever sought control of the region, even then only as a thoroughfare between the southern portions of Russia and the capital city of Kabul.

That night, my copilot was an unpopular guy by the name of Phil "Tits" Bogswell. Phil was another one of those guys who had plenty of hours to be signed off as a pilot in command but could never get recommended at the monthly pilot-in-command board. In this case, I had always given the thumbs-down myself, and there was no one pushing for him to be signed off. Phil was one of those obnoxious guys who didn't quite care about anything and had a relatively immediate *fuck-it* response to just about any situation requiring actual work or vigilance. He was vulgar; any conversation about women that came up was met with Phil's standard question, "Did she have big tits?," as if this sort of high school mentality kept him in with the gang. Phil had a way of repelling people physically by being overweight and bald, wearing beady-looking wire-rimmed glasses, and generally having a damp, pasty appearance. His handshake was always clammy and limp, and between his raunchy sense of humor and his child-molester appearance, he was especially easy to dislike. A handful of the other pilots even made a game of who could draw the best cartoon of Phil, and many amusing variants of a dumpy figure evolved on the whiteboard to the delight of almost the entire company, always being erased immediately with the laughter.

One person who would never lower himself to the point of engaging in the juvenile mockery but still held plausible disdain for Phil was Arturo Matos. Ever mindful of how hard he was working himself, Art took immediate offense to the existence of such a no-load and slovenly individual and wouldn't hesitate to remind Phil of his deficiencies as well as give him nonnegotiable guidance on how to improve. Making little effort to be discreet in their relationship, their many septic interactions throughout the year provided more and more subtle entertainment to incidental eavesdroppers.

Besides having to fly with Phil, which meant an added degree of babysitting for his careless flying, the weather was also not as favorable as Alicia the SWO[1] had promised. This was almost always the case, and pilots would have to interpret their own skies, often asking aircraft coming from the other direction what it looked like through the pass or what it looked like down by Ghazni, etc. Such was the case today; the visibility wasn't as grand as the SWO had predicted, but it was still workable. In the SWO's defense, mountain weather is extremely difficult to predict. Huge mountain ranges jam up weather fronts. In light of this reality, most of the pilots took the weather report with a grain of salt. Comically, one pilot who *didn't* was Bill Westergaurd, who on short order had come up with a cringe-worthy nickname for Alicia in particular: The Lyin' Bitch. This could sometimes add an unfortunate but giggly undertone to the briefing room when Alicia was giving the daily weather brief, which she didn't really deserve.

After we dropped off and picked up the manifested pax from the gravel bank, our small formation departed once again, conducted carefully in the black of night, at a low speed of only 100 knots within the confines of the valley, and then surfed our way down the breeze toward the narrow pass, with the rock walls seemingly close enough to touch. After what felt like huge invisible hands pushing our tiny machines toward the rock, we were summarily spat from the cleft, floated down, called the tower at Bagram, and landed. Easy mission.

It's difficult to fly into the Panjshir valley without considering the history or even imagining what it would be like to be a foot soldier charged with fighting over such daunting topography. Hyperventilation comes to mind, yet through history there have been countless attempts either to conquer or control Afghanistan. North–south traffic between the mass of Asia and the Arabian Sea would naturally funnel through Afghanistan. That part seems logical, but only the insanely ambitious would then decide the torturous path should be *owned*.

Not to recite all of history, or misquote Wikipedia even, but there are enough historical indicators and tales of endless struggle from Alexander the Great to present day suggesting that no outsider has come to Afghanistan on short order and changed anything. Most relevant, within the past three or four decades, Big Russia had been in there and had gotten their asses kicked, on a deployment that hadn't been from halfway around the world; it was much closer to being in their backyard. There we were, though, not just attacking the Taliban but attempting, as *yet another foreign entity,* to affect the thought process and lifestyle of Indigenous people who are as open minded toward a Western mentality as the mountains that surround them. It's such a long shot, really, which potentially made the point of Operation Enduring Freedom more a question of how to get out without making things worse, and less about fighting the war on terror.

Could blind obedience have been the main problem with this war? Hundreds of years ago, a strategy called "counterinsurgency" (or COIN) was developed, whereby, with a large-enough implementing force, an insurgency gets expelled from a region with military action, then the desirable remaining population, with a unified government, becomes empowered and strengthened enough to prevent the insurgency from returning. There have been successful counterinsurgency operations in history, with great amounts of bloodshed and political salesmanship, but there have also been many failed counterinsurgency campaigns. Each case seems to be a different sort, but like any war, success is in the numbers. If the implementing force is bigger than the insurgency, step 1 will happen. For step 2 to happen, the remaining government and population have to become stronger than the original problem, validation of which is revealed only upon departure of the implementing force.

So, our strategy in OEF would be to deploy troops down every goat trail and into every village, kill any Taliban we came across, and meet directly with the population and the elders of Afghanistan to convince them that if we work together to keep insurgents out of their homes and communities, a season of safety and prosperity will ensue. To sell it, we would bring in the money and resources for local improvements, in return for the network of elders and the spokesmen of tribes providing intel on who the bad guys were and where they would be. But low-level Army officers in the O-3 to O-5 range bear the burden of implementing this strategy, with decades less experience on how to proceed than the general who ordered it, and walk into little villages for meeting after skeptical meeting with the elders.

In theory, if the locals were uplifted by a new road or a new bridge or a new school and felt as though we would be effective enough to prevent retaliation, they could be convinced to sell insurgents down the river in order to keep getting coalition enrichment and protection. In return, the coalition could work within the populace, be more in touch with who's who, and be able to fight a more advised war against the bad guys on the basis of firsthand HUMINT. The recurring problem was that insurgents often lived within the community. Those insurgents had a family, and their children interacted with the other children. They were also farmers, and they shared their small crop with a few of their neighbors. Perhaps they weren't really insurgents, but their cousin was. Their cousin wasn't really an insurgent, but he was given favor by an insurgent whom he had allowed to stay in his shed one night. Someone had climbed over the hill from Pakistan and was friends with his son and traded them a few goats but also wanted to affect certain decisions in the valley. And so on. It's just ambiguous enough . . .

In this spiderweb, not everyone is somehow related to a bad guy. They are closely tied together, though, usually within only a few degrees of separation. So, the foundations of COIN balanced precariously on a biased, or perhaps only partially honest, relationship. An elder may want the new road and the new school, so he gives the immediate unit commander enough intel for the relationship to feel genuine. But he omits enough so his cousin (who at times had cooperated with insurgents to provide for his family) doesn't get in trouble. Or maybe he provides "new intel" on a house he thought the Taliban used, but it turns out to have been abandoned weeks earlier. Either way, real progress in COIN is tentative, especially with the Taliban (seasoned by *years* of outmaneuvering the coalition) threatening the locals if they cooperate.

Local commanders, realizing COIN is a game of numbers, ask up the chain of command for more help. If one company of forty or fifty troops is trying to negotiate in a community of hundreds, it is difficult to establish enough solid relationships or develop enough useful leads to effectively curb the season of harassment by the Taliban, especially as part-time diplomats and full-time warriors. The ratio was poor. Local commanders got reminded COIN was the mission. It would take time, but we were there to make it work, and eventually it should work, even if we had to add troops to prove it.

A unit commander is in Afghanistan for only a one-year deployment. They don't have the time to get embedded and comfortable, then make the kind of historical shift being asked of them. They have to trust that the unit commander before them had it started, and that they themselves will add to the progress and then get to hand it over to the next guy and so on, until over the course of many years it begins to work. But no individual commander wants to stand up and say, *Look, we're getting our asses kicked, we're always going to be viewed as outsiders, this is stupid, and we should go home.* Few with their own career or family in mind are apt to take that stand when they have such a short duration of responsibility. They could only get there, be vigilant until they got their mind wrapped around what the mission was, and proceed forward on pure obedience, to include quelling their own potential prejudices, and if disenchantment started to set in, their own relief was on the way. It was a challenging scenario for continuity to accumulate, let alone strike an infantry commander as being *God's Mission*, or create the passion required to become exponentially effective.

Still, the request went up. *We need more troops for counterinsurgency to work.* The president himself, who had to answer to the American people, was saying counterinsurgency would work, so no subordinate commander down to the lowest field-level commander was likely to object. Military programming creates obedience. *Get'er done.*

ROGER.

Soon the words "troop surge" were in the news and 30,000 more troops were deploying. What do you suppose the reaction of the local populace in Afghanistan was? If I lived there, I would have felt like they were a bunch of unwanted tourists in my hometown. All you have to do is imagine the roles being reversed to understand the tedium of the whole scenario. This time imagine the *diplomatic* version of Red Dawn: Suppose 100,000 Chinese soldiers in Texas were walking around trying to get a bunch of good ol' boys to embrace communism, and they were going to hand out free Chinese finger cuffs until it happened. Could it ever work? That's another dysfunctional example, but the essence of the cultural barrier is similar.

The question I wondered about, as a politically distanced utility pilot, was *if we were fighting the war on terror, why weren't we deploying the special forces, exclusively? Why didn't we shift over to drone strikes, exclusively?* Have a list of high-value targets and methodically pick them off. . . . The answer seems to be that the Taliban is so deeply saturated within Afghanistan, those more exclusive tactical options would be extremely difficult to execute responsibly from a distance; you'd never be able to identify the correct target from satellite imagery or UAV optics. The answer of who the bad guys are seems to float up only through the murky waters of HUMINT; times and locations are foreseeably diluted, and any action taken had to be locally executed and fairly immediate before an alerted enemy dissolved back into solution.

So, were we getting rid of terrorists who were a threat to US soil? Were we making sure there were no training camps in Afghanistan? Had we shifted over to a humanitarian mission, having noticed that whether the Taliban was a problem to the United States or not, they were pretty horrible to the people of Afghanistan? Or were we just determined to truly get rid of the Taliban? Whatever the answer was, it stood in front of a heavy machine; it takes roughly two-thirds of our Army just to support the actual ground combatants who go on missions. Looking at who the actual fighters are, they are significantly outnumbered by the chain of command, administrators, cooks, medics, chaplains, refuelers, transportation specialists, helicopter pilots, crew chiefs, drivers, and maintainers. Bringing in Big Army puts a *huge* machine in place, and it felt like an enigma for the mission we were there to accomplish, especially if the mass of Big Army has neither training in negotiating nor speaks Pashto. Once we hit a benchmark of eliminating al-Qaeda, should we have left?

CHAPTER 28
WALK TO THE NOISE

Day 254. A few nights later, I found myself paired up with Tommy Ingram. Tommy was another senior line pilot in the task force, so for both of us to be in the same cockpit was not only a low-risk crew mix, but also kind of fun because there was no need to monitor each other as closely as with one of the junior pilots. We constituted one QRF crew, Art Matos and Sammy Park the other.

It seemed like it was going to be a quiet August night. Several people were watching and rewatching a YouTube clip of Usain Bolt becoming the fastest man ever to run the 100-meter sprint, at the 2009 World Championships in Berlin. But halfway between dinner and breakfast the phone rang, and the TOC said they needed one Blackhawk for an urgent medevac chase aircraft, on a simple tail-to-tail flight down to JBAD and back. The QRF team is two crews and two aircraft, but with the medevac bird being one, only half of our QRF assets had to go. Tommy and I looked at the other crew, but Art seemed to be in the middle of chastising a depressed-looking Sammy Park for the font he had chosen for a route card, so we said, "We'll go," and received no objection from our sister ship. It was going to be kind of fun to interrupt twelve continuous hours of boredom, and the other crew didn't seem to be in the mood for it anyway.

Half the time, depending on crew mix, we could beat the medevac aircraft out to the threshold, which was the case that night. In the final minute of waiting for the medevac bird, we made small adjustments to the cockpit and got mission details and launch approval from the TOC. It was dark. The forecast was for 0 percent illumination, based on a new moon, and with a substantial cloud layer there would be no starlight. I also realized I had forgotten one of my mission essentials: my thermos! Contemplating ways either to go back for it or have someone bring it out to me, the medevac bird taxied up and announced REDCON ONE. *Crap.*

The mission was to go get a soldier who had a gunshot wound from a firefight up in Bostick, on the north end of the Kunar River valley, and was being transferred to Bagram for a higher level of hospital treatment. JBAD launched their QRF to get the soldier from Bostick, and Bagram launched their medevac to get the soldier from JBAD; hence the tail-to-tail transfer. The only logistical deficiency was that we all launched at the same time, with roughly the same distance to go. By the time Tommy and I got to JBAD, the JBAD QRF was just getting to Bostick, which we could see on the Blue Force Tracker. This was a common lack of timing on the part of the battle captain and meant we would be waiting.

The flight down to JBAD was typically quiet—no real population to speak of, so no lights on the ground, and no threat. It was about as rugged as terrain got, at least for part of the flight, so we went high, latched the flight director onto a waypoint at JBAD, and sat quietly for forty-five minutes. Despite the fact we were heading for an urgent transfer, our droning flight still had a sleepy component in the middle of the desert expanse between Bagram and JBAD. Our only source of entertainment was the Blue Force Tracker icon of JBAD's QRF slowly marching up the Kunar on one of the cockpit displays. By the time we were landing, we had figured out we would be waiting on the ramp for at least thirty minutes for JBAD's QRF to get back down to us. We thought about recommending to the battle captain that we continue up and make the transfer at ABAD (Asadabad), but it seemed as though there was already a plan in place with no confusion, so we decided to just wait.

We fired up our little auxiliary power unit to pick up the electrical load and brought the throttles down to idle, because the Blackhawk has transmission-driven alternators that trip off-line if the rotor rpm gets too low. We sat. The little blue icon was now moving south again, which meant we had twenty more minutes to wait in the dark, in the middle of a sleepy flight on what may have been the darkest night of the year. JBAD was a blackout airbase as well, so there was not so much as a single ramp light. And we sat.

I had it: "Hey man, you want some coffee?"

"Sure, buddy," Tommy replied in his typically agreeable way.

"We're supposed to be ready, but we do have twenty minutes, and the JBAD TOC is within 75 yards of where we are sitting," I justified. "OK, here I go. I'll be back in a few."

Out of habit more than anything, I took off my night vision goggles when I got out of the cockpit. That green light shining in my eyes for the last hour hadn't done anything to help my natural night vision, and I waited a few seconds for my eyes to adjust. The folks at JBAD had dozens of large steel shipping containers littering the ramp from a recent arrival, and I didn't want to walk into one of them. Why I didn't think to just put the goggles back on and focus in for walking is a good question, but I opted to Frankenstein my way forward, arms extended as I tried to slink along. It was the darkest ramp on the blackest night, but I didn't have too much time to waste.

Upon reaching the TOC, I opened the door to what must surely have been the most well-lit, brightest, freshly white-painted TOC in the whole country. *Why white?* How about something a little subdued? I suppose the supply chain couldn't bring everything in the Home Depot chip collection, so no one would be enjoying the cuddly named colors of the civilian world, like "Whispering Peach" or "Violet Indulgence." The logistics machine would have been far more concerned with the right amount of fuel and bullets than considering which glow to bask in when they threw some paint into the shipping container back at Campbell in 5-gallon buckets. So, it wasn't "Kitten Whispers" or even "Tuscan Sunset" in this TOC, just *white*. The name on the can could have been "Pinpoint-Pupil White," or maybe "I-Saw-the-Light White." The blinding display made me flinch as I stepped in unexpectedly, with each TOC watch stander examining me curiously. I heard one of the younger-looking guys say, "Oh shit," as if they had never seen a pilot walk through the door. It could have been the case, because we wear so much survival gear, that I had been mistaken for a swamp creature of some sort.

Shocked I was even standing there, one guy stood up and asked, "Can I help you, sir?"

I said, "I was just wondering if I could get a cup of coffee?"

After a momentary pause of chin tucking and furrowed brows, the TOC burst into a frenzy of action! Every single operator simultaneously abandoned their station, all shouting commands and reports: "I'll get the coffee!" "I got the water!" "Start the pot! Dude, go clean out that old filter!" This cacophony of urgent response caused the task force XO to emerge from his office, looking confused as to why there were no operators at their stations.

Responding to his perplexed glance, I sheepishly admitted, "I asked for some coffee."

The XO's face lit up before a triumphant proclamation: "I've got coffee cups!"

Well for Heaven's sake. I have never seen such customer service in my life. As my eyes continued adjusting, I noticed a large-scale Blue Force Tracker on the wall, recognized the Kunar River valley, and saw the small blue icon halfway back down to JBAD from Bostick. *Damn.* As the final soldier poured in the water, he said, "There you go, sir!" I said, "Thanks," and began shifting my glance between the unremarkable coffeepot and the blue icon marching steadily down the screen. Contrasting the TOC personnel who got it started, the Black & Decker coffeepot had little perceivable response.

The team resumed their stations, and at the disheartening rate of about a drop per second, the calcified plastic appliance began to function. With reservoirs of liquid, specifically engineered fluid pathways, heat being applied, and chemical reactions taking place, there was no stopping the pair of speeding Blackhawks that defined the amount of time available. Perfectly synchronized turbine engines screaming through the night sky would outpace the cheap coffeepot.

It was a delicate situation then—someone's life hung in the balance, and I needed to be at my station when they arrived to fly them up the next leg to Bagram. But the TOC also could not go without their due appreciation for such a considerate response to the coffee request. There was about half a cup of black coffee then. They had been so helpful. How shallow I would seem to just abandon the very thing I asked them for, which they, at the cost of their own responsibilities, had so generously facilitated.

The icon was within three minutes of JBAD, then *drip . . . drip . . . drip . . .* a life hanging in the balance; the dull tingle of negligence creeping up my spine; the loathsome coffee maker snorting and sneezing its pathetic way through two simple cups of water. I heard a muffled radio call, followed shortly thereafter by the radio operator announcing, "Sir, the QRF is Zulu," and the battle captain acknowledged, "Very well."

They still had to taxi in, I thought; that's at least a minute, and then any tail-to-tail transfer would take several minutes to shift the personnel over with the IV bag and resecure the patient in the next medevac bird. With Tommy being my copilot, I didn't even need to carry any responsibility or situational awareness to the cockpit. I could get my body back in the seat and he could take off within five seconds and we would be meeting every requirement. So, I needed only thirty seconds to walk back out. Just then, I heard the unmistakable sound of a Blackhawk taxiing by outside, and I couldn't take it anymore. I had to get back out there. With an inch of *very strong* coffee in the bottom of the pot, I poured half each into two Styrofoam cups, said, "Thanks, everybody," and stepped out of the brightest, whitest, most well-lit TOC into absolute blackness.

Shit. I stopped dead in my tracks, totally blind.

With only seconds to spare, I shifted into primal mode—*this is easy; just walk toward the noise.* Slowly at first, then speeding up as my plan worked, with half a cup of tar-like coffee in each hand, I walked at full speed into the broad side of a shipping container. With both cups of coffee exploding all over myself, I shouted, "Fuck!" at the container. Seeming even more urgent then, with scalded hands, I consolidated what was left of each cup into the less deformed of the two, which added up to about five sips. I felt my way back to the Blackhawk, climbed inside, plugged in my intercom system, and said, "Here's your coffee."

"Thanks, Buddy," Tommy said, not seeming to notice the deformities of the cup.

I sat in my coffee-soaked flight suit looking at dozens of steel shipping containers on the ramp through my night vision goggles for thirteen more minutes before the medics were ready, and we departed back to Bagram.

CHAPTER 29
IN GOOD HANDS

Day 275. A few days before Labor Day, I was on QRF, paired up with Todd Wolfe. Fantasizing only briefly for a quiet night, we learned at the update brief that there was a scheduled resupply mission into the Pech, beginning at 11:00 p.m., which would make going to the DFAC for *mid-rats* an impossibility. This fact coupled with a complete lack of enthusiasm guaranteed we would be eating Powerbars and cookies all night. Also of note: not giving the threat brief, but sitting with one of the Chinook crews, was Lt. Gilley. Heavy D had finally been convinced of the value in the S-2 staff having firsthand knowledge of the operating environment and mission, and it was no surprise the intelligence officer seemed to be the most attentive person in the briefing room. Ironically, while the intel brief described threat along the route as only moderate (baseline threat level for a mission into the Pech), it also included mention of new HUMINT suggesting the Taliban commander had an RPG specialist in the Korangal valley and was intending to attack COP Vegas during the day.

Here was a classic case of composite risk management kicking in; of course, this was a high-risk mission because of the historical threat in that neck of the woods, but now there was an additional variable. The backdrop to this discussion is that there was always the chance of an RPG in the Pech or Korangal. That's why it was the helicopter shoot-down capitol of the world. If we canceled every mission at the first sign of threat, we would have never been able to go in there. We had to, though, because of the number of coalition bases and troops stabilizing the volatile region who needed resupply: produce, frozen and canned goods, fuel for generators, water, mail, and, of course, ammo.

The first mitigating factor to green-light this flight would be that the mission was going to be flown at night; an RPG is a dumb-sighted weapon, and less likely to be wasted at night. The intel suggested plans for a daytime attack, so we'd stay out of there during the day. The next mitigating factor was providing a gunship escort; the sight of Apaches lingering around could cause all but the most hardened of insurgents to stay home. For those who would still come out to play, we would be present with brutal firepower. The final mitigating factor was my own component of the mission, two Blackhawks in the high orbit with a contingent of heavily armed Pathfinders, who could be rapidly inserted on the site of any downed aircraft to provide ground security. While there may have been additional threat, it had been compensated for.

Usually, the Chinooks would go into the Pech and start making runs back and forth from outpost to outpost, with the Apaches snooping around for anything suspicious. Both the Chinooks and Apaches were vulnerable, but the huge Chinook also had the nearly constant disadvantage of being low and slow for the many approaches and departures in the tiny valley. They don't have time to accelerate up to a speed where they would be hard to hit, so they make the required deliveries with a degree of fortitude. Meanwhile, the Apaches have a slightly more defensive posture, staying higher, flying faster, and generally maneuvering to be a hard target. They were also *looking* for trouble, and once in a while they found it, but the Pech and Korangal valleys had been stable for several months. Back and forth the Chinook had to go, between FOB Blessing, OP Restrepo,[1] and COPs Vegas, Honaker-Miracle, Able-Main, and Michigan,[2] and at their own discretion the Apaches would tactically buzz about.

Optimally, our task force can get UAS feed prior to any human-flown aircraft being in the valley: a remote-controlled aircraft way above the terrain, looking down with special cameras, feeding a video stream directly to the TOC, and allowing the operations folks to see if anything is suspicious. Sometimes the UAV[3] was there, sometimes it wasn't. They have the same potential maintenance and personnel management challenges a regular aircraft has, similar weather problems to sort through, and similar technical and connectivity problems to deal with. I let that portion of the threat brief float over my head, primarily because we hadn't seen any real trouble brewing in the Pech since early January of that year, when a helicopter had been shot with an RPG and made a flame-engulfed approach to the ground but landed on a stump and rolled over.

That night was another one of those bright nights with 100 percent illume.[4] Nights with a full moon and no cloud cover are some of the most dangerous. While bright illumination lights up the night vision goggles and makes the world look like broad daylight in green shades, it can also be bright enough for the enemy to see the aircraft with the naked eye. Flying under *low* illume is harder for the pilots because the goggles don't have as much light to amplify, but is a safer threat scenario because the bad guys' effectiveness is notably hampered by darkness.

This resupply package included two Chinooks, led by Chinook pilot Ryan Dechent in "BIGTIME 56," two Apaches under the call sign "OVERDRIVE," and two Blackhawks flying with our usual call sign of "HONCHO." We flew the typical route from Bagram to JBAD, or just north of JBAD, then turned north up the Kunar River valley to ABAD for hot gas at the FARP[5] before proceeding west into the Pech. BIGTIME would land at FOB Blessing to begin picking up netted sling loads and fuel blivets, OVERDRIVE would begin snooping around, and HONCHO would go high to the ROZ. It took an hour just to get to where the mission would begin, and while it's fun to listen to the radios on more-elaborate missions, the trip across the desert was as dull as it always had been. If you sit still in the dark for an hour, especially wrapped up tightly in body armor and harnesses, hearing only a dull rumbling noise outside your hearing protection, and gently bumping along through the night sky, this combination of factors is remarkably similar to what an infant feels when swaddled, to the same effect. Finally, we hit the FARP and went high, being ever mindful not to set the JLENS balloon free at Asadabad. The Chinooks and Apaches split up into teams so the Chinooks could independently resupply the various outposts, few of which could handle two Chinooks at once. Each Chinook then had its own escort, and an internal deconfliction plan was established between these teams to prevent any collisions during several trips back and forth to FOB Blessing. The bigger base supplied the smaller ones.

As bright as it was, the Duke and I decided to flip up our goggles and fly unaided to rest our eyeballs for a while. Just having the extra weight of goggles on your head adds fatigue to any mission, but the eye strain that comes with looking through the goggles for a prolonged period of time will also add so much fatigue to a flight that within the flying rules, NVG[6] flights are restricted from being as long as daytime flights by several hours. It is a relief to take the goggles off and relax the eye strain. Within a few minutes of taking the goggles off, we had dimmed down the cockpit lighting and our eyes were dark adapted. It was *unusually* bright out. I could clearly see the other aircraft down in the valley, along with the outline of the terrain and even much of the texture of the hillsides. We decided to fly in a racetrack pattern, three minutes heading west, a lazy turn, three minutes heading east, and another lazy turn, which equaled the same thing happening every eight minutes or so. That was pretty typical behavior in a holding pattern for an aerial standby asset.

Another quiet hour had gone by before one of the Chinooks got shot with an RPG.

BIGTIME 56 had just released a "triple hook" of sling loads at COP Vegas and was repositioning to offload passengers. Due to an unusual request made by the PZ[7] controller to drop the cargo in between some buildings, the Chinook had flown in and remained facing west to release the slings. Prior to landing for pax drop off, however, the flight engineer decided that the terrain and visual references of the LZ favored landing to the east, and recommended reversing direction. Dechent agreed, completed the pedal turn, and was sliding right to get over the LZ when the RPG round struck. The high level of illumination and the maneuvering that resulted from the special request of the PZ controller created the perfect combination for some pebble-chewing fuckstain to step out with his prized possession and take a potshot. This individual happened to be hiding near a Hesco barrier and, in RPG terms, was at point-blank range inside 20 meters.

The RPG round flew into the bottom of the ramp on the back of the Chinook, exploded, and continued through the sheet metal of the ramp to send shrapnel flying throughout the cabin. Hearing a sound like a howitzer going off, Dechent felt the nose of the huge craft pitching down before smelling cordite. Momentarily encumbered by chaos but realizing the machine was still flying, he decided to hastily return to FOB Blessing and land, even while noticing the controls were not responding normally; *there must have been hydraulic damage.* Even if they made it only to the valley floor, they would have been farther from the threat perched on the high ground near COP Vegas. Realizing the massive ship itself might be bleeding out, Dechent accelerated to a gutsy speed for the conditions and within minutes made a successful landing back at FOB Blessing.

The Apache pilot went into hyper-commo, asking if they needed the Pathfinders inserted or not. Several times we heard the question over the radio: "Should we call Honcho!? Should we call Honcho!?," with the eventual reply of no; they had landed safely and appeared to be out of harm's way.

Going from quiet, lazy circles in the sky to sudden radio chatter got my full attention, but my only response was to flip the goggles back down, which lit the entire area in a bright-green wash, and to push the big "D." The M-model Blackhawk has a "direct-to" feature that allows the pilots to type in any position, and the flight management system will create a GPS waypoint and fly directly to it. The call never came, though; the Chinook had landed within the walls of one of our own bases, so extra security was unnecessary. Landing an extra helicopter and releasing the Pathfinders was guaranteed to add confusion, which Dechent made a sound tactical decision against.

This event transformed the resupply mission into an emergency medical situation, as well as a modified downed-aircraft-recovery scenario. All personnel involved shifted immediately from a mindset of logistical efficiency to one of being effective first responders; this trait of our military force was ingrained from initial training, and reinforced through frequent recurrency training.

On the ground at FOB Blessing, as copilot John Wilson completed the emergency engine shutdown, Dechent proceeded into the back of the Chinook to assess the damage and check on his crew. It was immediately obvious that the crew of five, along with twenty passengers, had been through a horrific event. The ramp gunner, Valdemir Yazzie, had received whole-body shrapnel injuries and a mild concussion, having been the closest to the point of impact. Additionally, his ICS system had been knocked out, which in the darkness created the sense that he was unresponsive, though in reality he was incapacitated, but conscious and writhing in pain.

One of the passengers had what is referred to in ballistics lingo as a "through and through" neck injury, where something flew through one side of his trachea and out the other, and he needed immediate medical attention. Every seat in the cabin was affected, all the way up to the jump seat (closest to the cockpit) and beyond. Shrapnel even embedded into the thin forward bulkhead and soundproofing behind the pilot's seats, by which point most flying fragments had run out of energy; the pilots were unscathed. Most severely, some shrapnel had flown all the way through the cabin to hit forward door gunner Casey Church, completely severing most of his left gluteus, though somehow missing the femoral artery.

Church would later describe it as being hit in the hip with a sledgehammer, but in real time, after the explosion, he couldn't feel his left leg. Not knowing he was already in critical condition, he used his right leg to kick his left to see if it was still there, and it was. While waiting for a chance to say anything over the ICS system, Church lowered himself down to the floor. When there was finally a break in the chatter, he told the crew he was hit, but not sure how bad, that his leg was still there, but that he could no longer feel it. His hip was fractured, and he was in shock. He had massive bleeding, both obvious and internal, and was receiving emergency first aid from the passenger who had been in the jump seat, Lt. Sarah Gilley. On her first combat flight in a war zone, to gain insight into the exact medium her team supplied information for, she was absorbing a level of exposure she would never have hoped for. Reacting immediately to an urgent life-or-death scenario, Gilley took off her gloves and sank her bare hands into open, bloody muscle tissue to stop the hemorrhaging. Seeing this, Dechent was able to contribute to what otherwise may have been unstoppable bleeding, with a recalled packet of Quick Clot, which he was supposed to have turned in earlier that day. Throughout his experience, with increasing amounts of anguish and gauze, Church never stopped trying to get back up to his gun.

John Wilson made his way back from a shutdown cockpit and began administering first aid to Sgt. Yazzie, as the first medic from the aid station was running down to the Chinook. Shortly after the landing, the mangled ramp of the Chinook had drifted open, due to hydraulic damage, and gallons of hydraulic fluid had pooled behind the craft. As the medic tried to make a quick stop near the ramp, he slipped in the puddle and landed hard on his head. He made his own recovery but wasn't able to contribute to the immediate medical needs of the crew. More medics arrived with aid bags and stretchers then, and Church, Yazzie, and the civilian with the neck injury were carried up to the aid station. The rest of the passengers needed only first aid, but it became apparent that the aid station at FOB Blessing was not equipped to handle a scenario of this magnitude, and the "NINE-LINE" call was made for the medevac assets at JBAD to respond.

While Valdemir Yazzie and the civilian were medevaced to Bagram, Casey Church was medevaced through urgent means all the way to Walter Reed Army Medical Center in Bethesda, Maryland, via JBAD hospital and the Army's major hospital in Landstuhl, Germany. He had stayed awake and angry until he was inside the relative safety of the hospital at JBAD, angry mostly because he knew we shouldn't have been out there on such a bright night in the first place. Between the safety of the hospital and a morphine sucker a medic had given him on the medevac aircraft, he finally passed out and didn't wake up again for the next four days.

The other Chinook crew landed at Blessing to help, and pilot in command Rob Devlin, who was also a maintenance test pilot, began assessing the damage along with John Wilson, who had experience as a flight engineer before becoming a pilot. This combination worked well to decide on a hasty repair plan, and a DART package from Bagram provided additional tools, parts, hydraulic fluid, and crew chiefs.

After the crew and passengers' immediate medical needs were met, the crew of BIGTIME 56 completed a battle damage assessment and Dechent used a satellite phone to call Lift 6 to provide an update. After field-expedient repairs were made, Dechent and Devlin, the two senior pilots, decided to fly the damaged machine home, with John Wilson and Devlin's original copilot, Michael Saenz, flying the other Chinook home. All ships departed. BIGTIME 56 was flying, although the controls and subsystems were deranged and limited, including one of the digital engine controllers not working. Devlin would have to manually control engine rpm with a toggle switch to match torque with Dechent's control inputs throughout the flight. There was urgency to take off before sunrise at Blessing, however, because if the insurgency spotted a parked Chinook on the ground, it would have been an amusing target from the surrounding high terrain. FOB by FOB, in a white-knuckled flight, Dechent and Devlin limped the aircraft along, at each point deciding that it was working well enough to continue, and hoping the hydraulic repairs would hold.

The rest of us flew home quietly, adrenaline long gone, but with enough replay running through our minds to stay wired.

Finally, we descended into the Bowl, the sun was rising, and people were walking out on the ramp to look at the Chinook with its blood-stained sheet metal damage. A discussion ensued with Col. Dickerson about when to make the repairs to the Chinook; everyone was either coming down from an adrenaline spike, going to bed for the required amount of crew rest prior to flying the next night, or getting ready to begin the day shift. The night shift already had a busy night of maintenance, just in the normal course of operations. Furthermore, since the task force had two or three more Chinooks available than were needed for the next day's mission set, it seemed reasonable that the Chinook crew chiefs and maintenance team would be allowed a day to decompress, then begin untangling aluminum from the rivets and hydraulic fluid the following morning. Heavy D replied, "Tomorrow is another day," and since no one knew what tomorrow may bring, this combat asset would be repaired immediately. *Go put on some coffee.* I pondered this reaction, then appreciated it.

I had the deep fatigue only eight or ten hours of sleep could fix, along with unstoppable rumination of the evening. I imagined the individual with the RPG sitting behind the Hesco, waiting. He had acquired the RPG with the intention of using it. He had saved it for a special occasion. When he saw his huge target float into sight, he waited some more, and waited until he could send a fireball right through the back door. He hated us. He imagined his ability to be accurate with the weapon, imagined the explosion and percussion killing a group of humans. The thought steadied him; *he was a murderer*. Half a second after squeezing the trigger, he knew it was a direct hit. Was he thankful? Excited? Remorseful? Only he could know. It must have been mind-boggling then, after a direct hit, to see the massive ship absorb the round with little apparent effect before flying away. I was thankful he was not allowed the pleasure of knowing what happened inside the Chinook.

Replaying whether or not anyone could have seen this individual before he took the shot confirmed in my mind that the answer was still *no*. If someone wants to hide, they will be able to. Our only defense against RPG fire is speed and altitude. Door gunners would be lucky to hit anything; standing up in a moving platform while firing with accuracy is a tall order. If you can imagine standing in the back of a pickup truck bouncing through a pasture at 50 to 100 miles per hour, you can understand the challenge. The best they usually do is get the enemy to duck for a few seconds, and in that few seconds we could get 25 or 50 yards farther away. Depending on where we started, that could be enough to be out of range. Staying out of range in the first place or being too fast to hit is preferable to lighting up the door guns, but any of these generic tactical considerations go out the window during landing. The vehicle gets slower and lower until both parameters are zero. Resupply missions in the Pech were just vulnerable, regardless of the vigilance or skill of the crew. It was lucky the pedal turn on the LZ happened; had the shot been fired thirty seconds earlier, they would have taken it on the nose.

CHAPTER 30
SEA OF TEMPTATION

Day 276. The next morning, talk shifted with remarkable speed from Bigtime 56 to news of two of the most senior sergeants in the battalion simultaneously having an affair with one of the most junior specialists.[1] This unfortunate episode ended up being unfortunately juicy.

Apparently, in monotonous FOB life, both sergeants had simultaneously begun private affairs with the specialist, neither knowing of the other, with the specialist initially accepting each. After some time, conflicts in the affair caused the specialist to find things less entertaining than she had initially enjoyed, and she sought to conclude it. By then, however, she had been so enticing to the senior men that neither of them wanted the arrangement to end, each trying harder and harder to amuse her for continued favors.

Somehow the two men learned of each other, which, instead of causing each to flinch away from the situation with an urgent sense of damage control, somehow caused both of them to increase their efforts at winning favor over the other. The scandalous affair came to light after the specialist forwarded up the chain of command some video footage that one of the senior men had filmed of himself masturbating and emailed to her; it supposedly had been some sort of competition between the two men. It was an absurd and embarrassing lapse of judgment that ended up costing everyone involved a lot of status, rank, and marital stress.

There is a military rule of thumb about having a relationship with anyone more than three pay grades from your own, but that applies mainly to people in the same major unit. Any sergeant major would argue that point, that it's a unilateral violation across all units and branches and certain taboo. In normal circumstances, it wouldn't be a *moral* crime if a junior E-9 met a senior E-6 from a different base and developed a relationship, if they would not, in due course, ever have a chance to affect each other's career. In reality it happens quite often. I knew several successful couples in similar scenarios. Military folks are often attracted to one another. But if anyone involved is in the same unit (or, worse, in the same chain of command), it is not only inappropriate but also completely dysfunctional. Any other person in the same unit or chain of command would naturally wonder if favoritism or abuse was occurring; therefore it is corrosive to unit cohesion. A greater problem, in this case, was that both senior guys were (past tense) married family men. It was more than a violation of General Order #1, or even good military protocol. It was real adultery.

Before condemning the already damned, though, at least ponder the circumstances: While their behavior is inexcusable and shameful, the catalyst of their failure is separation from normal life. Some people live within the moral deficit that "whatever happens on deployment stays on deployment," but that wasn't *necessarily* their nature. Maybe they wanted to be faithful, but they were weak.

People sometimes allow themselves a minor infraction, rationalizing that slipping one's toe into the sea of temptation won't do any harm, especially if they don't let anything escalate. Some *innocent* flirting might be fun and relaxing, and sometimes that's all one needs to quell their sex drive for a year and maintain a grasp on normalcy. That person either did or did not expect whomever they were flirting with to respond, but it doesn't take much for two physically isolated people to suddenly realize that something sparked and is exciting, or to get from there to a point where a master sergeant is suddenly having fantasies about a specialist who responded to him. Then, through the same historical lapse of judgment the world sees often, compounded by loneliness, isolation, or boredom, the deal gets sealed. The master sergeant all but condemns himself. When his wife back home asks why they didn't get the normal amount of money in the DFAS deposit from Cleveland, there will be no comfortable explanation for why he got reduced in rank from E-8 to E-7.

Another family bites the dust.

That isn't the norm, thankfully. Most families do what they have to do to keep everything straight. The R&R program helps a lot with that, and so do letters, phone calls, Skype, emails, care packages, and the FRG. The Family Readiness Group (typically a group of wives led by the wife with the most senior husband and hosted by the unit liaison) keeps families informed back home. Sometimes the FRG gets information faster than the soldiers do! The need to keep families together by keeping both sides of the equation informed is a lot easier now than it would have been in previous wars, with today's many communication avenues. Often, there is this sense of *Thank God for the FRG.*

In this fight, it can feel more like *going to work* than being in combat. Not to discredit the actual combatant troops who walk on patrols or ride in dangerous convoys, and who are deployed to the more austere locations, but a great many of the support personnel of *Big Army* live in relative comfort for the year, almost completely removed from the threat. That fact can undermine any sense of purpose that an otherwise vigilant soldier might have started with, resulting in the perception by the dwellers of the large plywood village that they are on a pointless, yearlong camping trip. Everything can really seem pointless. People start looking for fun, and most of the fighting force are mating-aged people in reasonably good shape. It doesn't take too many weeks of celibacy combined with boredom before people's minds begin to stray from the straight and narrow. Normal dudes and dudettes just want to get laid.

I can relate, having recently enjoyed a fling with Emily. I had no qualms with the matter, though. Despite breaking Army rules, we were merely a woman and man stuck in the desert for a year with no chance of ever being in the same unit. Both single, both responsible, and both discreet. There was no moral crime. While the most-institutionalized senior leaders would've related my behavior as something akin to blasphemy, in the modern sense of social dating it wasn't. For others who were in the same unit (or married), it created a dreadful scenario for the leadership to deal with, and in turn a series of broad-sweeping rules became endemic up and down the full range of commands and across all spectra of military activity to avoid any form of courting imaginable.

A funny abstract is that it prevents only the most obedient of soldiers from getting into any trouble, and they wouldn't have gotten into trouble in the first place. For everyone else it's like being told to stay out of the cookie jar. The same thing is true for drinking, taking war trophies, viewing pornography, and using drugs. I don't know why the force commanders don't take psychological advice from an expert on how to deal with the matter, but they obviously don't. Perhaps they take advice from their office mates, the sergeant majors of the world, whose first embedded reaction is to rule with an iron fist: "You want them to behave?! Then we'll ORDER them to behave!" What people might respond to more effectively would be treatment as adults.

In my first submarine tour aboard USS *Hammerhead*, the new captain, a Navy commander by the name of Karl Hasslinger, had discovered this very strategy to be effective. Previous captains had set rank-limited rules for activity during the various liberty ports we would pull into. E-1 through E-3 had a radius of only 50 miles; E-4 through E-6, 100 miles; and E-7 and above, up to 250 miles. Capt. Hasslinger gathered the whole crew on the pier in Norway during a deployment and announced the new policy: "You are all men. Act like it. You have four days off here. Have fun. If you want to get on the Concorde and fly to Istanbul for the weekend, have a good time. If you're not back on Monday or you embarrass me, it's your ass. Dismissed."

The new policy worked: the junior guys who were typically the most careless and likely to embarrass the command placed value in the provision. The whole crew, for that matter, felt like a new level of trust had been established, and were responsible with not violating it. No one wanted the old set of rules back. There were no incidents.

That level of responsibility is not entrusted to soldiers enduring an extended deployment. There was one exception: In 2009 in Iraq, the theater commander authorized two beers per soldier, without too much resultant trouble during the Super Bowl, which was a welcome gesture. It resulted in a lot of stress relief for the troops, but only for one night. *Maybe it was a pilot program . . .* In the generic discussion of expected behavior, to take a group of adults and isolate them in a plywood village for a year with an ambiguous sense of purpose, while removing the normal devices of stress relief, is as nearsighted as telling all the convicts in a prison to remain inside their cells with the doors unlocked.

Why not adjust the rules but hold people accountable? The nearest sergeant major will quickly point out he doesn't need any more illegitimate, deployment-conceived pregnancies, any more drug overdoses, or any more people caught with contraband items causing trouble for him. But those things will always occur if humans are in the equation. The conclusion may be this: Fewer violations will occur if a controlled allowance is provided. There may be significantly fewer people caught with contraband drugs and alcohol, for example, if everyone from the Joint Chiefs on down realized that people like adult-level stress relief. A bar on post with a simple ID-card-scanner system, just like the one at the DFAC, would allow an individual one accounted drink if the database indicated the following day was their day off. It's an unlikely solution in a military choked with political correctness. At least one other country in the coalition did exactly that, however. The German base in Mazar-i-Sharif had a bar, and the pilots who flew up there got to enjoy it. Not at Bagram, and not at any other base with a majority US population.

Although we had the R&R system during a twelve-month deployment, follow-on units would be given only a nine-month deployment with no R&R. It ends up being an even longer stretch with no break. I wouldn't expect Army leadership to acknowledge the subtle psychology of the situation, and I can hear a stereotypical conclusion: "*We're here to support Operation Enduring Freedom, not open a goddamned bar*." So, people are left to invent their own stress relief, and, apparently, stress relief is required. How many cases of PTSD that we're trying to get our minds wrapped around could be managed to some extent by allowing people's normal coping mechanisms to exist?

The military's strict control of deployed behavior is a factor in the long-term mental health of our deployed troops. David Finkel's somber book *Thank You for Your Service* does a great job of capturing how poorly the Army and the VA have handled cases of PTSD and TBI, which, for combatants who frequently see violence, IEDs, ambushes, amputations, and blood and guts, ends up being a much-bigger struggle for them than the deployment itself. The absence of coping mechanisms is a factor.

With the suicide rate for active-duty military at an all-time high, along with the supporting epidemics of depression and PTSD, the military, in conjunction with MWR,[2] has done an excellent job with certain types of off-duty activity: There is no shortage of world-class gym facilities in the military, even deployed; the gyms are excellent. Miniature fast-food restaurants have been brought in to remind the troops of home and normalcy; at least four different common fast-food restaurants can be found in the form of a small food truck, with a fairly convincing experience—the Burger King tastes like Burger King, for instance. Even certain colleges have created pseudo-campuses on the major forward operating bases (another indicator of an ambiguous battle?). It's not too hard to find a chess set or a dartboard on the bigger bases, along with internet cafés, makeshift movie theaters, and libraries. So, it's not like there was no thought put into recreation. But there's a difference between goody-two-shoes recreation and badass-motherfucker recreation. Not everyone can right themselves with a game of checkers or some travel-sized Pizza Hut.

I can understand the hesitation with having a bar on base, but if it were treated with the same amount of control and regulation everything else was, it could be managed. I have to think that if the master sergeant had an opportunity to go unwind after work with a cold bottle of Sam Adams, there may have been an opportunity to quell his temptation toward the specialist and get his mind relaxed. Maybe the cook who died huffing whippets could have chilled out at the bar that night as well, or the guy begging anyone he could find to bust a nut on his face for two grand, or the guy who shot his buddy over at Catamount, or the frustrated ground commander who was told to go home during the unwinnable firefight. Could a cold brew curb the persistent rash of PTSD in the military? Certainly, the troops who lived through a bloodbath would have taken a beer if you offered them one; it's the most common go-to coping device in the military. Thirty years ago, it might have been cigarettes, but not today. Without an adult beverage, not only do troops have to process trauma in real time, but they also have to simultaneously process why they're not being allowed to grab a cold one for their nerves.

Another caveat to this discussion is the number of soldiers who go home after deployment and create a wave of embarrassing or expensive mishaps during their first month back. We miss beer so much, the only natural tendency when we get home is to buy a bunch of it and just go swimming! Instead of an allotment of beer to curb undesirable tendencies before we come home, though, the Army has created "reintegration training," where every day for the first week home, soldiers have to sit in class and listen to someone tell them not to drink too much. Totally annoying, but an analyst might argue it works: the troops don't get as hammered the night before if they have to show up for reintegration training at 6:00 the next morning. *Good for you, Army analyst. Now shut the fuck up.* Any troop coming home knows the work-around; after reintegration training ends at 9:30 in the morning, we hit it hard and get shit-faced drunk by noon, racing in earnest to make up for lost beer-drinking time during the deployment. Reintegration training probably does reduce short-term DUIs, but if we become day drinkers, does it reduce long-term DUIs?

It's a subtle thing, but a tall order—the people who could implement such a risky-sounding adjustment to the deployment formula are too close to the top of their careers to suggest something as unprofessional sounding as "just add beer." I know there are some who would find ways to abuse the privilege if it existed, and still get into the other kinds of trouble, but they are the ones drinking on deployment anyway. It's also likely, in the current leadership climate, that if one or two people did abuse the privilege of having a bar on the FOB, the local commander would default to mass punishment and shut the whole thing down. We are a beer-drinking, flip-flops and barbecue fighting force, though, and even a tiny dose of anarchy can go a long way toward good morale and discipline. Not that biting into a hot, greasy handful of Burger King french fries can't provide a measure of stress relief; it certainly can. It's just not the same chemical process as watching some babe undress or feeling an ice-cold mug of beer hit your mind.

CHAPTER 31
TACTICAL EXHILARATION

Day 291. After enough time on the night QRF shift, I decided to join the living and "reverse out" to a normal daytime lifestyle. Being on the night shift could be enjoyable, often quiet, and convenient for calling friends and family back home; our midnight was New York's 1:30 p.m., for example. After a while, though, it could get a bit owly. There's also something that stems from having to fly with night vision goggles on every flight that takes some of the fun out of it. The modern goggles are brilliant; the picture is clear and bright. Still, it's heavy, and after a while it just makes your eyeballs and your neck hurt.

Autumn was here, September had come and gone, the windy days had died down. I didn't feel like marching into the gloom of winter one night shift at a time, so I traded schedules with Jared Walsh, who was equally happy to get a break from the nitpicky administrative runs that daytime guys usually got peppered with. Swinging by his room in the early evening to arrange the swap, he greeted me with his standard "Hey there, feller," and I was delighted to share a drink with him after he thought it would be amusing to show me his hidden cache of alcohol. Good fortune found both of us on a day off, and there was seldom good-enough reason to deny an impromptu happy hour.

I knew that most of the guys in the company had a bottle of one thing or another tucked in here or there, but Jared had gone all "Escape from Alcatraz" with his own extensive stash, hidden cleverly behind a faux wall. Asking if I would care for a snort of something, I said, "Sure," looking around the room for likely hiding places. I had looked right at it without a clue, though; in between the studs separating his room from the adjacent room were the usual things; books, pictures, a stick of deodorant, and whatnot. But somehow, without any interruption of the lines, he was able to swing open a 2-foot-wide-by-7-foot-high rectangular section of the wall to reveal a secret vault, which he had engineered into the structure of the whole building! *Ah, brilliant.* The James Bond feature was loaded with contraband items, most notably an AK-47 and a loaded RPG! "Holy shit, dude!" I said in the same giggly voice I might have used observing a safe full of gold bars. It brought a smile to my face and caused immediate chuckles. It was clever enough to pass any inspection, even if the most ambitious lieutenant had come by with a magnifying glass. He must have built the faux wall almost immediately after being assigned to the space, before he cluttered the walls with the usual personal effects, flight suits, or gun belts.

Jared was one of those guys who kept his own counsel on most things and had found his own ways to cope with the boredom of deployment. He had also become notorious for diverting whole formations to the few stops in the country that sold local Indian naan. Sometimes the other pilots would get annoyed if he was the air mission commander, but other times everyone would be just as happy to add twenty minutes on to a flight to get a taste of the delicious, locally made, fresh, hot naan. Of course, this would have meant several hundred dollars of JP8 fuel for the taxpayers if things were accounted for that way. They really weren't, since during the hundreds-of-millions-of-dollars-per-day deployment there was a preallotted flying-hour budget whether we used it or not. One might also argue we were flying unnecessarily farther through harm's way to get the naan, but if the mission had taken us there officially, we wouldn't have blinked an eye about the threat, and everyone knew it.

After marveling at a notable collection of war trophies, which must have taken masterful guile to acquire, Jared offered me a shot of scotch to celebrate our shared appreciation of casual contempt. It was almost the warrant officer way, depending on who you asked, but in the operational sense there was never anything behind it. Every warrant officer I knew was always striving to do an excellent job, with most of them achieving it. Any projected attitude of being a rebel could almost universally be chalked up to low-level sarcasm. And the scotch? That was something different too, since many of us had settled for run-of-the-mill bourbon, some even stooping low enough to drink Old No. 7. The scotch had an air of being highbrow, even though in conversation, Jared didn't. His international street smarts were more sophisticated than mine, though, since he seemed to be interacting with his foreign surroundings much more intuitively.

I wasn't nervous to be in the room with it, but being that close to an RPG put me on guard. It was almost like someone had given me a chance to meet a member of the Taliban. The meeting could have been interesting, but I would have sensed evil. The pale green of the warhead and the wooden accents on a nicely finished mechanical item could have been good texture and tone choices for an interior decorator. Even the labeling font of the nomenclature seemed well chosen. But somehow, I got a vibe from the weapon that made my skin crawl. How he got it or why he'd want it, I don't know; it may have been simple fascination. I certainly understood that from buying the Lebel. As far as war trophies were concerned, or even if it would eventually just be a conversation piece in his den, the risk of customs finding it would have made it nerve wracking to sneak home, let alone an entire lifetime of trying to make sure it wasn't accidentally triggered somehow.

We agreed to swap shifts and parted company after savoring inappropriately tall shots of scotch, always delightfully exclusive and, for Jared, always the fifteen-year Glenlivet.

I strolled back to the CP to change our names on the flight schedule and informed the platoon leaders, then began the typical two-day reset. The first real challenge would be managing my circadian rhythm, which I had already fucked up for the night. I may as well live it up and make the rounds to anyone having parties or social hour, then by about 2:00 a.m., instead of digging down deep for vigilance to stay awake through the wee hours of the morning, I would succumb to sleep, avoiding caffeine in the meantime. Further, if I was able to wake up at 5:00 or 6:00 a.m. after what would have been only a nap, and stay up until 8:00 p.m., I would make it through the tough part of reversing out.

A day off on deployment could be painfully boring, and tonight was no exception. I would resign myself to hours of movie watching in my stateroom, punctuated by going to the gym. After dinner, I wandered back into the CP to find a giggly group of pilots trying to watch *Blackhawk Down* in the back room, and decided to sit in with them for a few minutes. Blackhawk pilots watching *Blackhawk Down* was similar to submariners watching *The Hunt for Red October*, or *Crimson Tide*. The current Hollywood could be especially generic with technical details. Real operator's skills are always founded first on the technical details of a thing, and those technical details never leave your mind. While the movies were certainly entertaining, it can be hard for an operator to look past the egregious technical faults and just enjoy it for the plot. Instead, the movie becomes a cheap facsimile, which gets heckled for every technical detail. Even *Blackhawk Down*, being factually based on a recent historical tragedy, was almost a comedy to this tough crowd.

I wasn't exempt from the atmosphere of cynical analysis, though it crossed my mind that I had been only one degree of separation from the guys portrayed in the movie: Two summers prior, we had flown missions for six months in the Bahamas supporting "OPBAT," the decades-long Operation Bahamas, Turks, and Caicos, an aerial-assist mission with the DEA to find suspicious activity in that part of the world. I had deployed and flown often with Capt. Rob Wolcott, who was Cliff Wolcott's son, Cliff being one of the pilots of Super 61 who died in

Mogadishu. Rob was twelve when he lost his father, but in his twenties by the time the movie came out. He knew many of the pilots and crew chiefs personally, having spent time together at the typical backyard barbecues any unit tends to enjoy, but found *Blackhawk Down* to contain greater parts of technical and historical negligence than anything emotionally provoking, even for him. It was the only real Blackhawk movie, though, *Firebirds* being mostly a horrible movie about Apaches, and *Team America* featuring only one Blackhawk. So, we watched it, with occasional points of nostalgia punctuating what mostly was a giggle fest.

After the movie, my friend Seth Hobbs and I decided to use residual tactical exhilaration to ruck-march around the perimeter of the airfield in full body armor and kit, a hike we estimated at 3 miles. Of course, this was a juvenile suggestion, from which neither of us had the maturity to back down. By the Air Assault standard, we should each be able to complete a 12-mile ruck march with 35 pounds on our back in three hours. On the basis of the math, 3 miles should take only forty-five minutes, and it seemed like a fun adventure in the night. We both got our rucksacks and met near the pavilion, after which a short discussion ensued about how to achieve the 35-pound standard. While we were standing there in the middle of several converging roads, the first and most apparent solution presented itself to be sandbags. *Perfect*, we both thought, picking up a sandbag to estimate the weight. The first sandbag we picked up disintegrated immediately, but we strolled around to find some that had been installed more recently than the Third Anglo-Afghan war. Neither of us knew the weight when we did pick one up, but, estimating 20 pounds, we decided on two sandbags apiece. We suited up and hoofed out directly for Disney Drive.

This ill-conceived stunt of physical prowess was immediately awkward and painful, and neither Seth nor I wanted to admit it was a struggle just to walk. This was probably just a warm-up period, I thought. The elevation of Bagram, being only 400 feet less than Denver, was a factor certainly contributing to respiratory struggle. Either that or we were just pilots not conditioned for ruck marching. It opened our eyes to the daily struggle a dismounted troop had to put up with on a foot patrol. It sucked, and we weren't even carrying our rifles. Pilots had the luxury of having to carry only an M9 pistol, which at that moment I was thankful for: only 2 pounds vs. the 8 pounds of an M4 rifle. Even 8 pounds doesn't sound like a lot but, if carried at the ready, would feel like lead within an hour. We marched on, pretending it was effortless, until it was obvious that both of us were hyperventilating and covered in sweat.

"Damn," Seth said, after twenty minutes.

"Yeah," I replied, for the first time conceding to our pathetic state, any facade of being gung-ho receding swiftly. Still, we marched on, soon realizing we were under the approach end of the runway, a quarter of the way around. On the east side of the base, the perimeter road took several turns toward the countryside, which we elected to follow, determined to walk the true perimeter.

Thirty minutes later, making blisteringly slow progress, we estimated our position at halfway around. I said, "Dude, this really sucks. I wish we could ditch these rucksacks and walk back without the pain and suffering." Capt. Hobbs agreed, but a rucksack is a hand-receipted item. If we abandoned them, we would no doubt owe the government hundreds of dollars apiece, and thus we felt condemned to finish our trek. I'm not sure if it was the hypoxia or the exhaustion that kept us from simply removing the sandbags and walking back with empty rucksacks, but neither of us thought of it.

On the dark side of the base, away from all activity, the perimeter road reached far enough into the country to give one a sense of what it would be like to evade on foot. Even though we were protected by rows of fencing and concertina wire, the desert was dark and cold, and each mysterious house that came looming into view across the wire felt at least a tiny bit suspicious. Only then did I realize that we were within just a few yards of recent suspected mortar-launching points on the threat map, and I noticed my hand had subconsciously checked for the presence of my M9, which would have been virtually useless in almost every circumstance. It was obvious I was no foot soldier, and I never hoped to be. I can sure appreciate the real troops, though.

After an hour and forty-five minutes, we passed the opposite end of the main runway, back under the main stadium lighting, and finally realized we could just pull the sandbags out of our backpacks. Laughing at our own stubborn lunacy, we somehow concluded we were within a quarter lap of finishing and should stick it out, so we marched on under the oppressive weight, drenched in sweat. Finally walking past the pax terminal, Seth said, "Come on, man. Let's weigh this shit."

"OK," I said, relieved to finally sling it down from my twisted, aching back.

Seth's rucksack landed on the scale at 83 pounds, to mutual giggling, "Holy shit, dude!" My rucksack also came in at a brutal 78 pounds, from which we finally realized the source of our struggles: sandbags are about 40 pounds each. We took one step outside the pax terminal and ditched the sandbags, finishing the final few hundred yards feeling light as a feather and comically idiotic, promising never to tell anyone how we spent our free time.

I walked home and shook the sand out of my rucksack before going inside, then stashed it under my bed, took a shower, poured a small glass of painkiller, and was able to doze off easily by three in the morning.

I had no sense whatsoever that the bloodiest battle of the year was about to begin, less than an hour away from my cozy plywood den.

CHAPTER 32
HIGH GROUND

October 3, 2009. Day 292. Problem was, the place was down in a ravine. Tactically, it couldn't have been any worse, and everyone knew it. Everyone knew it for *years*. Combat Outpost (COP) Keating was also the junction of two river valleys, so as a provincial reconstruction team (PRT) location, it was considered an important hub for local commerce. The possibility that it was also a funneling point for illegal smuggling traffic and other unwanted transients going to and from Pakistan prevented the coalition from abandoning the outpost years earlier. Effective counterinsurgency could happen only with a fully embedded force.

As far as the think tank was concerned, in the big scheme of variables contributing to the COIN mission, COP Keating was in a perfect spot. Knowing the COP was tactically vulnerable, observation post (OP) Fritsche was constructed several hundred feet above the PRT, giving COP commanders the sense that they had comms with the high ground and at least a partial overwatch advantage. In theory, that meant they would know when there was trouble coming, and be able to brace for it or even reach out with squad-sized elements before the outpost got pinned down.

It was ambitious on our part, and another case of an outsider being in Afghanistan and not fully considering the terrain. There is a powerful force in junior leaders to get the job done, no matter what the job is, with good ol' can-do spirit and determination. There can be an expectancy to get the job done from the top down, which causes hesitation on the part of ground commanders to say they *can't* get something done. Nobody wants to be the one to stand up and suggest that something is a bridge too far. Again, anyone's tour is only a year long. So, they have to get there, figure out what's going on, and try their hardest in good faith for several months before realizing they're up against a huge disadvantage. A period of sustainment prevails until they realize they're within a few months of going home, with no time to make a huge course change. So, it's not a total mystery that commander after commander served at COP Keating without pulling up stakes.

The problem that got overlooked yet again, by yet another superpower, was that the people living in the steep mountains of Afghanistan had been repelling foreigners for centuries, with total efficiency. It's arrogant thinking that some ground force commander is going to come huffing into their new temporary assignment up in the crags and convince an old tribe and their elders to become Americanized in the eight-month period they might have once they get their mind wrapped around the situation. It would take more time than we had to win the trust of the locals, and even more time to change their mindset or culture and convince them we could fix their Taliban problem. We tried anyway, and we surged all the troops we could to get the greatest saturation within the local populace, in an ambitious plan we would eventually abort. Not that I knew it at the time; I didn't. In real time, the most typical reaction to any suggestion is to ponder only briefly the big picture, then shift quickly into figuring out how to do it. But counterinsurgency?

A diplomatic task teetering so precariously on the cultural essence of a place is something even the most seasoned secretary of state would hesitate to engage in. In the current plan, we were sending active-duty soldiers in, with an interpreter, to convince the elders of a village we could fix their problems. Consider further how other nationalities think of us . . . now imagine "the Ugly American" in full body armor, proposing a diplomatic solution to tribal people with rifle in hand, and you have counterinsurgency. Could it work? Madeleine Albright might be rolling over in her grave.

During three years of mounting resistance before COP Keating got overrun, there had been enough ambushes and firefights and enough American soldiers killed for every FOB, COP, and OP in the valley to be named after a fallen soldier. It was like every street on Edwards Air Force Base being named after a fallen test pilot, or every street on Submarine Base New London being named after a late submariner. COP Keating itself had started as PRT Kamdesh, named after the local area, until Capt. Ben Keating was killed in the line of duty several stages of deterioration earlier.

Keating had been given an order to send an LMTV back down to FOB Naray along a risky and poorly maintained mountain road beside the Landay-Sin River, after the truck had barely made it to the COP in the first place. The large truck on the narrow road not only made for an easy target in a high-threat area but also threatened the immediate loss of the truck because of the road being too poor for such a massive vehicle. Being the kind of guy who wouldn't order a troop to do something he wouldn't do himself, Keating opted to drive the truck, with a squad patrolling ahead on foot. This proved to be a selfless but fateful decision after the road crumpled at a narrow spot and sent Keating and the large truck violently down into a rock crevasse.

After many convoys and smaller vehicles encountered one type of problem or another along the road, mostly ambushes and firefights, helicopter became the primary mode of transportation in and out of COP Keating for normal commerce. Counterinsurgency and patrols protecting the encampment continued to happen on foot.

Fighting the tide of poor reception, units assigned to COP Keating continued their efforts amid frequent attacks. As the endless skirmishes and potshots added up over the months and years, the defensive tactics and rapid-response posture of the tiny base down in the gorge may have been revealed a few times too often. In a battle described in remarkable detail in Jake Tapper's book *The Outpost*, a force of several hundred insurgents attacked simultaneously in the early hours of the morning on October 3, with little warning, and in a manner organized enough (or perhaps with enough expendable fighters) to get the upper hand on the American army for most of the day. This strategic attack included taking out OP Fritsche, which left COP Keating with no high-ground advantage. The battle between a few dozen coalition fighters and an estimated three hundred insurgents, including continuous small-arms fire, mortar rounds, and a staggering number of RPGs, would ultimately lead to the closure of the COP, since it finally became indisputable that the camp's physical position was indefensible against an organized attack. The fight lasted well into the evening, until a combination of will-power and airpower finally turned the tide in the coalition's favor, and any remaining insurgents retreated.

During the surprise attack, members of Task Force Destroyer, 3rd Squadron, 61st Cavalry Regiment, dug down with raw determination to kill hundreds of members of the Taliban, some of whom had been locals and some of whom had crossed in from Pakistan for the event. They fought through dire-enough conditions for one sergeant and one specialist to be awarded the Medal of Honor, but ultimately COIN had failed in the region. It had failed at the immediate cost of eight more American lives.

Two days after the battle was over, the heavily damaged post was shut down. It had been scheduled to be closed for months due to its undeniable weaknesses, but the assets had never become aligned for it to happen. Shutting down such an outpost creates a vulnerability during the process, when some amount of personnel and equipment have been removed and a reduced battle force remains waiting for the next lift; defensive positions are dismantled, sectors of fire are no longer monitored, and troops might even be inside packing their bags.

Optimally, a greater military presence would need to be brought in as the camp dismantled itself, to fend off any potshots and make up for a diminished defensive posture. This organized plan for dismantling COP Keating had been planned for several months prior, but only a hasty version of the plan ended up happening after the attack.

One theory suggesting why it hadn't happened on a more proactive schedule was that the search for Bowe Bergdahl had used every available asset for several days. Even if this had not coincided with the exact dates of the proposed COP Keating shutdown, it may have pushed normal commerce and resupply so extensively behind schedule that shutting down the COP took a back burner until it was too late.

The news of COP Keating reached me in the form of gossip: someone told me in passing as I lingered in our housing area on my day off. There was no bulletin for such things, only word of mouth. If you happen to work in the TOC, the report could come officially through the classified communication system linking tactical-operation centers. A lot of times we would catch wind of this kind of thing, and it felt like it was happening somewhere on the other side of the world. It really wasn't; the Landay-Sin River was only a few minutes' helicopter flight north of the Pech River, which we frequently serviced. Although COP Keating was serviced by a different unit, it was the same geographical area and in the same formidable terrain. It also reminded me that while vital to the success of the overall mission, helicopter pilots lived a life of luxury compared to the true combatant forces of our military. Their lives, and the conditions of threat in which they functioned, stood in stark contrast to my own plush existence. While part of me wished I could have been there, I wasn't. Without trying to armchair-quarterback the heroic response to the attack, it was still perplexing that the Taliban could get the upper hand on a US encampment. It had nothing to do with our response once it began, and everything to do with the preexisting variables prior to the engagement: At COP Keating, the enemy had the tactical advantage. They measured our response to various types of attack until they had a custom-tailored strategy, and they held the high ground.

In an interesting transition from counterinsurgency, having the COP attacked awoke the larger machine; normally dormant, or at least waiting in idle, a true US military occupation includes fighter jets, bombers, field artillery, UAV missile strikes, special forces, rangers, snipers, sappers, and every other type of combatant the greatest military on the planet possesses. In counterinsurgency, those devices are supposed to remain slumbering, but it doesn't mean we didn't bring them. As tiny battles or skirmishes pop up, the assigned unit would respond with as minimal a response as possible, without escalating, so as not to upset the precarious balance of diplomatic progress. Past a certain threshold, however, any US Army soldier's first loyalty is to his family, then to his country; if the Taliban punches us in the face hard enough, instinct will overcome obedience. We'll punch back harder than we got punched; we revved up the larger machine, and as soon as A-10s and B-1 bombers arrived, the fight ended. In flat analysis, we killed far more of them and maintained the terrain, so we won the battle. We prevailed after absorbing a surprise attack. Simultaneously, within the framework of counterinsurgency, we had lost. We decided to pull out of COP Keating, effectively yielding to the Taliban in that region.

Between the Pech River valley being the helicopter-shoot-down capital of the world and the continual troubles of COP Keating and other outposts in the same volatile region, all of Nuristan Province showed durable inhospitality toward the coalition and Operation Enduring Freedom. Time would slowly but surely see us responding with a subtle form of retreat; the troops would be centralized at the larger, more-defensible bases until the end of the campaign, the hands-on component of COIN would taper off in the region as ground troops receded, and we would eventually go home with a new campaign pennant on our guidon marking our occupation of the region, two more combat tour stripes sewn onto our sleeves, another unit citation, and another Air Medal.

CHAPTER 33
ROCK LABYRINTH

Day 312. There didn't seem to be any protracted concern over the recent situation at COP Keating. It hadn't marked progress or setback to any notable degree at Bagram at least, nor was there the typical knee-jerk reaction where the modus operandi became hastily constricted. It came and went like a third-page blurb in the paper; most people wouldn't even have known unless they went to the daily intel briefing, which did not state so clearly, "US ARMY GETS ASS KICKED BY TALIBAN, CLOSES OUTPOST." It was a definite setback, metrics of the entire theater must have noted, but whether it caused any doctrinal shift or altered the big schedule in the sky stayed out of focus at my level.

After reversing out, I settled into the daytime QRF shift and enjoyed a few days without so much as a trip around the pattern. As the heat and brutally abrasive wind died down, even the terrorists calmed for autumn. You could never bank on that, but there were definitely long periods of time when nothing happened at all.

The more nothing happened, the more we got into trouble of our own. Several of the crew chiefs developed extreme and painful cases of kidney stones from drinking too many Rip-its. A pilot with appendicitis was prescribed a course of Gas-X by the battalion PA and told to sleep it off. When his case became acute, another doc was able to correctly diagnose and send him to emergency surgery. He recovered after two weeks of local bed rest in his plywood room and returned to duty. A soldier was run over by a Humvee on the airbase when the driver wasn't paying attention. Several senior enlisted cooks got into a knife fight in the DFAC, causing a temporary shutdown and investigation. The pilots had a mustache competition that offended the first sergeant, and when it was over, they trimmed all their facial hair and left it in an oil sample bottle on his desk with a ribbon. Two pilots got into a fistfight over what music was playing in the planning area. Four pilots, including the company commander, flew up to the top of the ridgeline overlooking Bagram and got out of their helicopter, stripped off all their clothes except for their flight helmets, and took a picture. On another occasion, a crew chief acquired some golf clubs and golf balls somehow, and several people went back up to the ridgeline and began hitting golf balls off the cliff. A captain in the brigade who had deployed at the same time as his warrant-officer wife found out she had been very publicly having an affair with an Apache pilot, causing their immediate divorce. All manner of anomalous activity took place when there was no actual mission. Then again, maybe it took place all the time but was noticed only when there was no actual mission. Our deployed life easily paralleled the comic side of *M*A*S*H*.

I finally had a flight request to go down to JBAD and back, which I was happy to accept, only to have a near midair collision with a UAV in the traffic pattern. Looking out the side window, I saw the large, robotic-looking craft within five seconds of slamming into the side of our helicopter and yanked up on the collective for the UAV to skim under our landing gear by 20 feet.

In my best "calm voice" with the tower, I described my concern with traffic flow in the pattern and got a contrite "Sorry about that, chief" in return. Joint control over such vehicles has them at times being controlled by someone from an extremely remote location, with only a limited onboard camera to help guide them back onto a runway. Yet another party communicates with the tower and decides on what direction to fly on the basis of the GPS icon, and yet another party somehow retrieves and manages the contraption once it is on the ground. It was by then a fantastic capability that had the potential to deploy to locations a manned craft could not, and for a fraction of the price, while saving lives in the process; a UAV crash never kills the crew. The early days of integration in the sky with a bunch of unsuspecting, traditionally piloted aircraft, however, presented a steep learning curve. The drones always did have their own assigned altitude stratum, but there was potential conflict on the way up or down.

After another week went by, a mission none of us would ever hope for developed, and the daytime quick-reaction force got utilized for its doctrinal purpose: Red-Handed 56, a Task Force Odin antiterrorism aircraft operated by civilian contractors, had disappeared from the radar twenty minutes east of Bagram.[1] There were three people aboard, and the best information suggested they crashed up in the high mountains north of Kalagush. We would launch immediately for *no-shit* search and rescue, regardless of possible scenarios. Furthermore, the emergency was a degree more personal because Task Force Odin was Joe Puskar's unit, and Joe showed up to join us.

Most of the milk runs we flew all year had been at relatively low altitude. The elevation at Bagram was around 5,000 feet, Shank 6,000, Kiwi base 8,000, and occasionally we would pop above 10,000 feet MSL to get through a pass. All of that flying had usually been at less than 1,000 feet above ground level. Helicopters usually fly down low, and it's safe to say there are pilots who can't bring themselves to get too far from the ground even when their machines are capable of it. In the case of the M-model Blackhawk, the performance charts suggested altitudes up to 20,000 feet MSL, although performance becomes marginal. The factory test pilots had taken it higher than that, but the usable envelope was too small to even bother printing in the operator's manual. Jumping from Bagram over to Kalagush, a small base halfway to JBAD, we turned north and headed for the last known point on Red-Handed 56's flight path.

Kalagush itself was wedged up in a long draw, cemented onto a crag of sorts, and was home to a small Army artillery team. From that centralized spot, in theory they could lob 105- or 155-millimeter explosive rounds halfway across Nuristan Province if they were called for fire support. We continued north from there and within five minutes faced the steepest peaks of the Hindu Kush Mountains and began wandering around in earnest.

The terrain we were flying over was the most jagged, steepest terrain I had ever seen in my life. It ranged from 7,000 feet up to over 20,000 feet above sea level, with most of that elevation change taking place within a three-minute flight. Not just fifteen or twenty pronounced peaks, the Hindu Kush Mountain range was more of a texture than a ridgeline, covering thousands of square miles. The many random peaks were nameless, bunched tightly together, and looked impossibly steep even to walk on.

As we wandered around the labyrinth of rock spires and began searching for any sign of wreckage, it became apparent that this was going to be a challenging exercise of crew coordination. While being tempted to stare down into the rocks, the pilot on the controls had to maintain good discipline on basic flying; as our search had us climbing higher and higher, the maneuverability and power available dwindled proportionately with thinner air. Also, there were passes and peaks that lured us into areas with only one entry and exit point for our available power. If we flew through what looked like a tempting pass, in some cases we would soon discover that a tight and dangerous circle back to the same pass was the only chance of escape. With a flight of two aircraft, that could be fateful, because not only was any rapid, steep maneuvering hard to follow in between rock formations, it also tempted physics; any bank angle would point available lift in the wrong direction. Rolling the aircraft facilitated the turn, but it also took away that part of the thrust vector keeping the machine in the sky. Flying at times within only 100 feet of the rock, there was little room for vertical negligence.

Our sister ship discussed splitting up to broaden the search, which we did to a limited extent. Everyone acknowledged the danger of losing track of one another and then finding each other unexpectedly; we decided to separate the flight but proceed in the same direction and within visual separation of one another. The very nature of searching suggests slow, wandering flight, so in that sense assigning another pair of eyes to maintain contact with the other ship in the formation cost us that set of eyes searching the ground. That seemed OK at first because the terrain seemed hopeless. Not only was there a slim chance of finding the aircraft, but there was also a slim chance of an aircraft landing successfully in this terrain.

We wandered. We wandered to the extent of the fuel available, went to refuel, then came back and wandered some more. Suddenly there was a startling scene on a cliff face in front of us: a large, smoking, black smudge. Radioing the other aircraft that we would be circling and to give us a wide berth, we went back, and reported our initial observation to the TOC via SATCOM. Our excitement would soon dwindle; there was only smoke and charred rock. No wreckage, no fragments, and no obvious point of impact. Apparently, there had been an unrelated fire, which left only distracting evidence. We eventually cued the other aircraft to check out the same spot as we receded from it, and they arrived at the same conclusion. The location was marked on the search map in the TOC as a reference point, for successive flights to note. As we flew on, we found more and more distracting burn marks and later discovered they were either the result of illegal charcoal production for the market in Pakistan, or locations where evidence of illegal logging had been destroyed. There is a lucrative timber market in Afghanistan for pine, cedar, fir, yew, and birch.

After nine hours of searching, we realized our shift was ending and we would have to spend the last half hour flying back to Bagram to turn the helicopters over to the night shift. On the basis of the overall risk level of the flight, and the speculative nature of wandering around huge rocks in the dark, Lift 6 made the wise choice to discontinue the search until daybreak. Differentiating between aircraft wreckage and anything else in such terrain through the green wash of night vision goggles would be extremely unlikely. For the pilot, managing the aircraft at slow speeds in such terrain with reduced visual cues would also increase the risk level to such an extent that the most likely outcome of a nighttime search would be the addition of more aluminum to the rocks.

We flew back to Bagram feeling disappointed we weren't able to find the crash site or the wreckage, or the survivors, or whatever it might have been. There was a strong sense we were doing something important, occasions of which during the year had been few and far between. We shut down and were immediately approached by the night crew, who not only had their flight gear with them for staging but also wanted a complete debrief on what we had seen and what it had been like up in the mountains. We gave them the scoop with all the highlights and emotions and feelings about the matter, only to walk into the TOC to fill out the required mission-debriefing form with the same sad thing we write for most missions: "NSTR"—*Nothing significant to report.*

CHAPTER 34
SPONGY AIR

Day 313. The next morning, I woke up at 3:00, intensely alert, and looked back down into the rocks, somehow feeling like I could review yesterday's images from memory and still come up with something new. After a few seconds I realized I wouldn't find anything, nor was I going to fall back asleep. I sat up in bed for a few quiet moments in the dark, to what seemed like absolute silence, but after a few seconds sounds became apparent; a muffled turbine whine, a distant vehicle accelerating and then shifting, even gravel crunching under someone's nearby feet. I felt like I had heightened senses and was wasting time. I just wanted to launch again, but I'd have to wait three more hours. I doused this anxiety by turning on the light in my room and began the coffee-making ritual.

By 0320, I made peace with the fact that I had to burn time. I needed a mindless movie to pass the time and put the only movie I had into the computer and let it play. I settled back onto my pillow, staring at a screen I wasn't able to see. *What happened to that plane?* There hadn't been any significant weather on the day they disappeared; had it been a rare mechanical failure? Most of the time when anything crashes, it's pilot error, but could something else have happened to the plane en route? In the area where their signal had dropped off, they could neither have been climbing from an airport nor descending to one, so they would most likely have been straight and level, either en route to another airport or merely patrolling in the normal course of their duties, which would indicate it was not a critical phase of flight. They weren't in the middle of a complicated maneuver for the pilot to even make a mistake, and they weren't low enough to have carelessly flown into something. That means either they encountered severe icing or something went wrong with the plane. Icing hadn't been on the weather report that day, nor did their circumstance include any negotiating with ATC for higher or lower altitudes. Had they run out of fuel? That's not very common in a two-pilot aircraft. In fact, their communication record hadn't included *anything* with ATC, so it must have been a mechanical failure of some sort. Was it the same tragic scenario that resulted in the loss of Payne Stewart? *What happened?*

Task Force Odin was a relatively new entity in the wars; they had been created in 2007 as a response to the roads in Iraq being littered with IEDs. The team employs both manned and unmanned aircraft with an array of special sensors to detect the placement of improvised explosive devices, either through the activity of placing them or the signals emitted by their triggering devices. Further, those aircraft had been equipped with a laser-designating capability, allowing them to effectively identify targets for handoff and destruction by other platforms. They had racked up an impressive record in Iraq, keeping the roads safer for dismounted US troops, and recently had migrated into Afghanistan for the same mission. Red-Handed 56 was being piloted by a civilian subcomponent of Task Force Odin on a routine mission when their aircraft mysteriously dropped out of the sky.

A scene in *First Blood* of a helicopter hovering over a rocky landscape snapped me out of whatever trance I was in, and I checked the clock. It was only 4:00 a.m. then, two hours until takeoff. I turned off the movie and got up for a shower. I could get breakfast early and go in for map recon, figure out where we had been the day before and where Red-Handed 56 supposedly had been, and come up with a new searching plan.

The CP was oddly abandoned when I got there, and a quick check of flight plans indicated the nighttime QRF assets had launched down to Ghazni for a tail-to-tail medevac transfer and would be getting back to Bagram right at shift change. I sat down at one of the planning computers and pulled up the satellite imagery layer of Falconview, the software we used for mission planning. It was pretty easy to draw a line north from Kalagush and see where we had been, and to further plot the last known, best-guess location of the target. It was going to be one of those needle-in-a-haystack kind of searches. It looked like we had effectively searched about an eighth of the potential area where the aircraft could have ended up, depending on their altitude and speed. I created a crude hash graphic on the image and saved the file on the desktop for briefing later in the morning. We could be more organized with where we had been and cover different areas.

Finally, 0530 rolled around, and the other pilots and crew chiefs were filtering in for the morning. The night QRF aircraft had landed, and the cold-refuel trucks were topping them off. I went to the Lighthouse for a fresh thermos of coffee on my way to the TOC for the morning briefing and was greeted by Tony Harbiter, my copilot for the day. Tony was a senior instructor who for some reason had fallen out of favor with the battalion SP and only recently had worked his way back to being a pilot in command in the unit. For administrative purposes I was the pilot in command that day, but I could tell that the company SP and platoon leaders were stacking cockpits with senior pilots flying together on this critical mission. This wasn't unusual; crew selection was a common thing when missions were critical or dangerous, although it could be unfortunate for the junior pilots. These missions could be the most educational, and the newer pilots could even be the most interested and attentive, but they were often excluded either for safety reasons (in that the combined hour level of a "crew mix" wasn't high enough to satisfy the risk-assessment algorithm) or for simply being bumped by more-senior operators who wanted the action for themselves. The latter case was a morale-crushing shame, because the younger generation of pilots didn't develop as rapidly. In the former case, however, there could be cause for concern if one of the new guys didn't have enough hours to be safe and got paired up with a junior pilot in command. Sometimes crew mix could be essential, most notably if there was a low-illume goggle flight into either a technical area or a high-threat area where the success of the mission was imperative. In these cases, the crew is hand-selected for success, and the junior guys have to sit out, being allowed to build time only on more routine flights.

This practice is common, but maybe a sign of the times; new pilots in World War II were almost entirely younger than new pilots today, and many of them had phenomenal success with significantly less training than modern pilots. There's something about throwing a pilot in over his head that makes him grow up quicker. For some reason, either bureaucracy or the extra level of judging that goes along with flying a two-pilot aircraft, young pilots are not trusted to be the pilot in command for *years* now. It's a conundrum that breeds prudence and caution instead of intrepidity, the long-term result being that pilots never have to push themselves into situations requiring balance or risk. Then, if by chance they get into a tricky situation, they can find themselves lacking the guts to resolve something ambiguous without asking for permission or someone else's interpretation. This retardation of pilot growth and responsibility, along with inadequate training and experience operating "high, hot, and heavy," contributed to well over two hundred helicopter crashes within the Iraq and Afghanistan theaters alone, the gross majority of which were caused by pilot error.

Tony and I sat in on the daily briefing given by the TOC and received a report similar to what I had come up with a few hours earlier, with the only updated information being that the weather would be good again, there was still no threat in the area, and, furthermore, the Air Force would also be deploying a few Pavehawks[1] in the same province to add to the search. Various ISR platforms in different strata were searching as well, but I would tune out when the briefing covered where the drones would be, at an altitude I couldn't reach and without a radio frequency to call.

We were ready to go, and, knowing we might spend the next twelve hours in the cockpit, I turned to crew chief Kent Wallace to make sure we had food and water for the crew for the long haul. "Wa-*Lacheeee*," as we called him, had already packed enough food and water for both ships to evade on foot successfully for what looked like several weeks, and returned the monotone report of "Got'cha covered, chief." Sometimes you get to work with people who just let you smile.

I was eager. We had real purpose again today, we were alert and ready, and this was going to be some of the best flying of the year: daytime, good weather, requiring skill, and having immediate, tangible meaning. Much of what we did seemed pointless or only self-serving, and a lot of that was further dulled by the extra weight and fatigue of having goggles and battery packs clamped onto our noggins. It was going to be a clear, coffee-drinking, comfortable, and intense day. I was poised, and I was *on*.

Tony and I figured out that the call sign for the Air Force entity was "Pedro," and began trying to raise them, hoping to get some deconfliction in place before we got in there and found each other wandering around in close quarters. We reached them later in the morning and found they would be happy with an east–west boundary separation plan, which was accepted immediately as a pilot-to-pilot agreement. This was fairly common in real time; it wasn't unusual for functional details to be overlooked when two different agencies had to work together but did not attend the same briefing. It was also pretty easy to negotiate in the moment, as long as one agency didn't get territorial with the other or imply any sort of hierarchy. There may actually have been one, depending on who was assigned to a higher command, but we were lucky neither of us knew or cared about it.

As we proceeded into different geographical areas, the elevation continued up, up, up. Tony and I talked about the power margin, which was first and foremost our main concern for the day. Growing up closer to sea level instills a very dependent comfort level in many Blackhawk pilots. Sometimes, the 4,000 horsepower of twin turbine engines seemed like it could never be completely used up. Above 10,000 feet, however, the engine response time lags more, and the rotor rpm doesn't catch up to any demand as quickly. We decided to do an experiment, in an attempt to validate the power suggested in the small checklist we carried with us. According to the chart (I referenced as Tony flew), at the current temperature and weight we were flying, we should still have the power to hover out of ground effect at 10,000 feet. Concurring that this sounded reasonable, Tony agreed that if we could find an area at least 500 feet above the rocks, and with an escape route (meaning if we started to lose rotor rpm, we could dive down until we regained rpm), that we would try it. We found just such a spot, informed our sister ship over internal what we were doing, and began the deceleration.

For aerodynamic reasons, a helicopter uses the least amount of power when it is in straight and level flight at around 60 knots. A hovering helicopter creates so much disturbed air with vortexes and pneumatic curlicues around the disk that it uses more power to stay still than it does to go faster, up to a point; above 60, other elements of drag begin accumulating and eventually match thrust. Furthermore, if a helicopter is hovering close to the ground, it will use less power than if it is way up in the sky, because close to the ground the downwash has something to push against. Helicopters have three generic modes of flight: hovering in ground effect (IGE), hovering out of ground effect (OGE), and cruise flight. The mode requiring the most power of all is hovering *out* of ground effect. We would be out of ground effect anywhere above about 50 feet.

Tony and I continued the deceleration, and as the airspeed bled off and we were no longer able to outrun our own disturbed air, the power required to maintain the same altitude began steadily increasing. Using the GPS signal to determine when our ground speed was minimal, first we saw that we were keeping station with no altitude loss, and second that it was taking 99 percent of the maximum power available for the temperature and pressure. That would suggest that if we went up into air any thinner, we would no longer be able to hover out of ground effect. The chart was validated; we would not be able to hover above 10,000 feet. An additional technical problem is that the airspeed-sensing system on the Blackhawk, a simple tube pointing forward to measure the ram air pressure, is flawed at airspeeds below 40 knots (46 mph) because of the rotor downwash and the hanging angle of the fuselage at low speed. If we get into the disturbed air only at low airspeeds, but the airspeed gauge was flawed below 40, the only comfortable measure of safety was to stay above 40 knots indicated. That made flying slowly around to conduct the search and rescue extra challenging, because the pilot on the controls would also have to carefully monitor airspeed so as not to fall out of the sky. It was like flying in an airplane with a stall speed, since we would no longer have the luxury of simply hovering if we saw something.

We proceeded upward.

The logical geographical sequence of the search area, minus the areas we had already searched, pointed us uphill. By midmorning, we were searching areas well above 16,000 feet, with the number of distracting charred areas increasing. There must be a Sherpa-like group of industrious loggers and charcoal burners seeking out every area where they stood to profit. Each time we came across the charred and smoking slopes was another chance to get excited, look closer, fly slower, and get into trouble. It was mushy-feeling air up there, the control response was sluggish, and with all the fuel available for the powerful General Electric engines, we couldn't suck in enough air to maintain the necessary mixture. The engines couldn't produce maximum power, and the blades couldn't produce maximum lift. But this was search and rescue and generally considered to be one of those missions where someone might have to push the envelope. Additionally none of us were using the supplemental oxygen our regulations required; we didn't know we were going to be up there, but we weren't about to go back for it.

Every charred patch was damn distracting, but eventually we realized we couldn't spend too much time at any one of them. We had miles and miles to cover, and only a few hours left to do so. Every single thing we got to look at was fascinating, spectacular, and intriguing. None of it was aircraft wreckage. After a long, long day, with many breaks for hot refuel, our shift timed out and we had to go home.

NSTR.

CHAPTER 35
OPERATIONAL URGENCY

Day 315. After three days of no result, having spent a significant amount of time wandering the rocks, Tony and I surrendered our ship to a junior crew for the day and then sat outside on the bench to enjoy the morning's activity over cups of fresh black coffee. With a cautious brief to the oncoming crew involving eye contact and acknowledgment, we conveyed the importance of not getting too slow or too distracted, and off they went.

Soon thereafter, Bob Massey came up to us and asked if we could fast-rope some pathfinders onto the ground in the search area. I'm sure, sitting there, Tony and I must have looked like an easy target for a technical mission. Fast-roping was one of those things we could do (under the right circumstances) that often showed up in recruiting commercials and Hollywood movies trying to make the military look cool, involving troops sliding down a rope to get out of the helicopter. It was a great technique for certain applications; rooftop assaults in the urban environment, jungle insertion if you didn't own a jungle penetrator, or places where the ground just wasn't flat enough to get a wheel on. All of us were qualified to do it and practiced it often back at Ft. Campbell. It was really just another example of hovering but required a finer touch to not injure the individuals on the rope, and better situational awareness and crew coordination with the crew chiefs, because the pilots cannot see the rope. But one of the rules of thumb for fast-roping is that it requires OGE hover capability in the helicopter, because having a rope hanging down to the objective implies that the helicopter is staying high to avoid hitting something with the rotor system. Even over a building, most of the rotor system can be hanging out over free space, requiring extra power to create lift while saturated within its own huge loops of air current. It's a little bit like spinning your tires in the mud.

"No," we said, with a surprised expression, indicating not only was there no chance we would go out and try it, but there was no chance the Blackhawk was going to be able to do it. At least not above 10,000 feet, and the current search area was now well above 14,000 feet.

"OK, so you guys don't want it?"

With an expression like I just chewed on a clump of dirt, I said, "Bobby, we *can't* do it. Nobody else can either. It's just not in the numbers up there." I didn't know if the Blackhawk would even hover *in* ground effect, but the fast-roping thing was a nonstarter.

One of the other teams had seen something they wanted to get on the ground to look at. The whole search-and-rescue mission had become the latest excitement and was attracting a notable array of interested volunteers riding in the back of various flights, and as such, a bunch of extra eyeballs saw a bunch of extra things. It was good, but now the next step was a challenge. Like most hastily planned missions, in the true essence of the quick-reaction force, there was no extensive planning or consideration; there was no plan for what step 2 would be if we found the crash site.

Another factor in the subtle psychology of risk management is that we considered ourselves to be operating in the "life, limb, or eyesight" realm. In briefings or training on risk assessment and risk management, there is a clear delineation as to how much risk to manage (how many chances to take) outside the operator's manual, unit SOP, corps regulations, and Big Army regulations we typically operated in compliance with. If you have to save someone's life, you should break the rules if you have to. In other words, don't let someone go blind, wait too long with a tourniquet on, or bleed out altogether and come home defending how you stayed in compliance with the outdated, poorly worded, standard operating procedure. Sure enough, this was a search-and-rescue mission, which flipped on the *anything goes* switch with some of the participants, with no voice saying loudly enough after minute one or day one or day three that the crew of the doomed aircraft had most likely expired, so let's not gallop into thin air quite so intrepidly.

With a crowd of ambitious crash seekers accumulating daily in the mountains, it only stood to reason that more and more search-and-rescue ideas would surface. It's not unreasonable that the fast-roping discussion came up, and it's important to consider every idea in the decision-making process. Any pilot looking at the performance charts would easily come up with the same answer, though: the Blackhawk wasn't going to hover up there, any more than you could will it to the moon. As months of suppressed tactical frustration suddenly found an outlet through this exhilarating mission, the "operational-urgency" vector was marching across the graph with startling determination toward the edge of the envelope.

Someone in the task force voiced another available option: just fly in there with a Chinook. With greater power and lift, landing with the massive eggbeaters would prove more atmospherically plausible than fast-roping from the dainty Blackhawk. On the basis of the QRF force consisting of all Blackhawks, it had been only Blackhawks searching, plus whatever the Air Force had thrown at it. The Chinooks continued supporting the other elements of the war, which simply couldn't grind to a halt, such as daily resupply missions and normal commerce, but the Chinook company commander was ready and willing to support the mission in whatever way the ops officer asked. After a discussion with all parties concerned, it was decided the Blackhawks would continue the search but also start looking for a potential "heavy LZ," or location where a Chinook could land up in the rocks to get boots on the ground.

A fair amount of ambition continued to well up in the dedicated sense that somehow, through determination or tenacity, in flight or on the ground, we were going to find the missing aircraft. Hope of finding anyone alive tapered by the fifth day of searching, but there had been no decrease in the urgency assigned to finding the missing aircraft and crew. Task Force Odin member Joe Puskar had gone out on every flight, every day, searching for the aircraft and crew members he had known personally, from the original group put together at FOB Speicher in Iraq.

On the fifth day of the search, Joe caught just a glimpse of international orange on the ground, maybe, but wasn't up on a headset to tell the pilots. In a moment of hesitation, he let it go, thinking it was probably nothing, just like everything else he had seen for the last five days. He would replay that image in his mind for years after events of the following day unfolded.

CHAPTER 36
OPERATING ENVELOPE

Day 317. On day six of the search, as crew mix evolved to give everyone a chance to be part of the search, the two crews that went up included Bob Massey and Jasper Diego, flying Honcho 048 with crew chiefs Ron Ecker and Kent Wallace in the back, and Arturo Matos and Ronnie Allen, flying Honcho 062 with crew chiefs Trevor Morris and Victoria Burns, a pathfinder by the name of Cleary, flight surgeon Joe Puskar, and a civilian contractor operating a sensitive, airframe-mounted camera system that could aid in the search. Their ship had the most bodies of any aircraft yet in the search area. Additionally, by this stage of the search and rescue, air crews had learned that supplemental oxygen was indeed available from the aviation life support equipment team, and had begun to draw this required equipment prior to every flight into the high-altitude search area.

In a rare appearance on the Blackhawk flight line, Heady D's boss, Apache pilot and brigade commander Col. Ron Lewis, approached the two crews and reminded them to be careful on the unusual mission, as word of the high altitude and narrow power margin had floated up to his desk. While rare in person, Col. Lewis frequently escorted assault missions en route in his own Apache and was a common presence in the sky. To see him on foot on the Blackhawk ramp was unusual, and noteworthy; it's sort of like when you see an ambulance coming with lights and siren—you have to slow down, move over, and look. No one ignores the brigade commander, and if he was there, it meant *something*. Apaches had recently been sent into the search area for security and additional eyes, and it became known that the Blackhawks were flying up to altitudes the older generation of Apaches weren't able to reach. Any pilot would presume caution flying in thin air, but the colonel's message that morning was simple: "Don't become the main effort."

After they shared sideways looks with each other to acknowledge the colonel's special appearance on the ramp, their flight began as any other had, into good weather, out past Kalagush, turning north and slowing, searching for Red-Handed 56 as well as a heavy LZ.

Throughout the day, the search efforts covered some of the previous areas and as such began relatively low, around 9,000 feet. Progressively they wandered along for hours, looking around, climbing throughout the day. They eventually came upon the reference datum, a grid at which someone had seen *something* but didn't know for sure; hence the desire to get someone on the ground for a closer look. Circling out for nearby possible landing zones, suddenly one presented itself.

Perhaps not seen the day before, or maybe having been flown over from the other direction, this spot hadn't presented itself, but someone aboard Art's aircraft spotted a gravel wash. This particular feature may have even been a caldera. It looked big enough for a Chinook, and Ronnie stored the target grid in the fix-store feature of the cockpit software, while Art transmitted to Bobby that they had a spot they were going to check out and began the normal protocol for verifying an LZ.

"OK, let's check it out, but make it quick. We got about ten minutes left before we hit our reserve and need to head down to JBAD for hot gas."

"Roger that," Art replied in his typically all-business tone.

Having decades of experience landing on unimproved landing sites with a helicopter,[1] the Army has a long-established procedure for deciding whether a landing site is suitable. It starts with a "high orbit" or "high recon" to check out the big picture, see where the barriers are (tall trees or buildings), figure out the long axis and escape routes, see what the wind is doing, etc., followed by a "low orbit" or "low recon" to check for obstacles (power lines, antennas, or rock outcroppings), slope, texture, and the finer details of the terrain. Arturo, fully conscious of how closely he was to the edge of the operating envelope, decided to do several of each of these, considering carefully whether a Chinook would be able to land. It looked good.

Art was certainly a qualified assault pilot for selecting the LZ, in the sense that he had attended and participated in many planning and coordination meetings over an extensive array of terrain types and had developed an extensive number of LZ diagrams in his flying career.[2] One of the challenges when one group plans a mission or, in this case, recons a mission, and a different group is going to fly the mission, is communicating the extensive amount of detail that needs to be considered for a safe execution. Today's team decided to take a few pictures of the potential LZ to give to the Chinook pilots. In his experience, and most any assault pilot would concur, having some idea of the *scale* of such a photo would be extremely helpful to someone who hadn't seen it with their own eyes. In typically hard-to-interpret mountain photos, many of which contained misleading angles, it could be difficult to tell how much room there would be in the LZ. Further, if you get close enough to show the finer textures of an LZ, the only visible horizon in a photo may be the steep and misleading angle of a nearby peak. A scale reference would be extremely helpful.

Art decided to make a slow pass over the objective, escape route included, and have the other ship take a picture right as they were flying slowly through the frame. A Blackhawk on the objective would be a perfect size reference for the LZ diagram, as well as a means to measure the required heading for the approach, and almost everyone brought their own personal camera with them on missions. If they had yet to find the actual crash site of Red-Handed 56, at least they could come home and report success on locating a heavy LZ to include providing a user-friendly LZ diagram for the Chinooks. Art circled around now and got lined up for a slow pass at just over 14,600 feet. During the maneuver, to be useful as far as imagery is concerned, they would have to be less than 50 feet above the proposed touchdown point and going slow enough for someone in the other aircraft to be able to snap the shot. Reducing power and pointing the nose down, Art began the approach.

Having initially pointed the nose toward the far end of the objective on a path to overfly the gravel bank without having to change angle or power, some variable in the delicate equation shifted imperceptibly; with only the slightest power margin in the first place at that altitude, even a minor gust of wind could have done it. Maybe the geometric perspective had created an optical illusion of some sort, and they were lower than they thought. Maybe the very gravity of the mountain pulled them in, but something caused the approach path of Honcho 062 to steepen; they were no longer on a path to overfly. During a moment further confused by an emergency tone possibly emanating from Red-Handed 56's ELT,[3] which saturated the radios of their cockpit, and doing what any pilot's reflexes would command, Art instinctively pulled up on the collective, effectively increasing the pitch angle of all main rotor blades and sending more fuel into the engines. In every other instance of correcting an altitude problem in his life, this had worked, but at that moment nothing happened. The problem occurring immediately at that density altitude was that the finely tuned turbine engines had already been compressing as much of the thin mountain air as possible; no amount of fuel added was going to rev them up again, but the collective pitch increase began decelerating the main rotor rpm at a startling rate.

Over the rocks now, both pilots realized the main rotor rpm was sagging, which in plain language means *the big fan* was no longer pushing air down fast enough to hold up the weight of the vehicle. Almost any emergency in the cockpit might cause a pilot to pull up or back on the controls, but in this unique case that would exacerbate the problem. The pilots communicated to each other that rotor rpm was dropping, after which Art commanded Ronnie to take *step 2* in the emergency procedures checklist for the situation, which was to place the throttles into *lockout*, an override position allowing the pilots to add more fuel to the combustion chamber than the digital engine control had already calculated. Ronnie complied immediately, but because of a lack of ambient air molecules, overriding the engine controllers had no effect. The suffocating aircraft sank steadily toward the rocks.

Art had mere seconds to bank toward the escape route and get the rotor rpm back. But the only way for the engines to recover would be to unload them, which would mean complying with *step 1* of the emergency procedure: COLLECTIVE-REDUCE. In a mental dilemma between flying out of the situation and cushioning what seemed like an inevitable crash landing, Art banked slightly toward the escape route, hoping to make it over the cliff on momentum. By his own admission, the position of the collective never changed. Proceeding toward the brink under the ominous tone of the low-rotor-rpm horn, Art imagined a scenario of falling off the cliff out of control. It was the critical moment: if he went for it and the main rotor speed recovered, he got lucky and saved the day. If it didn't, they were dead.

About 100 feet prior to the cusp, Art spotted a patch of talus rock and decided to stick it. Even having used all remaining rotor system inertia to cushion the impact, the soft aluminum skin of Honcho 062 molded onto rock fangs like a ball of Play-Doh, and the main rotor blades slapped down to rock. No longer straining against the weight of the aircraft, the unloaded engines screamed back up to maximum power, and the tremendous torque increase ground the fuselage on the rocks like a lemon half being twisted against an old-fashioned juicer, and had to be shut down immediately so the aircraft wouldn't roll over from torque. At the initial moment of impact, the fuselage had snapped, providing an additional measure of crash energy attenuation, and a feature designed into the seats for crashworthiness extended the duration of g-force exposure substantially enough for everyone to be able to climb out of the wreckage without significant injury once everything stopped moving. Contrary to popular culture, the aircraft neither exploded nor burst into flames upon impact, which was not entirely luck; Sikorsky had, over many years of supplying helicopters to the military, developed breakaway fuel lines and self-sealing, crashworthy fuel cells that worked as advertised. Crashworthiness was an intentional design feature the Blackhawk demonstrated wonderfully.[4]

At that moment, within one search area, the number of wreckages doubled. The first-ever crash of a Mike-model Blackhawk had taken place at 14,657 feet, and seven members of the coalition became "the Main Effort."

CHAPTER 37
FALLEN ANGEL

In the quintessential *oh fuck* moment, company commander Bob Massey looked down in total disbelief as they circled the crash site, having only seconds prior heard interrupted moments of desperate shouting over the internal radio, followed by a troubling silence. Procedural compliance and muscle memory would have both pilots shutting everything down at combat speed, including fuel valves, battery switches, and all radios and crypto circuits, upon impact with the ground. By circling almost directly overhead, Bob and Jasper maintained visual contact and within a minute began to see people climbing from the wreck. After the several moments it took Art and his crew to come to terms with what had happened, they finally dug out a handheld radio from the survival equipment and were able to communicate again with their sister ship. Bob and Jasper listened to Art telling them he had crashed on the mountain, in a voice containing equal parts disbelief and agitation. After a short back-and-forth exchange, it became clear that no one was injured, and there was also no chance of getting off the ground again.

The *Aviation Procedures Guide* for the theater required any helicopter flying beyond line-of-site radio range with the TOC to have an escort. As such, almost every mission we flew was a flight of two aircraft. The whole point was to use the buddy system, and the most logical progression was that if one aircraft ended up on the ground for any reason, the other could simply swoop down and get the crew out of harm's way and back up into the relative safety of the sky. This could happen for a number of reasons and was a battlefield contingency. In the classic case of everything changing in an instant, though, this two-ship formation's day had gone from being a meaningful adventure to being a deflating mistake, but also a perplexing emergency. Not only was Honcho 048 low on fuel, but they were also circling over a crash site they already knew they should not approach. It was tempting, though; if they made a more cautious approach, intending to fly down into ground effect from the start, they might be able to pull it off if they shot for a smooth spot and successfully hit it with the Blackhawk's main landing gear and stout shock absorbers. But adding the weight of seven more passengers would doom them to being stuck on the gravel bank in a perfectly good helicopter. If they couldn't rescue anybody, what was the point of adding another aircraft to the crash site? They decided that not only was it too risky in the aerodynamic sense, but they could be more tactical by providing cover from the overwatch position. It was time to comply with another requirement of the *Aviation Procedures Guide*: make the "FALLEN ANGEL" radio call.

It was one of those calls you never want to hear on the radio, and having to *make* the call was suddenly a very foreign-feeling reality. Jasper Sol Diego hesitated just long enough to make sure he got it right. Verifying the exact grid and getting Bobby to concur that they were literally going to call in the cavalry, Jasper selected the SATCOM radio and stepped on the floor mic switch to transmit the code words to the entire theater of operations. There is an understanding among helicopter pilots theater-wide, regardless of branch: if you hear the words "fallen angel," no matter what mission you were on, you would drop what you were doing, fly direct to the scene, and save everyone's lives. That was part of the reason a downed helicopter became "the main effort"; all other agendas would be put on hold, and just about anyone within a 100-mile radius could be expected to show up without any direct guidance to do so.

As it turned out at that moment, Chinook pilot Ryan Dechent was in the middle of completing the black ring route[1] down by Salerno, along with Chinook pilot Josh McCurry, an old flight-school classmate of mine, over 100 miles away. Dechent heard the call over SATCOM and immediately dropped his pax and cargo at the nearest FOB and headed north with his flight. At the time, somewhat comically, they were flying the oldest Chinook assigned to the task force. For its various personality quirks and the last two digits of its tail number, it had acquired the nickname "The Dirty-30." At one moment, en route to Art's crash site, the main switch panel above the cockpit rattled out its last screw on the nonhinged side of the panel and fell open. As it swung down and bashed Dechent in the shoulder, a switch on the panel caused the wipers to turn on. In one of those *you've got to be kidding* moments, Dechent and McCurry flew a segment of the flight up to Honcho 062 taking turns between flying and repairing the panel. Amid this minor chaos, Dechent was able to reply over SATCOM that he was en route, to which a now hyper-focused task force commander came over the radio and told him to stand by; Col. Dickerson's position required several factors to be verified in the balance of risk assessment vs. assets, which in reality may have taken only two or three minutes, but even one minute would be an agonizing amount of time to wait. Dechent decided in classic assault form to blame the radios for not hearing that last part and proceeded at max speed. Almost immediately, though, Lift 6 came back over the radio, concurring the Dirty-30 should respond.

Simultaneously on the ground, at what would soon prove to be an adequate heavy LZ, Art and Ronnie Allen were taking the immediate action steps they were expected to take: zeroing all of the crypto keys, getting the survival equipment and first-aid kit out of the helicopter, setting up a defensive perimeter, dismounting the M240 machine guns to use once they secured the high ground, and generally being out of breath on foot from a level of hypoxia that hadn't presented itself while they were sitting down and flying. Even though they had been flying with supplemental oxygen, as soon as they took off their helmets, they also removed the nasal cannula connected to the bottle, and wanted to conserve what was left of their O_2 on the basis of an unknown scenario. Supplemental oxygen would not be required to *survive* at that altitude, but none of the crew were truly acclimated to be functioning well on foot, either. It was unknown at the time whether they would hike out or not, and some recovery O_2 may have come in handy.

At the moment they stepped onto the rocks, CW3 Matos would no longer be the pilot in command, and Capt. Ronnie Allen took over as the senior line officer on the ground, consistent with normal military protocol. On what had been a last-minute decision to go on one final flight, Ronnie had never even remotely considered the possibility he would now be leading a squad-sized element through an emergency evasion scenario. Soon, they realized there was no chance they would have to evade. This area was so remote that the threat of any insurgents was extremely low. They were already "up family" and had top cover, and their ride was on the way.[2]

Finally getting his moccasins on the ground outside the wire, Joe Puskar was the first to traverse to the high ground, already having secured his go bag and rifle. Being a medical officer, he couldn't take command of the scene, but being an authentic special-forces badass, everyone on the ground was thankful for his coincidental presence. In a transformation that happened while the aircrew was still scratching their heads and looking at damage, Joe had put on the kameez from his go bag, wrapped himself in a shawl, and topped it off with a traditional wool pakol and went to the ready with his rifle. In a moment already blurred by light hypoxia and disbelief over how completely destroyed the aircraft was, the civilian passenger with the fancy camera turned around to the startling realization that a member of the Taliban was suddenly upon them! Only Victoria Burns simultaneously remarking how fast Major Puskar had blended with his surroundings kept the passenger from shouting to the crew members to take cover.

As a pair of F/A-18 fighter jets appeared overhead, a pair of Apache attack helicopters also reported in over SATCOM that they were one ridgeline away if needed. The Apache pilots were maintaining a tactical balance as well; they lacked the power to get over the last ridgeline due to the fact they were carrying extra fuel tanks on their stub wings for an extended search time. If needed to provide more-precise air cover than the F/A-18s could provide, the tanks could be jettisoned, allowing the Apaches to get over the ridge but limiting their station time.

Meanwhile, nervously low on fuel, Bob and Jasper got a report that Dechent and McCurry were five minutes out. Looking south, Jasper spotted the huge craft, nosed over to such an extent that the figure-eight image created by the rotor system was visible from the front. As soon as Jasper said, "I see them," Bobby broke station and conducted a battle handover to Dechent with Honcho 062 in the rearview mirror. This worked out well, allowing Dechent and McCurry to pick up the low orbit without having to do any deconfliction. Simultaneously, Art popped a smoke flare and threw it to the flattest spot of the LZ for the incoming Chinook to observe the surface wind direction. Before Dechent and McCurry even completed the first orbit in what now had become a light falling snow on top of the mountain, Ronnie called up to Dechent, using the handheld radio, and in a moment of courageous humor deadpanned, "Bigtime Element, this is Honcho 062. The LZ is marked with yellow smoke and a crashed Blackhawk."

Dechent noted the smoke, as well as what appeared to be a distracting lone insurgent on the high ground with a rifle. Directing his gunners to monitor, he made the approach without incident and enjoyed a tentative feeling of success as the crew of Honcho 062 begin climbing aboard with as much sensitive equipment as they were able to strip from the Blackhawk. After sliding down the rocks from having effectively secured the area, Joe Puskar was the last one to board the Chinook, which departed easily to the south before returning to Bagram.

The crew of Honcho 048 made a direct beeline toward the small base at Mehtar Lam (sarcastically referred to as "the Meth Lab" by flight crews) on reserve fuel and as a single ship. Over 10,000 feet lower then, in significantly thicker air, Bob and Jasper decelerated and descended somewhat anxiously onto short final for hot refuel when the number 2 engine flamed out. In a moment of disbelieving humor, both pilots exchanged nervous and giggly cheers of "Holy shit dude" as the helicopter touched down at the pump under power of the number 1 engine alone.

In a JOC-level handoff, the Air Force assigned Predator UAV support for round-the-clock surveillance of the crash site until a decision could be made about how to recover the aircraft, which took several days; first, master aviator Gary Drake and senior maintenance pilot Manny Broussard flew back up as passengers in a Chinook to take a look at the damage. After less than twenty minutes of consideration, they deemed the aircraft unflyable due to the extent of damage to the main rotor blades and the fact that the tail rotor driveshaft was no longer in line. While new blades could have been brought up, there was no crane or lift capability with which to mount them. Further damage to some of the control tubes in the fuselage would have required extensive on-site repair work, with the craft still adhered to the rocks, and both the maintenance team and security detachment performing with notable deficiency under minor hypoxia.

A substantial amount of conjecture would be exchanged by pilots young and old for days and weeks to come about whether or not the craft could have been flown off the rocks after some basic repair. Some speculated that the rotor blades even in their damaged state would still generate lift, some stated that if it didn't have the power to hover up there in the first place, then it would stand to reason it would still not have the power to take off, and others concluded that if the aircraft were stripped of its heavy armor plating system and thousands of pounds of radio equipment and electronics, it could be flown out single-pilot in the cool hours of the morning. Either way, the two pilots assigned to figure it out were both seasoned enough, and neither felt like accumulating any more recognition or awards in an attempt to raise the Phoenix under its own power.

After the possibility of flying it out gained no traction, another Chinook flight took several shifts of crew chiefs and avionics technicians up to the aircraft to strip out the main engines, radios, gearboxes, hoses, passenger seats, and anything else that was easy to disassemble. Daily, the pile in the hangar grew, with parts being destined toward various manufacturers for recertification or scrapping. Some battalion- and brigade-level logistics meetings took place to determine if the brand-new, thirteen-million-dollar aircraft could somehow be saved by lifting it out as a sling load under another helicopter. It could, maybe, but not even by the powerful Chinook. Way down in Kandahar there was a massive Russian Mi-26 helicopter being operated by civilians that could potentially be leased, but by the time of this discussion, the crash site was already drawing unwanted attention; the network of insurgents and their cell phones had spread the news that there had been a lot of activity up in the hills. One suspicious-looking figure was even seen in the UAS feed lurking around the helicopter and eventually walking away from it with what appeared to be one of the seat cushions.

It was decided by the brigade commander, in the balance of threat, environment, damage, logistics, and other operational needs in the theater, that the machine was a combat loss. Two days later, to make sure the materials of Honcho 062 wouldn't end up being used by the enemy somehow, the Air Force dropped a 500-pound bomb on it, which we got to watch in real time on a monitor. Regardless of shift, and with more anticipation than the Super Bowl, every member of the company gathered to pay silent homage to one of our ships. The mute drone footage went from an obvious helicopter on the ground to an amount of light so intense the tiny camera bleached out completely. Contrast returned over three or four seconds, showing a massive gray smudge on the mountain, forever closing The Book of Honcho 062 with finality. Art left the room before anyone caught his reaction.

The day after the crash, the wreckage of Red-Handed 56 was located. Air Force Pedro elements had returned to one of the grids of interest and positively identified components of an MC-12 aircraft, including a tiny patch of international orange from the bottom of one of the seat cushions. Joe Puskar immediately realized from comparing the crash report location to his personal GPS datum that indeed it had been the orange material he had seen in his periphery the day prior to Art's crash. From then on, he held himself partially accountable for the crash of Honcho 062.

Few other topics were discussed for the following several days, and nothing was as captivating as the action on the mountain. Everyone had something to say about it, ranging from technical speculation to the complete analysis of Art's personality and aptitude. Since no one had been hurt in the accident, all measure of irony and judgment floated about freely. To those who had often fallen under excessive scrutiny from Art, it seemed like exactly what he had coming to him. Naturally, an amused Peter Griffin didn't hold back his own cheap analysis of the crash, offering to anyone who would listen that he wasn't surprised at all. In one case, the news was even celebrated: pasty-looking Tits Bogswell walked gleefully into a crowd with the classic shit-eating grin on his face to boisterously proclaim, "So, Art burned one in, eh?!" while pumping his fist. Crash survivor Victoria Burns was standing in the crowd, though. She felt that Art had actually saved them all and told Tits to *shut his fuckin' pie hole.* His awkward comment sank quickly with the unreceptive crowd, and Bogswell slunk out of the room like the snail he was.

At the compassionate end of the spectrum, another senior pilot who had crashed a Blackhawk once in his career made a special trip from Salerno up to Bagram to ask Art how he was holding up and to provide some welcome counsel, being familiar with the melancholy feelings of the experience.

With not too much else to do, but also being grounded during the subsequent investigation, Art mostly stayed in his room. The investigation took a long time, with lots of entities needing to look at the information, and then a decision had to be made concerning privileges and potential retraining. The time ended up being reflective for Art; he went from feelings of personal responsibility to feelings of abandonment, because of the thought that he was being investigated for doing what he was supposed to be doing.

Meanwhile, after the final destruction of Honcho 062, flights went back to normal, ring routes continued to be flown, and all associated excitement died down. It had gotten people's attention and may even have caused a few people to "tighten up their shot group" for the remaining time on station. Fortunately, it came and went without grinding the unit to a halt. There were no resulting safety stand-downs, there were no additional inspections, and there were no new rules or regulations put in place. Amazing.

CHAPTER 38
MISSION COMPLETE

Day 333. The end was near. Just as we came into the country in pressure waves and microbursts eleven months prior, fragments of the task force were now scheduled to fly home. My own date to leave was a mere two and a half weeks away by the time I found out. *Wait, I wasn't ready to hear that!* What a strange feeling came over me then, having conditioned myself to live at Bagram; I had made a point not to count down the days. I felt like I had a wisp of Stockholm syndrome.

Our replacing unit was showing up, day by day, and I felt like they were impostors. We had adopted the CP as our own and had become comfortable with its personality, the dust, the mold-encrusted coffeepot, the way the fridge rattled for a second when the compressor turned off, even the greasy trim around the tabletop. It was ours, and now these loud, energized, ambitious intruders were all up in our business asking us to explain how we'd been doing things. They wanted to sit in our chairs and use our computers; they were even bringing in new furniture.

My first thought was *What the fuck is this?! These guys don't have a clue about how to operate over here.* This went on for a few days and mostly made me feel trespassed upon, as if my girlfriend invited a new boyfriend to move into the apartment before I even packed up my toothbrush. After picking up on a conversation with some friends who had similar feelings, we shortly concluded that we *loved* these new guys, because as soon as they were comfortable, we were out of there! It was a transitional moment, and since not a single texture of the CP had changed since we took over, it prompted a flashback to the first few days after our own arrival. We had stood in this exact spot, looked at this exact scene, and acted clumsy and intrusive until the outgoing unit decided we had a handle on it and left. So, we shifted over to a new agenda: *Let's make these guys comfortable!*

We set up a mini marketplace on the back porch, where items we had made or bought throughout the year were for sale to the new unit. A good portion of deployed possessions are truly worthless back home and not worth shipping or packing up to transport. A variety of things showed up, including a great selection of homemade lawn chairs, crappy guitars, coffee makers, video games, end tables, and shelving systems. Few of these items sold, even at rock-bottom prices, since most of it was just junk that could be hammered together in an afternoon. Most of that stuff ended up just sitting there until we left for good, when by default it became free for the taking or was disposed of.

When I got to the point where I had one week left in country, I decided to stop flying. I thought about one last flight in Afghanistan, because it was one of the most beautiful and dramatic landscapes I had ever flown over. Only Alaska had been more inspirational in my flying career. After careful consideration, I realized I had seen it and seen it and seen it, and the image of gorgeous scenery was already imprinted into my mind forever. One more flight would just be one more time I'd have to turn on the vigilance and attention, suit up again, go through another brief, and draw another machine gun from the arms room. It wasn't just pure fun to go out, and I had been out there all year. I was too close to the finish line to muster up the appropriate mission focus, and I decided to shift into perpetual celebratory mode.

I figured if I wasn't going to be flying, I probably wouldn't be hanging out in the CP too much either, and maybe it was time to sign the planning table. It wasn't really a rite of passage, but hundreds of pilots had signed it, so many that reading it was difficult. I signed the huge plywood and Plexiglas monstrosity and felt a small measure of closure on the time I had spent sitting in this dismal room, and I found bittersweet satisfaction in walking out the door.

At one stage of packing, I decided to dump out my trusty go bag to use the backpack for the miscellaneous effects of my trip home. After removing the thermal underwear, I discovered I was lucky to never have used the go bag for its intended purpose; flying high in the frozen winter months had caused the V-8 cans to rupture, perhaps ten months prior! The salty and acidic tomato juice had thoroughly seeped into all the M4 and M9 magazines before hardening, and the congealed piece of modern art had been evolving for most of a year in the normal corrosive process. My extra ammo was a rusted, calcified, useless clump of verdigris in the bottom of the bag, and the bullets could not be dug out of the magazines with a screwdriver. Joe Puskar would have been disgusted.

I packed up my room, took my dad's paintings off the wall, and reduced my possessions down to one duffel bag and one backpack. One source of daily edification for me had been drinking coffee from the porcelain coffee mug given to me by the Irish bartender. I contemplated the safest path for its return and decided not to carry it home in my backpack. I would shift over to Styrofoam coffee cups to sacrifice myself for this war trophy and packed it carefully in a tuff box. If it was wrapped in several T-shirts and placed center mass in a tuff box, it would have an excellent chance of making it home intact, if the tuff box made it home at all.

That's a funny thing about packing to go home—when you pack those tuff boxes for deployment, if you pack them right, once you're in the austere conditions of the war zone those tuff boxes eventually arrive like chests of gold. They are full of comfort, security, and reassurance. When you send them home, and go home, you forget about them completely. When they eventually arrive, they seem like random boxes of dusty junk, and a chore to sort through and put away.

I checked my two tuff boxes through customs and into my company's shipping container, where it was sealed up with everyone else's stuff. I would get my possessions back in two months, when this container finally arrived back in the parking lot at Sabre Army Heliport in Tennessee, after completing the circuitous route that containers had to travel. The stuff would see ship, rail, and ground transportation on its way back, a long and anonymous journey among millions of other containers moving daily about the globe.

By the time we left Afghanistan, the new unit was in-briefed, schooled up, given indoctrination flights, and settled into the routine. There were no progress reports of success or achievement, no discussions about increases or decreases of manpower or firepower. *Nothing significant to report.* For utility pilots, it was pure sustainment. All they had to do was continue the normal commerce we had sustained for the last year.

Eventually, the day came for me and a handful of buddies to walk down to the pax terminal, get yelled at by the sergeant again, and sit around waiting for hours and hours. As we sat, the dominant story on the overhead television was news of a brutal series of car bombs in Baghdad, killing hundreds and wounding many hundreds. It was a disturbing feeling to see a place where we had been and to watch it in complete turmoil, but it gave me an ambiguous feeling about leaving; it made me feel partially like something wasn't done, and partially like I was glad to be leaving. If Bobby walked onto the plane and said, "Ten of us are going back to Iraq for a few weeks; are you in?," I knew that that would feel right, and I would immediately focus on the new task. I was daydreaming though. I was still sitting in the pax terminal, with no option. Iraq was just frustrating. Finally, we walked single-file like ducklings into the back of a cavernous cargo plane with seat pallets. None of it caught my attention. They could have told me to tether in to a tie-down ring, and that would have been fine.

It was a sentimental feeling as we taxied out, knowing the taxiways, the runways, the radio calls—everything, really—and realizing my expertise with the place would never be utilized again. Where we were on the airfield was clear in my mind's eye as we taxied along; there are no window seats in the back of the huge transport, because there are no windows. I knew where we started, and could feel what turns we had taken, and knew when we were holding short. It crossed my mind that if I had been clever enough to save a flask of bourbon, it would have been a perfect time to celebrate. We were only days from real life, though, so it wasn't necessary.

Once the huge craft made the obvious turn onto runway 21 and began to shovel on the coal, smiles crossed every face, and giddy friends elbowed each other with glee. Once again, the plane rotated and the wheels left the runway to a cabin full of cheers, and the obvious venting of stress was so unanimous that the entire crowd seemed to deflate and turn inward. I was leaving the Bowl for the final time. Not too much else seemed to matter, and with no windows to look out, I resigned myself to the intense whine of the huge engines and the thought that I had left Bagram for good.

We made the same trip out we made going in. After being informed we were crossing the wire out of Afghanistan, several people cursed their way out of their body armor; others thought *Fuck it* and remained sardined in. We landed in Manas, Kyrgyzstan, again, and this time I wasn't as lucky with a quick turnaround time and had to spend four days in the ironic-feeling Russian suburb. Anything is fine, though, when you know you're on the way home. Typical with deployed military experience, there was always a lot of waiting.

It was impossible for me not to flash back to my time in the submarine force, which also included many long hours, and many years pondering our main adversary, Mother Russia. Kyrgyzstan was part of Russia for most of the twentieth century, although they had gained independence and became their own state again as the Soviet Union dissolved in 1991. While much of the population was Muslim, Russian was still an official language, and the look of the place was very Russian, with attractive but heavy-handed architecture. I learned that Kyrgyzstan was the poorest country in central Asia, which meant they wouldn't have money to change the appearance of any of their bridges or buildings and, by that measure, struggled to truly break from their Russian identity and create a new image. Even the much closer, neighboring China seemed to have little effect on the cultural essence of the place. It felt Russian and felt ironic to me; sixteen years earlier and 3,000 miles north, I had stood at the chart, carefully and quietly navigating a nuclear-powered attack submarine in the Barents Sea, sometimes looking at the northern coast of Russia through a periscope. I remember wondering what it would feel like to walk on the soil of the country, to taste the food, or to see the people. Being in Kyrgyzstan for four days finally gave me a sense of it, and it was difficult to fully let go of early programming: I was loitering in *enemy territory*.

Eventually, enough of my unit was assembled to fill up a World Airways DC-10, and we began the long series of flights back to Ft. Campbell, Kentucky.

Prior to landing, we had to put that goddamned body armor back on. There is a ceremony for the families who have come to greet their returning soldier, and for some reason it had become a requirement to get off the plane looking like you just stepped off the battlefield. I don't know if that's supposed to make the families feel like the trip was important and it was really dangerous the whole time, or to make the colonel feel like he was really commanding a bunch of warriors from the second they left American soil until the second they returned, but either way, it was total shit. It's certainly not for the soldiers. Body armor should be packed up into a container just like the other heavy shit and sent home on a boat. Instead, some dumbass who is more concerned with appearances than practicality decides to make travel-weary soldiers put on one last parade at the end of their long trip, brain buckets and rifle to boot.

After that, we filed into an open gym and had to stand in formation before even getting to greet our families and listened to some other goddamned colonel that we didn't care about, or some chief of staff or whoever the fuck he was, speak to himself over the PA system, trying to somehow associate our return with more-glorious returns of the past. It was damn phony and really reaching; it was obvious to everyone present that the deployment had no great historical significance, but he was trying to dress it up. It just wasn't going to be the cover of *TIME*, though. It was just lame. I mean, who the fuck thinks their underthought, overwritten speech is even going to be remembered? They ought to just let the families greet the troops when they get off the plane.

Finally, we got to reunite with our families. My parents had flown in, friends who had come home earlier were there, and it was good to be home. After the logistical tedium of turning in our rifles and pistols and the ballistic plates from our body armor, we finally got to step down from the freight train and walk away with our families. We were home before Veteran's Day. The deployment was over.

My parents drove me to my house, and I showered and put on some jeans and a T-shirt. Pulling open the drawers of my dresser brought the smell of clean laundry in antique hardwood, which was no portal; it was real. It didn't transport me anywhere. It was just goodness where goodness should be. My mom had made sure there was cold beer in the fridge of my house, and taking that first swig was the beginning of my recovery from the absurdity of being deployed. For a few minutes the living room of my house appeared to be a different size and shape than I remembered, but the smell was right. The paintings on the wall were right. That was my couch, I knew.

I really was home.

EPILOGUE

After completing the deployment, the members of Task Force Eagle Lift received the Army Superior Unit Award, as well as the Lt. Gen. Ellis D. Parker Award for being the best Aviation Combat Support Battalion in the Army.

Lt. Col. Rob "Heavy D" Dickerson was promoted to full bird colonel during the deployment, and successfully led the task force through more than 42,000 flight hours as LIFT 6. Following his deployment to OEF, he enjoyed brigade command, leading members of the 16th Combat Aviation Brigade at Ft. Lewis, Washington, followed by two years at the Pentagon on the Joint staff. He finished his 30 year career at the United States Military Academy at West Point, returning home to Michie Stadium, as the deputy athletic director.

Ryan Dechent received the Distinguished Flying Cross for his achievements during what was his third deployment; namely, the successful handling of his Chinook after being hit with an RPG round in the Pech River valley. The award was further validated by Ryan being the first responder to the fallen-angel radio call, cuing him to pick up the crew of HONCHO 062 after they crash-landed. He was universally considered to be the quintessential heavy-lift pilot and after a fourth deployment went to Ft. Rucker to work for the Directorate of Evaluation and Standardization (DES), flying all over the world to make sure other Chinook pilots were operating efficiently. After serving as a battalion-level standardization pilot and deploying for a fifth time, he went back to DES and became the first-ever Chinook pilot promoted to the Directorate SP position, giving him purview over all helicopter operations in the United States Army.

Casey Church recovered from the shrapnel injury, after eight months at Walter Reed Medical Center. With reconstructive surgeries numbering in the thirties, and the need to walk with a brace, he was medically retired from the Army. His decorations include the Purple Heart.

Sarah Gilley received the Army Commendation Medal with V Device for her selfless actions to save Church's life, and she continued after deployment to SERE school before serving a three-year tour with the "Night Stalkers" at Ft. Campbell, Kentucky.

Pech resupply missions were no longer flown on nights with 100 percent illumination.

Arturo Matos remained under investigation for the rest of the deployment until he was eventually let off the hook for the crash. There was no punitive action taken against him. The crash was recorded as pilot error due to Art flying into a situation demanding more power of the engines than they could possibly generate at that altitude. He went home with only one final Blackhawk flight in Afghanistan, a routine flight as a copilot. He was eventually reassigned to be an instructor at the helicopter school in Ft. Rucker, Alabama. By his own admission the entire episode was a humbling experience; not only did he recalibrate his sense of self as it concerned flying, he also went so far as to have the tail number of Honcho 062 tattooed on his arm as a lifelong reminder. By this measure, he achieved more humility than most.

Bob Massey, our company commander and the air mission commander in the search for Red-Handed 56, was stripped of his privilege to be an air mission commander, having not intervened to prevent Art from making a slow pass over the mountain while balancing within such a narrow power margin. Even if they *had* gotten a great picture, it wasn't worth the risk they were taking to get it, which is debatably something the air mission commander could have affected. Shortly thereafter, Bobby was awarded the Bronze Star for a successful deployment as the G Co. company commander and continued on successfully with other assignments.

Maj. Joe Puskar moved on in the normal course of things. He continued to be the exception, a tremendously capable and dynamic individual contributing in good faith to the outcome of any scenario he could.

An investigation about the Red-Handed 56 C-12 crash concluded that the crash was caused by a malfunction in the fuel system, which, combined with the cabin-heating system, developed into a disastrous cockpit fire. Few worse scenarios for a pilot can be imagined.

Todd "the Duke" Wolfe, who could never get signed off to be a pilot in command by the instructors of Golf Company, was eventually signed off during the deployment by a battalion-level check pilot. He became a safety officer and a flight instructor before being accepted to the US Navy's prestigious experimental test pilot school, and he worked the rest of his military career as a test pilot in airplanes and helicopters.

The gregarious Pete Latham continued on successfully to higher and higher positions, eventually serving as a battalion-level standardizations pilot before retiring.

Phil Bogswell went on to another unit and eventually was signed off as a pilot in command, only to later have that status stripped for harassing his ex-wife by hovering menacingly over her house with a Blackhawk, causing over $10,000 in soffit and shingle damage.

I returned home, enjoying most of a year at Ft. Campbell before moving on to my next assignment. After a month or so, our shipping container arrived, and everyone was summoned to the parking lot. Seals and padlocks were removed, and the creaky doors were swung open. It really did look like a big pile of junk. I got my two tuff boxes, hauled them home in my truck, and carried them inside, at least. The next morning as I made coffee, I had an amusing thought; I popped one of the tuff boxes open and dug around a bit. I could smell the deployment—it took me right back, and I found the heavy mass wrapped in T-shirts. My plan had worked; the Irish coffee mug was intact. A quick rinse brought it back online for the morning, and as I closed my eyes and took a sip from the same cup as I had in Afghanistan, I was transported vividly to my plywood stateroom, the quilt, the paintings, the smells, everything. The coffee tasted better, and when I came back realized I was misty-eyed. I missed my plywood stateroom and the chemistry I had been part of. I took a deep breath and made the rational decision that I'd rather be home.

The rest of the junk sat for weeks.

Six months after my return, I took leave to Raton, New Mexico, to visit the uncle I had mailed the Lebel rifle to. He had taken it to the gunsmithing school at Trinidad University and had a chamber casting made, verified there was no damage to the chamber or barrel, and test-fired it. It operated perfectly, and during my visit we spent a few hours at the Wittington Center, putting the Lebel through its paces with several boxes of 8 mm ammo from an online source. It was a soft-feeling and lovely little rifle by today's standards, not ranging out much past 400 yards with iron sights, but reverent-feeling that in its day it commanded the battlefield.

I spent the last four years of my military career as a Blackhawk instructor at Ft. Rucker, then retired. I finally got married to the Duke's sister, Ami, and we started a family. I opened a small fabrication and machine shop and went back to flying occasionally as a private pilot. I became a civilian again.

I am proud to have served, and I served alongside some great people. If I could go back to my plywood stateroom and begin planning and launching assault operations again, I'd be there, alive and well, and executing my duties with a level of tactical precision you can scarcely comprehend. Hot black coffee, fuel for the mission, rpm in the green. Crew, passengers, and mission equipment: SET. *Pitch pull in five.*

Blackhawk Helicopter Commander.

END

September 11, 2021, morning: In the desert near Payandeh Kheyl, following the departure of all coalition forces, a Taliban lieutenant leans the Chinese Type 56 rifle given to him by a late uncle against the back of a weathered Adirondack chair. He sits down, enjoying a skillfully brewed cup of hot Kahwah tea as the sun rises. The air is crisp; the view is inspirational. He ponders a day of controlling the locals in a land with almost no regulation whatsoever.

ACKNOWLEDGMENTS

Special thanks goes out to the dozens of Comancheros, Black Widows, and Kingsmen who banded together for a year to become the G Company "Reapers," who contributed to this work at bars and barbecues with beer and war stories that add up to its sum. The events recalled here are told differently by each individual who was there, but distill down into one common version that is reasonably agreeable.

Thanks to Rob Dickerson for enthusiastically providing as much information as I asked for, lending a perspective of leadership that many chapters needed, and for running the unit effectively in the first place, with total professionalism and devotion to duty. *Mission first, people always.*

Thanks to Ryan Dechent for the detailed summaries of the RPG incident in the Pech River valley, and the recovery of the crew of Honcho 062, along with a helpful amount of proofreading of the related chapters.

Thanks to Arturo Matos for his humbled account of the final flight of Honcho 062.

Thanks to Sarah (Gilley) Blatt for her account of being on board the Chinook during the RPG attack, as well as contributing significantly to the accuracy of the intel and threat discussion.

Thanks to Casey Church for his detailed account of what it's like to experience and then recover from an RPG blast.

Thanks to Milton Duran for a helpful conversation about the duty of protecting the airbase from mortar fire with continued patrols and vigilance as the commander of F Co.

Thanks to Rob Wolcott for his vulnerable and captivating account of losing his father in the Battle of Mogadishu, and for his perspective on civilian-military relations.

Thanks to Dennis Wolfe, Sue Wolfe, Douglas Gunn, Mark Havill, Eric Havill, Steven Havill, John Carter Cash, Andrew Lee, Conor Whitehead, Jack Clift, Pete Latham, Phil Cramer, Mike White, Martin Kickliter, Steve Armstrong, Todd Wolfe, Stanley McChrystal, Chris Bachuss, and Mark Robinson, for their encouragement and generous help in the editing of this book.

Special thanks to my wife, Ami, for the continued support and encouragement, for living with this process the longest, for her own many days of editing and formatting, and for believing in it with so much sincerity that I stayed inspired. Thank you to our children, Matilda and Henry, for being so unbelievably charming and precious that I was motivated to work harder toward a difficult goal.

The concert for the troops referenced during the flight into the Panjshir valley was recorded *live* and is available on the internet under the title *Peculiar Little Show* by Spike Nicer.

ENDNOTES

Chapter 1
1. Soldier slang term for the Kevlar helmet.
2. The wire is a reference to the border in this case. It is also a reference to the barriers that surround every coalition base.

Chapter 2
1. Illume is military slang for illumination.
2. A "Hesco" is a large wire-mesh bin with a heavy lining that can contain several yards of dirt for the sake of erecting temporary but heavy barriers, invented by Jimi Heselden.
3. Army battalions have several departments to handle the main categories of administrative function, generally referred to as the *staff* shops: S-1 is admin, S-2 is intel, S-3 is operations, S-4 is logistics, S-5 is civil-military operations, and S-6 is communication.
4. Slang for dining facility. Pronounced "Dē-fac."

Chapter 3
1. Command post.
2. The Blackhawk tail section has a hinge built into it, allowing the tail cone to fold in half to reduce the storage footprint. The main rotor blades can also be swept aft with a "blade-folding kit" for this function, which streamlines all four blades over the tail for storage on a special rack.
3. Air mission request.

4. The BFT is an electronic system based on encrypted GPS transmitters and receivers, allowing every component on the modern battlefield to be observed and communicated with, by every other component on the battlefield. Coalition forces are represented by blue icons. Threat forces are potentially represented by red icons if the system gets populated with that information.

5. There is a numerical designator in the Army for the commander, the XO, the command sergeant major, and several other positions, but universally "the 6" is the commander. Reaper 6, Eagle Lift 6, Thunder 6, etc.—the holder of the most responsibility.

Chapter 5

1. Forward operating base. Pronounced "fob."
2. Jalalabad.
3. Military slang for passengers.

Chapter 6

1. Tactical operation center, the battalion level nerve center, typically pronounced "tock."
2. Common Missile Warning System (commonly pronounced "SEE-mos").
3. Readiness condition—REDCON 1 is ready to take off. REDCON 2 is some lesser degree of readiness; for example, engines still at idle.
4. Standardization instructor
5. Space available. Passengers not on the manifest.
6. OH-58 Kiowa Warrior is a light observation helicopter with guns.

Chapter 7

1. Staff weather officer, typically an Air Force person assigned to work with an Army aviation unit.
2. Hot refuel or "hot gas" means to refuel the helicopter with the engines still running. This is a common practice for helicopters, which typically take a long time to start up and shut down but need refueling often during a long mission. Cold gas means the helicopter is parked somewhere and a tanker truck comes to it for refueling.
3. Satellite communication. One of the two forms of over-the-horizon comms on an M-model Blackhawk. The other form is texting through the BFT.
4. Return to base.

Chapter 10

1. Rocket-propelled grenade.

2. Three different-sized military trucks, all with a variety of potential functions. The HMMWV is more commonly referred to as a Humvee, which had replaced the old Army Jeep. The LMTV is a medium-sized truck that generally replaced the old Army deuce-and-a-half, and a HEMMT is a very large truck, modifiable to fill a variety of different functions; for example, it could be a tanker for refueling operations.

3. Typically, the Beretta 9 mm.

Chapter 11

1. Rip-its were a canned energy drink provided to troops by the Army. They were nearly as ubiquitous as water bottles, and due to their fun-sized 8 oz. cans, many soldiers drank them nearly continuously.

2. Midnight rations: a Navy term for the midnight meal.

3. The pathfinders were the most-tactical combatants assigned to an aviation unit. Having no actual flying role, they carried a different collection of skills, which made them very useful on the ground for dismounted recon, LZ prep, or tactical security.

4. Exfiltration; extraction. Getting the troops back out.

5. Restricted operating zone. Essentially, an invisible box in the sky.

6. Interior Communication System.

7. Jalalabad.

8. Joint Land attack cruise missile defense Elevated Netted sensor System.

9. Pickup zone.

Chapter 12

1. M4 is a small, collapsible version of the M16 machine gun, and the M9 is a pistol.

2. Combined arms is the effective cross-pollination of the different disciplines within a branch to achieve a more effective result, combining infantry with artillery, for example.

Chapter 13

1. Meal, ready to eat.

2. Aviation life support equipment: a variety of mission-related items, largely developed into the aviator's outfit: helmet, first-aid kits, tourniquet, basic navigation equipment, basic survival equipment, etc.

3. Squad automatic weapon. Basically, a souped-up .223 machine gun that can be belt-fed.

Chapter 14

1. The word "deliberate" in the Air Assault culture meant the full-blown, detailed, fully planned, extensively briefed, and meticulously rehearsed offensive action where troops are inserted in maximum-threat situations to gain the upper hand in a conflict..
2. Stability and support operations.
3. The pivotal moment of an offensive action reaching the objective.
4. Release point: The final point on a tactical route where everyone focuses on the objective and operators become hypervigilant.
5. Human intelligence: Word of mouth.
6. Auxiliary power unit: A small turbine engine that drives an alternator to supply basic electrical loads when the main engines aren't running.

Chapter 15

1. Code words for a disabled aircraft on the ground outside the wire with no security.
2. Huge cannons that would destroy any location we transmitted the coordinates of.
3. Unmanned aerial vehicle; a drone.
4. Fighter jets I could call if I wanted them to blow shit up.
5. A blood chit is a piece of durable material with information printed in various regional languages, offering a reward for the safe return of whoever was holding it. Intended as a bargaining tool for captured soldiers.
6. Intelligence officer.
7. Troops in contact

Chapter 16

1. Interior Communication System.
2. Auxiliary power unit.
3. The Blackhawk typically has four basic communication radios: FM1, UHF, VHF, and FM2. Additional configurations allow for speaking via other bands; for example, SATCOM or high freq.
4. Unmanned Aerial System.
5. Joint operations center.
6. Rules of engagement.

Chapter 18

1. The Spectre is a special C-130 with a lot of guns on it.

Chapter 19

1. Slang term for someone who never leaves the FOB.

Chapter 21

1. Nap of the earth; typically, not more than 25 feet above obstacles or vegetation.
2. Ballistic Protection System; armor; high-performance polyethylene fiber and ballistic steel.
3. Man-Portable Air-Defense System.
4. High explosive, antitank.
5. Aircraft survivability equipment; BAPS, flares, chaff, self-sealing fuel tanks, etc.
6. Intelligence, surveillance, and reconnaissance; UAVs.

Chapter 22

1. Boots on the ground is casually used Army lingo for anyone legitimate enough in the tactical sense to be "in the action" or "in the threat," directly. It is similar in the conversational sense to Navy usage of the phrase "at the deck plate level."

Chapter 26

1. Grid is short for grid coordinates. It represents the exact landing location, using a military (and metric) X/Y coordinate system similar in usage to latitude/longitude.
2. High-value target.

Chapter 27

1. Alicia the SWO was not only the squadron weather officer for the day. Her undeserved reputation for always being wrong about the weather soon became the subject of the cult song "L.B.SWO," popular among helicopter pilots. The song was included in a local concert for the troops put on by singer/songwriter Spike Nicer.

Chapter 29

1. Observation post.
2. Combat outpost.
3. Unmanned aerial system or vehicle; drone.

4. Slang for illumination.

5. Forward arming and refueling point.

6. Night vision goggles.

7. PZ/LZ: pickup zone / landing zone.

Chapter 30

1. Both "specialist" and "corporal" are variants of E-4 rank in the Army.

2. Morale, welfare, and recreation.

Chapter 33

1. The MC-12 EMARSS (Enhanced Medium-Altitude Reconnaissance and Surveillance System) variant of a Beechcraft King Air.

Chapter 34

1. Air Force version of a Blackhawk.

Chapter 36

1. An *improved* landing site has been leveled with excavation equipment, often paved and painted, usually features a windsock, typically is cleared of obstacles, and sometimes is published in the many reference materials a pilot can research prior to landing at the site. An *unimproved* landing site is any other place at which a pilot may consider landing, is a total mystery, may be unsuitable, and requires the pilot to perceive all variables on approach.

2. An LZ diagram is a piece of paper with a picture of the landing zone, sometimes taken during a reconnaissance flight but often taken from satellite imagery, along with as much information as can be generated during the planning process, such as elevation, latitude/longitude (or grid), and approximate size, to be referenced in the cockpit prior to landing.

3. Emergency locator transmitter.

4. Unlike the AH-1 Cobra and the UH-1 Huey predecessors of the Vietnam era, the AH-64 Apache and the UH-60 Blackhawk had to meet the crashworthiness certification requirements of the time (1970s), with design elements including landing gear capable of absorbing more than 10 g of force, plow beams fabricated into the cabin floor, and energy-attenuating seats.

Chapter 37

1. A ring route is a standard route flown on a predictable schedule for normal, scheduled resupply. At this stage of the war, they had been color-coded.

2. Family refers to the radio frequency assigned to the entire battalion or task force.

ACRONYMS

9-LINE:	The format used to call in an urgent medevac (e.g., line 1 is location)
ABAD:	Asadabad
AIR BATTLE:	A radio frequency in the UHF band for coordinating all air assets
ALSE:	Aviation life support equipment
AMR:	Air mission request
APU:	Auxiliary power unit
BAF:	Bagram airfield
BFT:	Blue Force Tracker
blivet:	A huge, reinforced bladder capable of holding thousands of gallons of fuel
blood chit:	A bargaining tool if captured
brain bucket:	Slang term for the Kevlar helmet
C2:	Command and control
commo or comms:	Communications
COP:	Combat outpost
CP:	Command post
DART:	Downed-aircraft recovery team
DFAC:	Dining facility
EXFIL:	The opposite of infiltrate; or extraction
family:	The battalion's internal frequency
FARP:	Forward arming and refueling point
fire support:	US artillery teams ready to destroy anything you ask them to
FOB:	forward operating base
fobbit:	Someone who never leaves the FOB
freq:	A radio frequency
grid:	A location
hardstand:	Army lingo for anything made of concrete or paved
heavy:	Anything related to the Chinook; heavy lift, heavy PZ, etc.
HEMTT:	Heavy expanded mobility tactical truck
HHC:	Headquarters and Headquarters Company
high element:	US fighter jets patrolling the skies
HMMWV:	High-mobility multipurpose wheeled vehicle or Humvee
hot gas:	Getting refueled with the engines running
HUD:	Heads-up display
HUMINT:	Human intelligence
ICS:	Intercommunication system
IED:	Improvised explosive device

illume:	Illumination
INFIL:	Infiltrate, or to insert the troops
intel:	Intelligence; information
ISAF:	International security assistance force
JAF:	Jalalabad airfield
JBAD:	Jalalabad
JOC:	Joint operations center
jumbotron:	A really big TV
LMTV:	Light medium tactical vehicle
M4:	A modified M16 (.223 or 5.56 mm automatic assault rifle)
M9:	A semiautomatic 9 mm pistol made by Beretta
mid-rats:	Midnight rations; a meal at 0000
MRE:	Meal ready to eat
MSL:	Mean sea level; altitude above sea level
NSTR:	Nothing significant to report
OP:	Observation post
OPSEC:	Operational security
pax:	Passengers
PT:	Physical training
PTs:	Physical training clothes
QRF:	Quick-reaction force
REDCON ONE:	Readiness condition 1. Ready in all regards for takeoff.
RETRANS:	A Blackhawk or other airborne platform with the ability to retransmit radio traffic
ROE:	Rules of engagement
ROZ:	Restricted operating zone
RP:	Release point
S-2:	Intelligence officer
SASO:	Stability and support operations
SATCOM:	Satellite communications
SAW:	Squad assault weapon
SOP:	Standard operating procedure
space-A:	Space available pax
SWO:	Staff or squadron weather officer
TAC:	Tactical
TIC:	Troops in contact
TOC:	Tactical operations center
UAS:	Unmanned aerial system
UAV:	Unmanned aerial vehicle
UHF:	Ultrahigh frequency or "uniform." Also COMM 2.

Massoud's Tomb
Panjshir River
Bagram
Tagob River
Naghlo Dam
Kabul
Airborne
Shank
Catamount
Good
hazni